THE WORLD'S MOST INFLUE

FASHION
DESIGNERS

Madame Grès, 1937

Issey Miyake, 2002

THE WORLD'S MOST INFLUENTIAL
FASHION
DESIGNERS

HIDDEN CONNECTIONS AND LASTING LEGACIES OF FASHION'S ICONIC CREATORS

NOËL PALOMO-LOVINSKI

A & C BLACK • LONDON

CONTENTS

A QUARTO BOOK

Copyright © 2010 Quarto Publishing plc

First published in the UK in 2010 by
A & C Black Publishers
36 Soho Square
London W1D 3QY
www.acblack.com

ISBN: 978-1-4081-2760-5

Conceived, designed and produced by
Quarto Publishing plc
The Old Brewery
6 Blundell Street
London N7 9BH

QUA: WIFD

Editor & designer: Michelle Pickering
Art director: Caroline Guest
Illustrator: Terry Evans
Picture researcher: Sarah Bell
Indexer: Dorothy Frame
Proofreader: Claire Waite Brown

Creative director: Moira Clinch
Publisher: Paul Carslake

Colour separation by
Pica Digital Pte Ltd, Singapore
Printed by 1010 Printing International
Limited, China

10 9 8 7 6 5 4 3 2 1

INTRODUCTION

This book is aimed at the student and lover of fashion as a way to help navigate the past, understand the present and recognize new pathways for the future of fashion design. We are in an exciting time in the world of fashion, as ideas of technology, sustainability and identity are changing to meet the needs of the creatively burgeoning 21st century.

FASHION WITHIN SOCIETY

For those interested in design, it is important to appreciate the place of fashion within society's framework of identity, expression and creativity. Only by understanding and exploring what designers are trying to articulate can their innovations be learned from and truly appreciated. Society has afforded clothing and fashion design with a meaning and significance that can be best appreciated when a designer exhibits skill, business acumen or intellectual exploration, commenting on who we are and our place in the world.

INNOVATORS OF STYLE

There are few design fields in which the designers are expected to create such a wide variety of novel ideas in such a short period of time. The ephemeral nature of fashion means that it often reflects the moment-to-moment changes in politics, art and culture, as well as the larger historically proven zeitgeist. To navigate the fleeting trends of fashion, many designers have developed a consistent style or brand identity. These brand identities allow consumers to ally themselves with designers who share their style concerns and best express their own personal identity.

This book is divided into themed chapters. Each chapter examines a group of designers with related approaches to style or fashion design, in order to assist in the understanding of the intricate balance that makes up the international fashion industry. The designers have been chosen not only for their contributions to aspects of fashion, but also for the sustained and inventive way in which they have achieved these innovations.

STARTING POINT

There are undoubtedly numerous designers and couturiers who deserve a place in the pantheon of major contributors to fashion but who are not included in this book – there is simply not enough room to include them all. However, this book does provide a starting point to help you navigate a map of exploration and investigation into the larger scope of influential fashion.

The structure of the book

The 50 designers featured in the book have been organized into six themed chapters, according to the designers' approach to style, fashion design or the fashion industry.

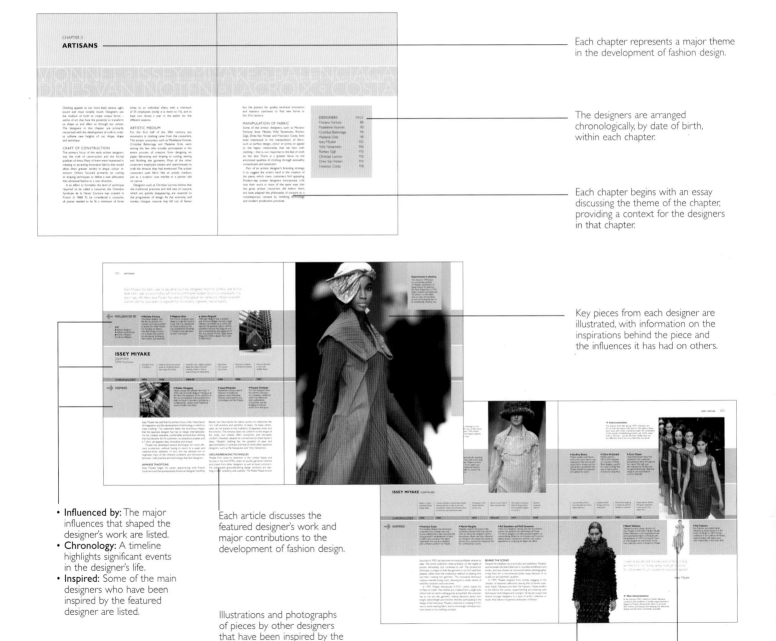

Each chapter represents a major theme in the development of fashion design.

The designers are arranged chronologically, by date of birth, within each chapter.

Each chapter begins with an essay discussing the theme of the chapter, providing a context for the designers in that chapter.

Key pieces from each designer are illustrated, with information on the inspirations behind the piece and the influences it has had on others.

• **Influenced by:** The major influences that shaped the designer's work are listed.
• **Chronology:** A timeline highlights significant events in the designer's life.
• **Inspired:** Some of the main designers who have been inspired by the featured designer are listed.

Each article discusses the featured designer's work and major contributions to the development of fashion design.

Illustrations and photographs of pieces by other designers that have been inspired by the featured designer are shown.

THE FASHION INDUSTRY: A BRIEF HISTORY

The international fashion industry has gone through several changes throughout its relatively short life span. The fashion industry as we know it today only began in the mid-19th century. Charles Frederick Worth was a British fabric merchant, who moved to Paris in 1845. A keen businessman, Worth saw the possibilities in creating a need for his fashion fabrics. Before Worth, wealthy women would hire seamstresses, and all fashion innovation and changes in style were slow. Worth began to create unique gowns for his wife and other young women, whom he hired to walk in public places to garner attention. He quickly gained a reputation, and his gowns were worn by Empress Eugenie of France, as well as all the noble ladies of court.

THE BIRTH OF HAUTE COUTURE
Soon, other designers followed in Worth's footsteps, and haute couture ('high sewing') was born. Worth's two sons, Gaston and Jean Philippe, joined the family business, and in 1868 Gaston helped to establish a guild of fashion designers, now known as the Chambre Syndicale de la Haute Couture. This governing body still dictates strict rules for anyone wishing to be considered a couturier. To be a couturier, a designer needs to have a showroom or atelier in Paris, with private clients who have at least one to three fittings per piece. The couturier is also obliged to show a collection to the press twice a year, consisting of at least 35 full looks, and must employ at least 15 people.

EMERGENCE OF READY-TO-WEAR
Until World War II, Paris couture reigned supreme, and it was standard practice to buy toiles (test garments) from Paris couturiers and copy them, so that Paris dictated fashion to the rest of the Western world. During the Nazi occupation of France, many couturiers stayed open, both to help morale and to supply jobs. Even so, Paris was cut off from the rest of the world, so for the first time, other countries were forced to rely on their own talented designers.

In the United States, the adaptations of French toiles for American customers had always been more functional and less ornate than the originals. Without the influence of Paris, the newly emerging American design aesthetic began to develop into an emphasis on mix-and-match ready-to-wear. The American look was more casual than that of Paris, and was distinctive for its relaxed, sporty fit.

BALANCING COUTURE AND PRACTICALITY
After the war, Paris again exerted its style leadership, but the advantages of ready-to-wear clothing continued to prove desirable in the fast-paced postwar era. By the 1960s, there was a new emphasis on youth and quick change, and haute couture began to lose its power of style leadership to the rapid pace of ready-to-wear.

Prêt-à-porter, meaning 'ready-to-wear' in French, was extremely controversial to the Chambre Syndicale. Many designers chose to create both couture and ready-to-wear collections, because it was increasingly difficult to make money from couture garments alone. The Syndicale fought against granting membership – and therefore the right to be considered a couturier in the strict sense of the word – to

↓ Maison Worth
Charles Frederick Worth was the first couturier to dictate to his customers what they should wear, and to present himself as the utmost authority on women's dress. Worth developed the practice of creating garments, or 'models', that he showed on young women selected for their likeness to Worth's wealthy clients. These models were seen twice a year or by special appointment, such as in this 1890s illustration showing ball gowns being chosen.

designers who participated in ready-to-wear, because it was felt that innovation, fit and technique would be diminished in importance. In fact, designers continued to create couture collections for the chance to be innovative, as well as to keep the techniques of couture alive.

INTERNATIONAL INFLUENCES

'Fashion capitals' were developed to add cachet to each country's contribution to fashion. Milan became known for its printed silks, superior wool suiting textiles, bright colours, precise tailoring and ornate handwork. London fashion existed on two sides of the style spectrum – conservatism on the one hand, and experimentation and even shock tactics on the other. London spurred on the youthful look that defined the 1960s, yet never lost its associations with legendary Savile Row tailoring. New York became known for an overall clean aesthetic, with saleable, practical pieces for everyday use. Paris continued to set trends and lead the way in the techniques of couture. Although the Chambre Syndicale was forced to concede that couture houses might exist outside of Paris, this did little to diminish the cachet of Parisian fashion.

In the 1980s, Japanese designers began to show in Paris, and irrevocably shook up international fashion, bringing new philosophies on silhouette, image and concept to the dialogue of fashion. In the late 1980s and early 1990s, Japanese designers were particularly influential on an emerging group of Belgian designers, whose approach to what fashion means in the contemporary context in turn affected other designers in New York, London, Milan and Paris.

LICENSING AND MARKETING

Throughout the 1960s, 1970s and 1980s, the fashion industry expanded exponentially as designers explored licences, marketing and diffusion lines (secondary lines of merchandise that retail at a lower price than a designer's principal, or 'signature', lines). Licences allowed designers to contract their names to other manufacturers. The practice of licensing had begun in the early 20th century with cosmetics and fragrance, but was now widely expanded. This meant that designers could get a large percentage of their profits from manufacturers, who used the designer's name to sell a variety of items, such as accessories, coats, decorative arts and occasionally even cars.

Initially, designers often did not exercise a great deal of care in the quality or look of their licensed products. Some designers lost control of their names in business deals, and others had the overall image of their name tarnished because of shoddy workmanship. Eventually, designers began to exert tighter controls in every facet of the merchandise.

Savvy marketing and advertising techniques helped designers to differentiate themselves in an increasingly competitive market. Eventually, these practices developed into lifestyle branding, which meant that there was a unified image or look to all of the designer's collections, including all the licences that were offered. Designers produced style narratives that created value for customers – value that was divorced from the actual product. In other words, a generic T-shirt suggested style cachet because of the brand that was displayed on the chest, rather than the inherent qualities of the actual T-shirt.

THE FUTURE OF FASHION

Today, many designers use their clothing collections, either couture or ready-to-wear, as a way to achieve notoriety that in turn sells product. Designers create a brand or image through innovations of style in their collections, but in reality the profit comes from the licences rather than the catwalk collections. If there is no brand cachet attached to the designer's name, the licences are not as valuable.

In a marketing arrangement that goes full circle, it is the licences that fund the collections, which in turn generate enough attention to sell the licences. This business practice means that designers are able to push the boundaries of innovation and suggest the future of fashion.

CHAPTER 1

DESIGNERS AS CELEBRITIES

Many fashion designers have used innovative approaches to marketing to create high value and prestige for their products. In many cases, they were effective at cultivating a successful brand image using methods that preceded modern advertising strategies – methods that are now common practice in nearly all business sectors.

PERSONAL CELEBRITY

Clothing, accessories and advertising methods have historically been coordinated to tell a story that a prospective consumer can literally buy into. Designers often place themselves within these narratives, using their own personal connection to the world of glamour as a branding strategy. By taking advantage of their unique position in the world of fashion, they are able to elevate themselves to the level of celebrity, where their fame becomes a large part of what creates value for the consumer.

The ability to recognize the potential for capitalizing on personal celebrity began at the turn of the 20th century. Early designers, such as Paul Poiret, focused on publicizing their work in competition with other couturiers on a relatively small scale compared to today's standards. Media and technology were limited, so Poiret often resorted to holding fashion shows and grand fetes in the public eye, or commissioning illustrations of his work to disseminate among his clientele. Young wealthy women could wear clothing by Poiret and be recognized for their new, modern way of living.

STYLE AND STATUS

Today, designers must compete on an international scale, creating a unique vision of fashion while providing an overwhelming amount of choice. Designers such as Karl Lagerfeld, Ralph Lauren, Calvin Klein and Tom Ford have excelled at creating celebrity identities that match their product. These celebrity designers carefully craft their image and use the allure of the fashion industry and the fashion press to advertise to the general public. Designers appeal to consumers by suggesting that if they buy designer clothing, wear designer perfume or co-opt a celebrity designer's style, they will be recognized for their own style and status.

BRANDING

Branding has now become essential for economic profit. The designer and the highly publicized fashion shows help to create an image that a group of consumers want to belong to. Even if these consumers cannot buy the high-priced clothing, they can buy the bags, glasses, shoes, hats, scarves, T-shirts, fragrance, cosmetics, jewellery or hosiery – or anything else with the designer's name on it. The sales of these lesser-priced items fund the high-profile catwalk pieces.

NAME RECOGNITION

Isaac Mizrahi exemplifies the 'friendly' celebrity – the newest incarnation of the celebrity designer. Mizrahi offers helpful hints to women with bodies that do not look like those of the models on the catwalk, but who want to attain fashionable glamour. Mizrahi has also created collections for department stores or in collaboration with mass-market companies, making him a household name. The goal of celebrity designers such as Mizrahi is one of creating name recognition and a desire to be associated with the designer's aesthetic.

Paul Poiret came to prominence at the cusp of the 20th century, and helped to define what a modern fashion designer would become. All that was exciting and magical about Paris at that time can be seen in Poiret's style legacy, which has become a rich source of inspiration for both designers and artists.

INFLUENCED BY

KEY
- ● fashion designer
- ◆ fashion house/brand
- ■ artistic influence
- ❖ cultural influence

● **Jacques Doucet**
Poiret worked for the established couturier and then set about destroying all the conventions on construction, proper dress and silhouette that he had been taught.

● **Charles Frederick Worth**
Worth represented the height of luxury and affectation in the burgeoning world of fashion. He was a dictator of style, often ordering his clients to wear particular colours. He was able to command this authority by creating sensitively crafted gowns that exhibited restraint and grace, yet were powerful in presence (right). Poiret rejected several precepts that Worth promoted, such as the wearing of corsets and formfitting gowns that controlled the shape of the body. However, what Poiret did extract from the 'father of couture' and his time working at the house of Worth was a sense of showmanship, theatricality and the idea of absolute tastemaker.

PAUL POIRET
French
(1879 Paris)

	Born April 20th in a rundown neighbourhood of Paris.	Couturier Madeleine Chéruit buys 12 designs from Poiret. He begins working for Jacques Doucet, where he creates a mantle for the actress Réjane that becomes very popular.		Having risen to head of tailoring, Poiret leaves Doucet to fulfill his military service.	Joins the house of Worth to create the practical garments that are worn with Worth's opulent evening gowns.	Founds his own house, moving premises several times over the years as his success and wealth mount.
CHRONOLOGY	**1879**	**1898**		**1900**	**1901**	**1903**

INSPIRED

● **Elsa Schiaparelli**
Schiaparelli met Poiret and was warmly encouraged by the established couturier to pursue a life in fashion. From him, she learned the importance of utilizing the energy of artists and pursuing the exhilaration of fashion.

● **Ralph Lauren**
Poiret was the first designer to do what Lauren has perfected: lifestyle branding. Like Poiret, Lauren offers decorative arts as well as a host of other products for a complete lifestyle vision. (Left: Ralph Lauren chair.)

● **Christian Dior**
The young Dior saw Poiret in Paris, and remembered the exuberant and artistic values by which Poiret lived and worked. Although the shy Dior would never be a showman like Poiret, a sense of the dramatic found its way into many of Dior's collections.

The dawn of the 20th century brought about massive transformations in Western society: a loosening of morals; experimentation in literature, art and design; and a revolution in thoughts, ideas and values that had seemed steadfast throughout the 19th century. What developed eventually became known as modernism, and Paul Poiret was there to witness and absorb those exciting changes.

Many designers of the time experimented with loosening the confines of women's dress, but Poiret gets most of the credit because of his superior skills in self-promotion. Poiret's designs did away with both the petticoat and, more radically, the corset. Along with Madeleine Vionnet, Poiret shifted the focus of crafting a garment away from pattern-drafting towards draping. This radical change of emphasis meant that the fabric hung or draped on the figure, rather than the body being forced to conform to the shape of the garment.

PATRON OF THE ARTS
Paris was the centre of the art world at that time. Poiret socialized with many well-known artists, including Constantin Brancusi, Robert Delaunay, Henri Matisse, Francis Picabia and Pablo Picasso. Poiret was a patron of the arts, and often held gallery shows in his atelier. He considered himself an artist, saying, 'Am I a fool when I dream of putting art into my dresses, a fool when I say dressmaking is an art? For I have always loved painters, and felt on equal footing with them. It seems to be that we practise the same craft, and that they are my fellow workers.'

Indeed, Poiret's primary marketing strategy was to promote his dresses and other products as works of art while presenting himself as an inspired artist. He travelled to Germany to visit the Wiener Werkstätte studio run by Josef Hoffmann. This collective of artists adopted some of the

Exotic mystery
This 1922 Paul Poiret ensemble interprets the Japanese kimono for a Western audience in sweeping lengths of velvet with chinchilla trim. The high collar and wide-brimmed hat give the model an air of mystery. Although offering a strikingly simplistic silhouette, the richness and plentitude of fabric suggest wealth and status for the Poiret customer.

→ **Neoclassical interpretations**
Paul Iribe's illustrations for the promotional brochure *Les Robes de Paul Poiret* in 1908 have become synonymous with the couturier. Poiret was attracted to Iribe's artistic style that highlighted the relative simplicity, bright colours and exoticism so appealing to Poiret's customers. The pieces are both luxurious and modern in their shape, texture and neoclassical silhouette.

INFLUENCED BY

KEY
● fashion designer
◆ fashion house/brand
■ artistic influence
❖ cultural influence

■ Denise Poiret
In 1905, Poiret married Denise Boulet, who became his primary muse. He said of her: 'My wife is the inspiration for all my creations; she is the expression of all my ideals.'

■ Neoclassical dress
From 1906 to 1911, Poiret's primary silhouette was inspired by neoclassical dress. This allowed him to rid the female figure of the corset and petticoats, and move away from the restrictive movement of earlier fashions.

PAUL POIRET CONTINUED

	1906–11	1910	1911
	Creates garments inspired by neoclassical dress that allow women to abandon the corset and petticoat. Commissions artists to create lavish promotional booklets for his designs.	The Ballets Russes performs Schéhérazade in Paris, inspiring Poiret with the rich fabrics and colours of the costumes. He introduces the hobble skirt, which allows the wearer to keep the ideal silhouette but inhibits her ability to walk.	Establishes a perfume and cosmetics company, and a decorative arts company. Hosts a lavish Eastern-themed fancy-dress ball that he uses to promote his new harem trousers.

CHRONOLOGY

INSPIRED

● John Galliano
Within Galliano's collections for the house of Dior as well as his eponymous line, a main source of inspiration is the time period when Poiret had the most influence on fashion. Galliano responds to the luxury of the period, and the haptic sensations that come from the exquisitely crafted garments that Poiret perfected. Both designers seem to be fascinated by the dichotomy of the modern woman – fearless and independent, yet tender and sensitive – and focus on the earthy delights of sensuality and sexual freedom.

● Ralph Rucci
Rucci delivers phenomenal craftsmanship with a sense of the dramatic. Like Poiret, Rucci is interested in the rich relationship between art and fashion.

→ **Smoky allure**
For his Autumn 2009 show for the house of Dior, John Galliano sent models down the catwalk with bee-stung lips, smoky eyes and clear references to the signature Poiret fur collar and loose fitted jacket.

utopian principles and philosophies of William Morris and the Arts and Crafts movement, but also utilized aspects of technology and the modern era. In 1911, Poiret was inspired to open his own art school, where young girls with artistic inclinations produced decorative arts, overseen by the textile artist Raoul Dufy. Poiret used the school as a marketing tool to justify the idea that all creations should be untainted and unrestrained by commodity culture.

LIFESTYLE BRANDING

Paul Poiret helped to establish the practice of what is known in the contemporary fashion world as lifestyle branding, as seen in the marketing strategies of designers such as Ralph Lauren or Calvin Klein. Poiret is credited with creating the first designer fragrances and cosmetics in 1911. He produced several different fragrances throughout his career, all with

'I am not commercial. Ladies come to me for a gown as they go to a distinguished painter to get their portrait put on canvas. I am an artist, not a dressmaker.'

Paul Poiret

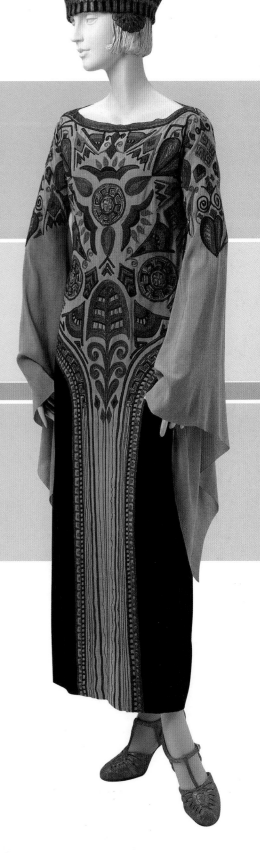

→ **French orientalism**
The French had long had a fascination with anything 'oriental', and Poiret continued this tradition. This 1923 dress by Poiret mimics the embroidery and shape of a caftan, and the hat is a type of turban. By interpreting this wholly utilitarian garment of the Middle East and North Africa, Poiret afforded women both ease and luxury.

● **Madeleine Vionnet**
Although a primary competitor, Vionnet shared Poiret's focus on draping as a major form of construction, as well as his abandonment of the corset.

● **Lucile (Lady Duff Gordon)**
The British fashion designer, who emphasized the emotionalism of her gowns, is credited with developing the first fashion show. As a contemporary of Poiret, she would undoubtedly have had a great impact on his notorious presentation style.

❖ **World dress**
Throughout his career, Poiret was inspired by the colourful and exotic costumes of the Ballets Russes, Asian dress such as the Japanese kimono, the Greek chiton, and North African and Middle Eastern caftans and turbans.

Tours North America, addressing women in lectures, negotiating distribution deals and acquiring the title 'king of fashion'.

Advertises reduced-price copies of his dresses in Vogue, calling them 'genuine reproductions'.

Unable to adapt to the new utilitarian aesthetic after WWI, Poiret closes his business.

Dies, impoverished, on April 30th.

1913   **1916–17**   **1929**   **1944**

● **Calvin Klein**
Poiret often used his personal life as a marketing tool, and promoted his wife, Denise, as his muse, something that Klein followed when he launched the fragrance Eternity to celebrate his marriage to Kelly Rector.

● **Alexander McQueen**
McQueen created dramatic shows in which the model or the clothing became a piece of art. Poiret considered himself an artist, and McQueen most assuredly agreed.

● **Romeo Gigli**
Gigli's collections are noted for their use of rich, textural fabrics and colours, and a sense of exoticism in the form of cocoon coats and draped dresses that echo Poiret's work.

personally designed or commissioned bottles. Clothing customers could also furnish their homes with the decorative arts and textiles from his art school.

KING OF FASHION
Poiret was seen as a celebrity and called the 'king of fashion' in the United States, a title given to him after a publicity tour in 1913. Indeed, his dresses were copied so much that Poiret was forced to create his own reduced-price copies in 1916–17. The illegal copies of his dresses meant that he was unable to collect on his creations, as well as diluting the impact of the original. However, Poiret was unable to adapt to the changes in fashion after World War I, typified by Coco Chanel's pared-down, sleek clothes. He died penniless and in obscurity, but his contributions to marketing and artistically crafted clothing will never be forgotten.

Karl Lagerfeld is a walking contradiction – skilfully balancing old and new, always changing, yet able to hold fast to the unique qualities of each of the brands that he so effortlessly designs. Directly involved in many aspects of fashion, from design and marketing to photography and advertising, Lagerfeld has become a powerhouse of design, helping to define 20th- and 21st-century style.

INFLUENCED BY

KEY
- ● fashion designer
- ◆ fashion house/brand
- ■ artistic influence
- ❖ cultural influence

● **Mariano Fortuny**
Fortuny was a man of many talents who sought to explore alternative outlets for his creativity, such as painting and photography, which is similar to Lagerfeld.

● **Thierry Mugler**
Mugler was one of the first designers to photograph his own advertising campaigns. Lagerfeld has since copied Mugler's lead, and expanded into fashion photography. (Right: Lagerfeld photographing a model on a bridge in Paris.)

● **Pierre Balmain**
Lagerfeld worked for the designer who famously said 'dressmaking is the architecture of movement', which seems to have clear connections to Lagerfeld's style for all the houses for which he designs.

KARL LAGERFELD
German
(1938 Hamburg)

CHRONOLOGY	1938	1952	1955	1955–63	1963–83
	Born September 10th in Hamburg.	Moves to Paris to attend high school at the Lycée Montaigne.	Wins first prize for a coat design in an International Wool Secretariat competition.	Works as assistant to Pierre Balmain for three years, then as design director for Jean Patou.	Freelances for houses such as Fendi and Chloé, becoming design director of both. Founds his own line, Impressions, in 1974, but it does not last long because of lack of funding.

INSPIRED

● **Anne Valérie Hash**
Hash was an intern at the house of Chanel and shares many of Lagerfeld's philosophies about couture, namely that it should be modernized. Both designers are also fond of Regency-era dandy Beau Brummell (right).

◆ **Viktor & Rolf**
The design duo admire Lagerfeld's business ingenuity and branding acumen, as well as his virtuosity in design.

● **Marc Jacobs**
Jacobs has certainly learned from Lagerfeld how to integrate pop culture into a designer collection. Lagerfeld has also paved the way for designers such as Jacobs to branch out into international markets.

● **Tom Ford**
Ford has said that Lagerfeld is the only other designer before Ford to have succeeded in working for so many international houses at one time.

The contradictions of Karl Lagerfeld pervade all aspects of his life, from his personal image to the many fashion houses and projects that he has taken on in his widely diverse career. Lagerfeld cannot walk down the street without being thronged for autographs, yet he hides behind his dark glasses, white ponytail, and starched Beau Brummell collar, or his signature fan of an earlier persona. Lagerfeld does not share any aspects of his personal life.

MANIPULATION OF IMAGE
Understanding what it means to be a fashion celebrity, Lagerfeld has developed his image and style of dress in order to become a character rather than a real person: 'I don't want to be real in other people's minds; I want to be an apparition.' Clothing is a mere by-product to the larger idea of brand, so when Lagerfeld quips that 'Now I am like a

personage who is nearly unrelated to fashion', he is commenting on the manipulation of image that is now more important than any product created in the luxury market.

Understanding this significant fact is what makes it possible for Lagerfeld to be so successful at designing up to six different collections, multiple times a year, without ever being accused of copying himself.

CEMENTING A BRAND
The name that Lagerfeld is most closely associated with is the house of Chanel, which he resurrected in 1983. Lagerfeld understood what had made Chanel successful in the past, and what was needed for this success to continue. His formula serves the needs of Chanel's more conservative customers, who take the Chanel suit at face value, but also infuses the house with a younger, more adventurous image.

Architecture for the body

Although Lagerfeld is a chameleon from one fashion house to another, what is consistent is his preference for graphic and architectural qualities. The Karl Lagerfeld Spring 2010 collection features structures that suggest the figure underneath, but deny the natural form. The silver motifs offer an alternative to the signature black and white that Lagerfeld so often uses, but are no less graphic or full of impact.

→ Lagerfeld as muse

In the Autumn 2009 Chanel collection, Lagerfeld makes reference to his own personal look, inspired by Beau Brummell, and combines it with a subtle Elizabethan reference in the signature Chanel tweeds. This not only reinforces Lagerfeld's own celebrity but also extends the Chanel oeuvre.

 INFLUENCED BY

KEY
● fashion designer
◆ fashion house/brand
■ artistic influence
❖ cultural influence

● Paul Poiret
Poiret was a celebrity designer who used his image and life to create a brand before the term was invented. Also like Lagerfeld, Poiret was a virtuoso in combining rich and ornate sources of inspiration to create a fantasy world for himself and his customers.

● Coco Chanel
Chanel has had an overwhelming influence on Lagerfeld, as he continues to play with and manipulate her early ideas of dress. Lagerfeld appreciates her innovations in fashion, but also her savvy business sense and intuitive understanding of branding.

KARL LAGERFELD CONTINUED

	While continuing as design director of Fendi, Lagerfeld also becomes artistic director of Chanel.	Launches ready-to-wear for Chanel, as well as his own labels Karl Lagerfeld and KL.	Begins photography as a professional career, creating his own advertising campaigns as well as editorials for major fashion publications.	Designs for German clothing manufacturer Klaus Steilmann.	Becomes design director for Chloé once again.
CHRONOLOGY	**1983**	**1984**	**1987**	**1987–95**	**1992–97**

→ INSPIRED

◆ Clements Ribeiro
The design duo use kitsch and pop culture in their work, effortlessly bringing diverse inspirations into a single collection. This coat dress from Spring 2010 (left) references not only the ubiquitous Chanel but also Lagerfeld's interpretations of Chanel that use graphics and pop culture to reinvigorate the label. One can also see references to the 1960s and pop art, which have been important style influences for many years.

● Julien Macdonald
Macdonald worked for Lagerfeld at the house of Chanel as director of knitwear. He credits Lagerfeld with teaching him about women of status and culture.

● John Galliano
Galliano sent out a Russian-inspired Autumn 2009 collection for his eponymous line after Lagerfeld's Pre-Autumn 2009 collection of the same inspiration for Chanel.

Lagerfeld has attracted a great deal of attention by pulling together the hallowed Chanel name with pop culture images inspired by rap, street culture and current trends. Chanel herself said, 'Fashion passes, style remains. La Mode is made of a few amusing ideas, which are used in order to be used up and replaced by others in a new collection. A style should be preserved even as it is renewed and evolved.'

Each season, Lagerfeld examines an aspect of Chanel's image, style, personal life or favourites, such as the camellia flower, and offers a seemingly unlimited number of variations and explorations of the classic Chanel style. By continuously revisiting the icons of the house and Coco herself, Lagerfeld has successfully cemented the brand to become one that is effortlessly recognized. As Lagerfeld says, 'I remember Voltaire's line: Everything that needs an explanation or description is not worth it.'

STRANGENESS IN THE PROPORTIONS

For all of his understanding of the constancy of image, Lagerfeld also abhors routine and boredom: 'I love change; I am attached to nothing.' Lagerfeld has worked at several esteemed fashion houses during his career, but leaves when he is no longer interested, or when he feels that he is limited in what he can achieve within the parameters of the house.

Lagerfeld created his own fashion house to explore a more personal aesthetic that centers on an architectural, often asymmetrical, and multilayered structured look. Lagerfeld, who is fond of quoting the many books he has read, says, 'Marlow said: There is no beauty without some strangeness in the proportions.' He has recently sold his own line and the diffusion collections that bear his name to Tommy Hilfiger, either for reasons of boredom or as a nod to the need to limit his output.

➜ Fendi fur

Karl Lagerfeld has been able to revolutionize the use of furs for the house of Fendi. By treating furs as fabrics, Lagerfeld has extended their use, technique and application so that they are no longer associated with the traditional mink coat. Lagerfeld has styled furs for the 21st century by using futuristic symbols, such as the geometric shapes and exaggerated shoulders in this piece from Autumn 2008.

● Jean Patou

Lagerfeld worked for the house of Patou early in his career, and was inspired by Patou's connection of activewear to couture to create his own youthful interpretation of the long-standing tradition.

● Vivienne Westwood

Westwood was one of the first designers to embrace pop culture as a primary source of inspiration. It was not until the latter part of the 20th century that Lagerfeld really explored kitsch.

● Yves Saint Laurent

Although the two designers were contemporaries, Saint Laurent successfully blurred the line between couture and ready-to-wear, and was the first major couturier to play with a variety of inspirations, paving the way for designers such as Lagerfeld.

Fulfilling a lifelong goal, he opens a gallery in Paris that exhibits photography, art, books and clothing. Launches the Lagerfeld Gallery label.

Tommy Hilfiger acquires Lagerfeld's signature lines, with Lagerfeld remaining creative director. The Costume Institute of New York's Metropolitan Museum of Art presents a show on Chanel, featuring the work of both Coco and Lagerfeld. Launches K. Karl Lagerfeld, a denim and T-shirt diffusion line.

1998

2004–06

● L'Wren Scott

The American designer is making a name for herself by creating beautiful gowns and feminine suits that reinterpret historical references and reveal the influence of Lagerfeld through shape and styling.

⬅ Ruff and ribbons

This outfit from L'Wren Scott's Spring 2010 collection is preeminently feminine, hugging the female form in berry and sweet pink, but alludes to Regency-era style icon Beau Brummell, as brought back into prominence by Karl Lagerfeld. The ruff and ribbons, combined with the tailored 1940s-style suit, are similar in approach to Lagerfeld's reinvention of historical references, making them wholly new and fresh looking.

'I work by instinct without asking myself too many questions.'

Karl Lagerfeld

Ralph Lauren has made millions by using iconic imagery and aspirational symbols of success to create a globally recognized label. The strong marketing and brand development that Lauren pioneered has helped to alter the international fashion business.

INFLUENCED BY

KEY
- ● fashion designer
- ◆ fashion house/brand
- ■ artistic influence
- ❖ cultural influence

● Adrian
Adrian used symbols from American heritage to promote a uniquely American way of dressing. Just as Adrian used gingham, patchwork and pilgrim hats, Lauren uses Ivy League, American West and Hollywood's golden age (right) to create Americana.

● Madeleine Vionnet
Although Lauren's technical prowess does not even approach Vionnet's mastery, he is clearly inspired by her bias-cut pieces and the attention to the figure that they bring.

● Mainbocher
In the 1930s, Mainbocher was known for his uncomplicated yet preeminently elegant clothing. Many of Lauren's eveningwear pieces borrow Mainbocher's aesthetic.

● Halston
Halston had a clean aesthetic, and was the first designer to deal with licensing agreements and marketing – business practices that Lauren perfected.

RALPH LAUREN
American
(1939 New York)

	Born Ralph Lifschitz on October 14th in the Bronx, New York.	Rejecting the standard thin dark tie, Lauren designs wide ties in flamboyant and colourful prints. Selling them under the label Polo, they are immediately popular.	Becomes the first designer to establish a shop-within-a-shop boutique for men in Bloomingdale's department store in New York.	Launches womenswear collection. Opens a store in Beverly Hills, California.	Launches the Polo shirt in 24 colours, as well as Polo accessories.
CHRONOLOGY	**1939**	**1967**	**1969**	**1971**	**1972**

INSPIRED

● Isaac Mizrahi
Mizrahi has developed a look that is often based on the golden age of Hollywood, so similarities between Mizrahi and Lauren are inevitable.

● Michael Kors
Kors often uses the same symbols of Americana as Lauren, such as nautical or equestrian, as well as bright colours and bold graphics.

● Carolina Herrera
In her Autumn 2008 (left) and Autumn 2009 collections, Herrera featured colours, silhouettes and details – such as from European-style hunting clothing – that are also often present in Lauren's collections.

● Tom Ford
Ford has cited Lauren as a model for his own ventures into marketing, branding and the luxury markets. Ford has also borrowed aesthetic ideas from Lauren, bringing Americana to Italy and Paris.

Ralph Lauren is the first to say that he is more of a stylist and a marketer than a designer: 'I'm not a fashion person. I'm antifashion. I don't like to be part of that world. It's too transient. I have never been influenced by it. I'm interested in longevity, timeliness, style – not fashion.' Lauren's clothing revolves around repeating themes, creating a consistent brand identity that is recognized the world over.

ASPIRATIONAL SYMBOLS
Lauren's astounding success is based on his ability to communicate basic human desires, and translate them into lifestyle branding and product. Lauren has allowed the middle-classes to look as if they belong to the upper-classes, notably in the 1980s with the preppy look. He says, 'I was always inspired by those kind of prep-school people and their clothes, by classic things, by the way those people looked and dressed.'

Lauren has a knack for employing symbols and iconic images that suggest attributes that are universally attractive. Symbols of the Wild West, Native Americans or even the Great Depression hold a sentimental value and represent basic human qualities of fortitude, perseverance and nobility. Lauren suggests upward mobility and aspirations by utilizing images of the British gentry, Hollywood or East Coast privilege.

A TOTAL LIFESTYLE
Lauren's success lies not only in his use of aspirational imagery but also in his development of an overarching marketing strategy and branding to create a total environment. An example of the total environment can be seen in his Madison Avenue flagship store in New York. The interior of this French Renaissance mansion, built in 1890, was

→ Depression chic

This look from the Spring 2010 show not only recalls Ralph Lauren's major contribution to film costume in the form of *The Great Gatsby*, but also uses the reference as a metaphor for contemporary financial difficulties. In Lauren's unerring American optimism, the collection suggests that no matter what the situation, we always find a way to be chic and stylish.

'I'm not designing clothes, I'm creating a world.'

Ralph Lauren

• Jean Patou

French designer Patou popularized activewear as daywear, and stuck to clean, simple lines and unadorned silhouettes – all of which Lauren is identified with.

• Claire McCardell

Like Lauren, McCardell was interested in making clothing that functioned well in the day-to-day world.

• Coco Chanel

Chanel and Lauren have many things in common -- they both changed womenswear by borrowing from menswear; they were not interested in altering the world of fashion, but rather in creating wearable clothes that functioned well; and they each built an empire on their straightforward approach to fashion.

Designs trendsetting costumes for the films The Great Gatsby and Annie Hall.	*Begins the now famous and often copied multipage advertisements in which the clothing is not highlighted as much as the image.*	*Launches Polo Sport, a fitness collection.*	*Introduces the Purple Label, Lauren's take on Savile Row tailoring.*	*Polo Ralph Lauren goes public on the New York Stock Exchange.*	*Launches the Blue Label, a reinterpretation of his classic Polo womenswear, and then the Black Label, a high-end interpretation of Polo Sport.*
1974–77	**1979**	**1993**	**1994**	**1997**	**2002–05**

• Tommy Hilfiger

Hilfiger has a clear association with the business practices of Lauren, as well as his aesthetic and branding. In fact, Hilfiger was caught in legal wrangling early in his career, because of the similarities between the two designers' product.

• Brian Reyes

Reyes featured equestrian style and a hint of British tweeds in his Autumn 2008 collection, both of which Lauren has also reinterpreted throughout his career.

• Derek Lam

Lam's Spring 2005 collection featured a romantic prairie look (left) that was often seen in Lauren's collections during the 1980s.

← American navy

The nautical look has become a tried and tested theme, and was cemented by Ralph Lauren. Here, Tommy Hilfiger creates an updated version for Spring 2010 that carries a sense of breezy freedom.

remodelled to display not only Lauren's clothing collections, but also his interior decorating and home products, fragrance and accessories, all of which reinforce the sense of belonging to an exclusive world.

For those not able to visit the flagship store, the lifestyle advertisements do the same thing. Lauren was the first to take out multiple-page advertisements that read like a photo album, offering a glimpse into a better place: 'The multipage ads are like movies, broad strokes of excitement, multi-dimensional; if I could have made the models speak, I would have.' To drive the idea that these dreams are attainable, non-models were often used to create a suggestion of reality. Ralph Lauren has expanded well beyond clothing to create a total lifestyle.

Calvin Klein perfected the use of controversial advertising to stimulate sales of items that are as benign as white underwear or plain denim jeans. His business model has set the standard for today's fashion companies, in which licences are the primary moneymaker and the actual collection of clothing by the designer is used as an image or brand.

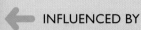

INFLUENCED BY

KEY
- ● fashion designer
- ◆ fashion house/brand
- ■ artistic influence
- ❖ cultural influence

● Halston
Calvin Klein was said to be fascinated by Halston, a celebrity designer who used his image as a branding tool. From Halston, Klein understood the power of courting celebrities and being seen about town (right: Halston with Bianca Jagger and Liza Minnelli at Studio 54 in New York, 1978). Halston introduced his signature fragrance in the 1970s to immediate success; Klein recognized this as an important business move and strove to duplicate it. The two designers also had a similar aesthetic of clean, unadorned silhouettes that became the hallmark of American design.

CALVIN KLEIN
American
(1942 New York)

CHRONOLOGY	1942	1959–62	1962–64	1968	1973–75
	Born November 19th in the Bronx, New York.	Attends New York's Fashion Institute of Technology.	Works as design assistant for suit and coat manufacturer Dan Millstein, but leaves to work as a freelance designer after a disagreement.	Forms eponymous company with school friend Barry Schwartz, producing men's suits and coats in the moderate price range. Women are also attracted to Klein's clean-cut style.	Wins Coty American Fashion Critics' Award for three successive years.

INSPIRED

● Narciso Rodriguez
An assistant to Klein for many years, Rodriguez was expected to be the natural choice as successor when Klein withdrew as creative director after the sale of his company. Rodriguez instead opted to launch his eponymous collection and venture beyond the established Klein aesthetic. Rodriguez was clearly shaped by his time in the company, always producing wearable, subtly coloured collections (left).

● Dries Van Noten
Several of the latest collections of Van Noten feature soft cashmere coatings and an emphasis on the interchangeable separates and blazer jackets that Klein was known for.

● Thakoon Panichgul
Panichgul's soft grey coats and light blousy dresses suggest the clean, elegant, but casual look that Klein helped to popularize.

Calvin Klein is a true New York designer, having been born and raised in the Bronx, and attended school at the famed Fashion Institute of Technology. Klein has helped to change irrevocably the way in which business is done and money is made in the fashion industry, both in New York and internationally.

Klein learned from a long line of fashion designers who had used licensing as a way to generate funds for their primary collections. Fellow American Halston and French designer Pierre Cardin had done much to pioneer the idea of licensing, but neither had understood the use of exclusivity or branding to the extent that Calvin Klein eventually achieved. Klein strictly reserved artistic control over all products and advertising bearing his name, which achieved an overall distinctive look for the company.

CREATING A HALLMARK LOOK
The collections of clothing were the primary focus in the beginning of Klein's career. Along with several of his contemporaries, such as Perry Ellis, Halston and Giorgio Armani, Klein wanted to create wearable clothing for an increasingly female workforce. Klein focused on soft tailoring, neutral colour palettes and interchangeable pieces that helped women look professional but not stuffy. He used luxurious fabrics, such as cashmere, silk and Italian wool suitings, in silhouettes that were largely unadorned for an easy elegance. The formula worked well and became the hallmark look of any Calvin Klein collection. Having a narrowly defined look helped to establish a known brand identity, and inspired loyalty from customers who knew what they were going to get.

← **The New York look**

In this 1972 look, Calvin Klein created a quintessential New York aesthetic that defined American fashion for well over 30 years. Interchangeable separates that are easy to wear, sharp in simplicity and borrow the best elements of menswear helped to create a wardrobe for the professional woman newly defining her position in the workforce.

● **Giorgio Armani**

Contemporaries of each other, both designers strove to create clothing that utilized soft tailoring and a neutral colour palette. Both also used a strong brand identity to keep loyal customers. In 1994, Klein poached Gabriella Forte from Armani by offering her the position of president and chief operating officer.

● **Paul Poiret**

The two designers' aesthetics could not be more different, but Poiret achieved many firsts that Klein would undoubtedly have learned from, including the use of one's personal life as a marketing tool.

Licenses jeans to Carl Rosen's company Puritan. More than 200,000 pairs are sold as soon as they hit store shelves.

Introduces TV commercial in which a teenage Brooke Shields suggestively says, 'You want to know what comes between me and my Calvins? Nothing.'

1978   **1980**

◆ **Akris**

The Swiss company that shows in Paris, helmed by creative director Albert Kriemler, has a long history of creating saleable and wearable clothing that borrows a great deal from Klein, from the neutral colour palette to the unadorned silhouette (right).

'I don't feel this sense of life achievement. While I recognize that we've managed to do a few good things, I'm still looking at how to do it all better, and how to get to the next place.'

Calvin Klein

→ Activewear as daywear
As seen in this Spring 1992 swimwear look, Klein's work helped to dissolve the boundaries between activewear and daywear, reflecting the increased importance of physical fitness and controlled beauty that is so much a part of our contemporary society.

 INFLUENCED BY

KEY
● fashion designer
◆ fashion house/brand
■ artistic influence
❖ cultural influence

● Coco Chanel
Chanel used menswear as a primary source of inspiration, and did not radically change the look of her collections from season to season, in the same way as Klein. Chanel is a symbol to all designers of practical, wearable clothing.

● Claire McCardell
McCardell, the developer of the American look of practical yet elegant clothing, has undoubtedly inspired the quintessential 1980s and 1990s designer Klein. McCardell's influence can be seen in Klein's collections, from the wearable sporty looks to the well-made construction that answered the needs of the women of the time.

CALVIN KLEIN CONTINUED

CHRONOLOGY	Hires Bruce Weber to photograph men in his new underwear collection, resulting in an unprecedented erotic portrayal of men in advertising. Introduces women's underwear shortly afterward.	Creates a controversial, but successful, underwear commercial suggesting group sex.	With the underwear business proving too successful to handle, Klein sells it to Kayser-Roth Corporation, but retains artistic control.	Obsession perfume advertisements with blurred pictures of a sexual encounter help to sell $50 million of the fragrance in the first year alone.
	1982	**1983**	**1984**	**1985**

→ INSPIRED

● Tom Ford for Gucci
Calvin Klein blazed the way in sexual and provocative advertising that also supplied a consistent brand identity. Ford has used similar tactics with great success as the designer for Gucci. (Left: Controversial Calvin Klein Jeans advertisement, 1995.)

● Tommy Hilfiger
A contemporary of Klein, Hilfiger has been influenced by Klein's use of celebrities to promote his fashion collections, as well as connecting to the rap music industry as a branding tool. Klein premiered a similar association with the music world by using the 1990s rapper Marky Mark for his underwear advertisements.

COURTING CONTROVERSY

Klein quickly learned that associations with celebrities, licensing agreements and controversial advertising would offset any boredom that might come from such a predictable look. In 1980, 15-year-old Brooke Shields appeared in Klein advertisements, suggestively posed with quotations such as 'Reading is to the mind what Calvins are to the body' or 'You want to know what comes between me and my Calvins? Nothing.' The ads caused an immediate uproar, and helped to generate $12.5 million in royalties for Calvin Klein in 1980 alone. Klein defined his advertising strategy for the remainder of his career by saying, 'The only way to advertise is by not focusing on the product.'

In 1986, Klein was married for the second time, to employee Kelly Rector, a beautiful brunette. Not long afterwards, Klein launched the fragrance Eternity, with advertisements featuring models who resembled Kelly and Calvin. Eternity is one of many successful fragrances, but is unique for its use of the designer's personal life as a way to sell the product.

Calvin Klein was also one of the first designers to gear advertisements towards the X generation, eschewing the use of supermodels popular in the 1980s in favour of the young waifish model Kate Moss, and creating the successful unisex fragrance ck one and the diffusion clothing line ck Calvin Klein.

→ Leather adventure

In this Spring 2000 Klein ensemble, the light blue leather jacket references not only motorcycle jackets, imbuing women's clothing with a sense of adventure, but also suggests scuba wear, reinforcing the activewear element that is so often seen in Klein's work.

● Norman Norell

Norell was an important American designer who combined the elegance of French collections with the practicality of the American market. Klein would have certainly understood the need to balance these two important components.

● Hubert de Givenchy

The French couturier epitomized the clean, unadorned look that Calvin Klein strove for. Although Klein never created gowns like Givenchy, he did produce dramatic eveningwear along the same lines as Givenchy's many dresses for Audrey Hepburn films.

● Ralph Lauren

Lauren went to the same school in the Bronx as Klein, but was five years younger. Klein paved the way for Lauren, who created a business empire based on marketing and branding the American aesthetic.

1987	1988	1991	1994	1995	2003
Sale of his business to manufacturing company Triangle Industries is stopped because of the financial crash of the late 1980s.	Introduces Eternity perfume to celebrate his marriage to Kelly Rector.	Launches the perfume Escape.	Launches ck one, a unisex fragrance, with advertisements featuring a young Kate Moss.	Advertisements for Calvin Klein Jeans are accused of being suggestive of child pornography.	Calvin Klein, Inc. is sold to Phillips-Van Heusen Corporation, one of the world's largest apparel companies. Klein withdraws to an advisory role.

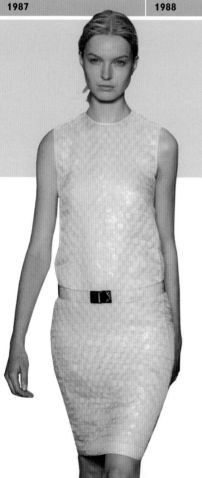

● Francisco Costa

After working with Klein since 2001, the Brazilian designer took over the helm of Calvin Klein Collection womenswear in 2002. Costa has taken this luxury tier of the Klein brand in a different direction, but still epitomizes Klein's unadorned look. Costa has been criticized for venturing too far into the artistic side of fashion, wanting to explore ideas of texture and, most importantly, shape. The latest collections are more closely tied to Klein's branded look, so it will be interesting to see if Costa can balance innovation with brand identity.

● Italo Zucchelli

Under the leadership of Klein for six seasons before becoming head designer for Calvin Klein Collection menswear in 2004, Zucchelli has continued the clean look of the Klein aesthetic.

← House rules

In his Spring 2009 collection for Calvin Klein, Francisco Costa replicates the Klein aesthetic perfectly by offering a clean, wearable dress that is young and sporty as well as professional.

SELLING AN IMAGE

Calvin Klein, Inc. is now an international business, with stores and products all over the world, selling items for the home, underwear, fragrance and clothing in a wide range of price points. In today's market, clothing companies no longer rely on the clothing to sell, but rather to provide an image that the customer can buy into. Licensing such a wide range of products allows the consumer to buy into the image, even if they cannot afford the designer clothing. Calvin Klein may not have invented this business strategy, but he did success-fully negotiate it and is therefore a major influence on all other designers.

Tom Ford's legacy has been to define the end-of-the-20th-century aesthetic by propelling the luxury market to dizzying heights. His work for the house of Gucci refined and influenced the marketing and branding practices of international companies, and created trends that can still be seen today.

 INFLUENCED BY

KEY
● fashion designer
◆ fashion house/brand
■ artistic influence
❖ cultural influence

● **Halston**
Not only has Ford adopted much of Halston's famous knit dressing and jewellery work with Elsa Peretti, but he has also modelled himself on many of Halston's early business innovations. Halston was a pioneer in licensing, and recognized that being a designer meant dealing with the business just as much as being creative. Halston also used his urbane and debonair looks as well as his active social life as marketing tools.

● **Ralph Lauren**
Lauren was a pioneer in lifestyle branding, creating a desire for membership into the luxury club defined by a WASP aesthetic. Ford took the idea and adapted it to the new Gucci international brand.

● **Karl Lagerfeld**
German-born Lagerfeld took over the iconic French house of Chanel as well as French Chloé and Italian Fendi. Lagerfeld set a precedent that Ford followed when he went to Italian Gucci.

● **Marc Jacobs**
Ford worked for Jacobs at Perry Ellis, undoubtedly learning from him that traditional American design could be limiting, and that a new aesthetic was needed to create worldwide success.

TOM FORD
American
(1961 Texas)

Born August 27th in Austin, Texas. Ford cites his mother and maternal grandmother as primary style influences.	*Initially pursues acting, but then attends New York's Parsons School of Design. Transfers to Parsons Paris and works as an intern in the house of Chloé. Returns to New York and works for ready-to-wear designer Cathy Hardwick and then Perry Ellis.*		*Moves to Italy to work for Gucci, eventually becoming creative director.*	*Creates an advertising campaign, with photographer Mario Testino, that puts an almost bankrupt Gucci back on the map.*
CHRONOLOGY	**1961**	**1982–90**	**1990–94**	**1995**

 INSPIRED

● **Donatella Versace**
After her brother Gianni's death, Donatella was forced to create a new look that was reminiscent of the Versace aesthetic, but also uniquely her own – just as Ford was actively exploiting so much of what her brother had established.

◆ **Dolce & Gabbana**
Dolce & Gabbana have used sex and shock advertising to their advantage while utilizing the amazing textiles and dressmaking traditions of their native Italy. Ford paved the way for straddling the two sides of fashion.

● **Alessandro Dell'Acqua**
The Italian designer has shown several luxurious yet blatantly sexy pieces that are reminiscent of Ford (left).

● **Stella McCartney**
Gucci and Ford helped McCartney launch her eponymous line. She has undoubtedly learned a great deal of solid business practices from the American designer.

Tom Ford epitomizes the concept of globalized fashion, combining all that is best from both sides of the Atlantic. Ford learned a business-savvy and pragmatic approach to fashion from his American predecessors, such as Halston, Calvin Klein and Ralph Lauren, and brought it to a European company to create an international marketing trend that has directed the fashion industry since the mid-1990s.

LUXURY AND LIFESTYLE
Tom Ford recognized the connection between luxury and lifestyle, and understood the draw of confident sexuality. He created an aura of luxury and refined living that so many craved after the recession in the late 1980s and early 1990s. Ford makes no excuses for his particular aim of financial success: 'I've always wanted to make beautiful things in a realistic manner. I am a commercial designer. I am proud of

that – and, by the way, I believe that can be harder than being a fantasy designer. As for impact on my peers that has never been important to me. Impact on the customer; yes obviously. I think about the customer.'

The fact that Tom Ford is also attractive has helped to cement the power of the Gucci brand. Ford understood his own appeal and used it to his best advantage: 'People criticize me a lot for being so identified with the brand. But all designer brands were really built on the personalities of their designers… Designer brands are aspirational.'

A NEED FOR FAMILIARITY
Tom Ford came to fashion at the right time, as people's fears and concerns about the oncoming 21st century surfaced, countered by society's attraction to the rapid growth of technology and globalization. Ford astutely understood that

← Modern glamazon

This Autumn 2006 look by Tom Ford for Gucci epitomizes Ford's formula of utilizing historical or cultural references, such as the 1980s disco era, while changing the proportions and creating a sexualized glamour to meet the needs of a contemporary market.

↓ Gucci cool

Frida Giannini's 2009 collection for Gucci pulls from the developed system of aloof and cool sexuality developed by Ford, and references Ford's use of jewel-toned fabrics to create a feeling of richness and luxury.

• Gianni Versace

The Italian designer was one of the first to use nudity and brazen sexuality paired with a type of rock 'n' roll aesthetic, which Ford took and expounded upon.

• Calvin Klein

Ford has been influenced by Klein's use of sex in advertisement campaigns as well as by his clean, largely monochromatic aesthetic.

• Helmut Lang

Ford has stated that he admires the slow development of Lang's vision, and is no doubt influenced by Lang's clean silhouette that often exhibits a sinister sexuality.

Gucci buys a controlling stake in Yves Saint Laurent and appoints Ford creative director. Saint Laurent leaves after disagreements over Ford's direction. Gucci buys out Rive Gauche (YSL ready-to-wear line) and Ford takes over as creative director.	Presents last collection for Rive Gauche before leaving Gucci.	Forms Tom Ford company, collaborating with Estée Lauder to create beauty products and fragrances. Launches Tom Ford sunglasses.	Presents a men's collection and opens a New York flagship store.	Opens boutiques in Switzerland and Canada. Directs his first film, A Single Man.
2000–02	**2004**	**2005**	**2006–07**	**2008**

• Alessandra Facchinetti

The Italian designer who immediately followed Ford at Gucci lasted only two seasons because she did not depart from the aesthetic that Ford created.

• Frida Giannini

As Ford's successor at Gucci after Alessandra Facchinetti, Giannini has needed to negotiate the phenomenal success of Gucci's comeback with her own aesthetic. There are many references to Ford's iconic luxe looks, from monochromatic dyed fur to matt jersey dresses with inserted jewellery. Although Giannini continues to focus on luxury, she has made a concerted effort to define a new, more contemporary sense of it.

the dominant aesthetic of revivals in the 1990s was based on our desire to forget the unpleasantness of the rapidly changing world around us and rely on the known and familiar. As Ford said, 'We seem to have some deep seated need for familiarity, and at the same time, an obsession with newness.'

'A fashion designer's job is to take a feeling that is in the air and turn it into something tangible that people can buy, to be able to tap into that zeitgeist and figure out what sort of physical thing can be created that people can buy into.'

Tom Ford

Isaac Mizrahi has expanded his career well beyond being merely a fashion designer to becoming a celebrity who provides style guidance to the masses. His bubbly personality aside, Mizrahi speaks from a solid understanding of the everyday woman's clothing needs.

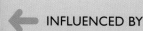 **INFLUENCED BY**

KEY
● fashion designer
◆ fashion house/brand
■ artistic influence
❖ cultural influence

● Claire McCardell
Mizrahi is steeped in the American look that McCardell created of practical, comfortable, but elegant clothing. References to 'McCardellisms', her signature design touches, have appeared throughout Mizrahi's career.

● Halston
Halston helped to refine the American style first conceived by Claire McCardell into a more contemporary aesthetic. Like Mizrahi, Halston was also a celebrity designer who appeared in the media, influencing style and trend direction.

● Adrian
Hollywood has always been an undercurrent of Mizrahi's style. Adrian was very fond of gingham, which is also a Mizrahi favourite, as featured in his collections for Liz Claiborne (left). In 2001, Mizrahi created the costumes for a Broadway revival of *The Women*; Adrian was famous for designing costumes for the 1939 movie version.

ISAAC MIZRAHI
American
(1961 New York)

	Born October 14th in Brooklyn. His father is a clothing manufacturer.	Attends performing arts school before studying at Parsons School of Design. Works as a design assistant at Perry Ellis and then Calvin Klein.	Launches his own label. Runs advertisements featuring himself in his studio. The house of Chanel invests in his company.	Launches IS**C diffusion line. Releases Unzipped documentary about developing a collection.	After erratic sales, Chanel withdraws financial support, forcing Mizrahi to close his company.
CHRONOLOGY	**1961**	**1974–85**	**1987–92**	**1995**	**1998**

 INSPIRED

● Behnaz Sarafpour
The young New York designer has the same love of 1950s glamour that Mizrahi has displayed so prominently in his career, as seen in Sarafpour's Spring 2005 collection (right).

● Christopher Kane
Kane's Spring 2010 collection centred on the use of gingham, a Mizrahi staple.

● Michael Kors
Kors has followed in Mizrahi's footsteps to become a celebrity designer. Kors is a popular judge on the television fashion show *Project Runway*.

● Phillip Lim
Lim has an aesthetic that combines the dressy with the casual, and the luxurious with the simple – echoing Mizrahi's design philosophies.

Mizrahi has always had two primary creative interests in his life: acting, films and theatre on the one hand; style, colour and designing clothes on the other. He has often flipped back and forth between fashion and performance, but always manages to combine the two in his work.

Mizrahi's fashion sense is influenced by the films he grew up with. In the 1995 *Unzipped* documentary about Mizrahi's development of a collection, one of the designer's primary influences was the 1922 documentary film *Nanook of the North* about life in the Arctic. Film and theatre help to inform Mizrahi's aesthetic, which is consistently recognizable, despite the many shifts of his career.

AFFORDABLE FASHION
The tradition of affordable fashion, introduced by designers such as Claire McCardell, has clearly influenced Mizrahi. This,

combined with his love of performance and his flair for Hollywood glamour, has made the designer into a style guru and media personality. Mizrahi has written several style books, appeared on numerous talk shows, judged others in style competitions and also hosted his own shows.

There are many designers, such as Ralph Lauren and Tom Ford, who use their own celebrity to enhance the aspirational branding of their products – that is, to create a premium, high-cost brand that people can aspire to own. Isaac Mizrahi has become a household name as a designer who is more concerned with reality and the everyday needs of working women. Indeed, Mizrahi's work with discount retailer Target cleared the way for many other designers, including Proenza Schouler, Jonathan Saunders, Patrick Robinson and Alexander McQueen, to design for the mass-market chain.

← Think pink

Although Elsa Schiaparelli may have first popularized the colour pink, Mizrahi has brought it into contemporary culture. This Autumn 2008 look is a nod to Bonnie Cashin's love of mohair, but is uniquely Mizrahi in colour and styling. The silhouette is from Mizrahi's favourite era: the 1950s and the age of Doris Day.

↓ Easy-going couture

Oscar de la Renta brings Mizrahi's brand of spontaneous and easy-going style into the world of couture in this Spring 1999 ensemble. The combination of a man's-style shirt tied at the waist with a 1950s-style circle skirt suggests elegant party scenes from the 1950s era.

● Bonnie Cashin

Influenced by Cashin's clean, uncomplicated designs and skilled use of fabrics, Mizrahi even created a mohair skirt with the same hooks at the waist that Cashin made famous.

● Calvin Klein

About his time working for Klein, Mizrahi said, 'I learned a lot about tailoring, about eliminating. I got to observe someone in his prime.'

● Gianni Versace

Mizrahi cited Versace as one of the 20th century's best designers. Versace's colour sense, pop culture references and sense of fun are all seen in Mizrahi's work.

● Perry Ellis

Ellis was a staple contributor to the solid American aesthetic of comfortable but stylish clothing in the 1970s and 1980s. Mizrahi served as an assistant at the company, and said of Ellis, 'He was my master. Without knowing it he was my mentor. He was incredible.'

Hosts his own television show, first The Isaac Mizrahi Show and later ISAAC. Starts designing for discount retailer Target, launches a couture collection and does dress makeovers on Oprah Winfrey's talk show.

Returns to New York Fashion Week with a ready-to-wear collection. Publishes his How to Have Style guidebook.

Becomes design director of Liz Claiborne. Hosts The Fashion Show, a fashion-competition television show.

2001–05   **2007–08**   **2009**

● Brian Reyes

There were several cute, brightly coloured dresses with corset boning across the midriff in Reyes's Spring 2010 collection, a look that Mizrahi first popularized.

● Oscar de la Renta

In his early and mid-1990s collections, Mizrahi was at the top of his game. His use of brightly coloured and patterned fabrics, inspired by 1950s Hollywood, influenced the collections of other American designers, such as De la Renta.

INFLUENTIAL AESTHETIC

Mizrahi has often had an unstable career, launching and then cancelling collections, and taking a complete break from the public eye after his company went bankrupt in 1998. Through it all, Mizrahi's aesthetic has been consistent, whether designing his couture collection, a line for Target, or his own ready-to-wear collections. Mizrahi's work is often characterized by silhouettes that are reminiscent of the 1950s and 1960s, with bright, bold colour combinations.

Mizrahi's influence is as wide-ranging as his many projects, and can be seen in numerous ways – other designers trading on their celebrity to become spokespeople of style in the same way as Mizrahi; young designers influenced by Mizrahi's love of all things American; and the many women who buy his clothing at Target or Liz Claiborne and refer to his advice books for style guidance.

'The constant, nagging, crazy question in my life is "What is style?" I don't know who first posed it. I don't know the definitive answer, or if I'll ever answer the question once and for all. The answer is always changing; that's the challenge of my life, chasing that answer.'

Isaac Mizrahi

CHAPTER 2

DEFINING WOMEN FOR A NEW GENERATION

COCO CHANEL ○ CHR
GIORGIO ARMANI ○ P

The 20th century has been referred to by many historians as the women's century, because at no other time has there been so much change in equality and position for women over such a short period of time. Clothing is a sartorial representation of women's status in society, and is essential in the discussion of feminism.

FREEDOM FROM CONSTRAINTS

At the beginning of the 20th century, a burgeoning spirit of modernism fostered changes in women's status within society, and women's dress was transformed by the abandonment of corsets and petticoats. To encourage independence, couturiers such as Coco Chanel strove to free women from uncomfortable clothing that constrained movement. Later, designers such as Adrian and Claire McCardell created clothing that symbolized women's strength and ability during World War II.

RETURN OF THE CORSET

After the restrictions of the war, women wanted to feel more feminine again, and Christian Dior was there to help them do just that. Dior's New Look of 1947 led a major trend to return to 19th-century values and aesthetic choices. Corsets and high heels now looked less like signs of oppression, and more like symbols of femininity and glamour. Throughout the 1950s, women were encouraged to return to domestic life to provide comfort after the war.

WORK CLOTHES FOR WOMEN

Soon, however, women began to voice a desire to have additional opportunities outside the home, and feminists began to encourage women to consider a career in addition to family life. Scientists also developed the birth-control pill that meant that women no longer needed to be constrained by the idea of marriage or children. In response to the limitations of Dior's look, Chanel came back into the picture in 1954 to create clothes for working women.

In the 1960s and 1970s, Mary Quant, Halston and Yves Saint Laurent continued to promote wearable work clothes for women who were neither prim nor prissy, but sexy and independent. In the 1980s, when women were challenging the

glass ceiling of business, designers such as Claude Montana, Giorgio Armani and Donna Karan created clothing that fashion historian Anne Hollander referred to as the 'new androgyny', in which women took on more masculine dress to suggest equality.

GENDER EQUALITY

As women became more powerful in their sense of self, and more confident in their own sexuality and its inherent power, designers such as Azzedine Alaïa and Jean Paul Gaultier began to use sex and gender equality as major subjects in their work. Miuccia Prada, Ann Demeulemeester and Marc Jacobs became attracted to the sexual allure of feminine intellectualism, and Stella McCartney appealed to sophisticated women with moral concerns for the environment.

Throughout the 20th century and beyond, all these designers have reacted to larger social issues and gender politics that have affected women. Their clothing has provided women with the ability to shape a new definition of themselves and the time in which they live.

Coco Chanel transformed the fashion world of the first half of the 20th century so completely that her designs are so ubiquitous as to be invisible. The creator of knit dressing, twinsets, short evening dresses, the little black dress and many other ideas, Chanel has influenced fashion irrevocably. Her name has been widely known since the house of Chanel's inception, a feat no other company can claim.

 INFLUENCED BY

KEY
- ● fashion designer
- ◆ fashion house/brand
- ■ artistic influence
- ❖ cultural influence

❖ **Menswear**
Chanel was a pioneer of the look that we now take for granted, and for which no other designer before her can really take credit. Other designers may have used style details from menswear for women, but not to the extent that Chanel did. This innovative look was primarily based on Chanel's close observations of men's dress, and the comfort and ease that it afforded. From a borrowed lover's sweater that she belted, to sailor pants worn at Biarritz, Chanel adapted all the best parts of a man's wardrobe and created practical, wearable, yet incredibly feminine clothing.

● **Jean Patou**
Patou was known for his activewear clothing and his creations for female tennis stars. Chanel considered him a great rival, but was nevertheless influenced by him. (Right: Chanel's activewear-inspired designs for a performance of *Le Train Bleu* by the Ballets Russes, 1924.)

COCO CHANEL
French
(1883 Saumur)

CHRONOLOGY	1883	1899–1909	1909–14	1915
	Born Gabrielle Chanel on August 19th in a poorhouse.	*Sings in a café in Moulins, where she picks up the nickname Coco. Starts an affair with Etienne Balsan. He gives her the use of an apartment in Paris, where she begins a hat business.*	*Now in a relationship with Arthur 'Boy' Capel, Chanel expands her business with his financial backing. Adding sweaters and dresses to her hat collections, she opens a second shop in Deauville.*	*Officially enters couture, opening a shop in fashionable Biarritz. After a year, she is so successful that she is able to repay Capel.*

 INSPIRED

● **Claire McCardell**
McCardell was most certainly inspired by Chanel's emphasis on knit dressing, comfort, usability and practicality. Both designers were known for their aesthetic interest in basic simplicity, with added metal and leather accessories.

● **Elsa Schiaparelli**
Chanel's success in knitwear inspired Schiaparelli to create her own versions, with much success. Schiaparelli also started out in ready-to-wear, as did Chanel.

 Individual flair
Coco Chanel, pictured here in one of her own three-piece knitted cardigan suits in 1929, had a reputation for being difficult, singularly ambitious and stubborn – yet how else could a woman of this time achieve so much and with such a unique vision of feminism and clothing?

Coco Chanel was a modern woman, who set the stage for much of what women today take for granted. Fiercely independent, with a drive and ambition normally seen only in men at that time, Chanel was demanding, egotistical and ruthless. In a dismissal of conventional morality, Chanel had a variety of lovers throughout her life, allowing them to finance and further her career. For all of these reasons and more, the woman as well as her design contributions are of continual fascination in contemporary times.

REVOLUTIONARY TRENDSETTER
Having been abandoned at an early age by her father after her mother died, Chanel took life into her own hands. She relied on her intelligence, pointed charm and personal drive to achieve a multimillion-pound business in her lifetime. The fact that she was able to revolutionize women's clothing,

→ Chanel's comeback

In 1954, Chanel adapted her clothing that had revolutionized fashion in the 1920s to meet the needs of the new working woman. The practicality and usability of the skirt suit meets the needs of women so well that it is still in use well over 60 years after its introduction.

● Paul Poiret

Chanel was a harsh critic of Poiret's sense of the dramatic and elaborate dressing. She used his clothing as a meter of what hers must not be.

❖ School uniforms

Many of the iconic looks of Chanel are based on the severity and plainness of the school uniforms that she wore as a child. One of her favourite looks was a white starched collar with a navy sweater and a bow in her hair.

Introduces Chanel No. 5, the first perfume to use synthetic ingredients mixed with organic ones. Chanel designs a simple bottle and names the perfume No. 5, because it is the fifth sample she smells and five is her lucky number. Originally given as a Christmas gift to her best customers, it goes on sale the following year.

1921–22

● Halston

A major portion of Halston's collections were based on knitwear and an uncomplicated idea of easy elegance. Also similar to Chanel, Halston employed celebrities to create unique jewellery for his collections.

● Yohji Yamamoto

An unlikely comparison, Yamamoto plays with menswear on the female form, as did Chanel. Also like Chanel, he is interested in the way that clothing interacts with the figure, and the sensory experience of clothing on the body.

as well as create one of the eternally best-selling fragrances, is only part of her incredible influence over fashion and female designers alike.

Although women are a minority within the history of fashion, they do have a unique advantage over men in that they wear the clothes and understand them better than anybody. As so many female designers after her would do, Chanel used herself as a source of inspiration and as her own first model. Throughout her career, Chanel started trends by wearing them, satisfying her customers with a duplication of her own look. She did not approve of Paul Poiret's ornate and dramatic sense of style, feeling that it did not allow women freedom of movement or comfort. She eschewed the corseted silhouettes, giant hats and long tedious skirts that were so popular in the early 20th century.

'I, who love women, wanted to give her clothes in which she could drive a car, yet at the same time clothes that emphasized her femininity, clothes that flowed with her body. A woman is closest to being naked when she is well dressed.'

Coco Chanel

INFLUENCED BY

KEY
- fashion designer
- fashion house/brand
- artistic influence
- cultural influence

■ Misia Edwards
Edwards was a socialite and artists' patron who had an incredible influence on Chanel throughout her life. Edwards educated the naive young woman in matters of society, art and culture, undoubtedly helping to create the mystique of Chanel. (Left: Edwards was one of the models for Henri de Toulouse-Lautrec's poster for the magazine *La Revue Blanche* in 1895.)

● Christian Dior
Dior so infuriated Chanel with his reinstatement of corsets and rigid construction that she is said to have come out of retirement at the age of 70 to provide women with an alternative. Although their philosophies and techniques differed, however, their clothing does share simplicity and refinement.

COCO CHANEL CONTINUED

CHRONOLOGY	1924	1931	1939
	Enters into a contract with Pierre Wertheimer, owner of Bourjois perfumes, to manufacture and distribute No. 5. Wertheimer retains 70% of Parfums Chanel; Théophile Bader, owner of Galeries Lafayette department store in Paris, 20%; and Chanel only 10%.	Samuel Goldwyn invites Chanel to Hollywood. She is interested in dressing the stars on and off the screen, and sees the business opportunities in attracting the mass market.	France enters WWII and Chanel closes her house. She is the only designer who does not reopen during the war, and remains in retirement until 1954.

INSPIRED

● Yves Saint Laurent
Chanel said, 'Fashion should not come from the street, but it must reach down into it.' The same quote might also have been said by Saint Laurent during the creation of his Rive Gauche ready-to-wear collections.

● Karl Lagerfeld
Lagerfeld has been the artistic director of Chanel since 1983, invigorating the company to become one of the most influential voices in contemporary fashion. Lagerfeld continually mines the iconic archives of Chanel's style. Each season, the symbols of Chanel, such as her favoured camellia flower (left), the Chanel No. 5 bottle (right), quilted handbags and the Chanel suit, are manipulated to create a fresh perspective on image, style, luxury and chic dressing.

STARTLING SIMPLICITY
Chanel started her fashion career as a milliner, creating hats that were simple yet elegant. Due to constraints of space and money, she began to create sweater dresses in basic colors of navy, black, grey and tan. The simplicity was startling, yet in the wake of World War I, the new ideas of dress seemed more appropriate and signalled a true start of the modern age.

Chanel had a distinct sense of the new type of woman who would come to define the 20th century. She popularized tanned skin for a look of athletic health, short bobbed hair and the wearing of trousers and knee-length skirts. Later in her career, when she made a comeback in 1954, Chanel again addressed the needs of the burgeoning career woman, providing her with comfortable knit dressing that predated the business suit we know so well today.

FINE CRAFTSMANSHIP
Chanel had no formal training in design, besides any sewing skills she picked up in school. Her sense of practicality dictated that dress design was a functional task, and was not to be confused with an artistic or political statement. As Chanel said, 'We are artisans. I am only a craftsman that works with her hands.' She demanded that the construction and feel of her garments be focused on comfort, usability and the finest craftsmanship.

← Benefits of tweeds
Chanel discovered the benefits of tweeds in the 1950s. This dress from 1957 has a soft graphic quality, and is decorated with white braid to suggest a more lithesome silhouette that calls attention to the hips in order to keep the dress looking appropriately feminine.

● Cristóbal Balenciaga
Balenciaga was known for his incredible skills as a couturier and the elegant starkness of his pieces. Chanel acknowledged his genius publicly, and was undoubtedly influenced in her own aesthetic choices.

● Madeleine Vionnet
Vionnet shared Chanel's focus on creating uncomplicated clothing that did not impose a shape on the body. Chanel's eveningwear (left) was unquestionably influenced by Vionnet's bias-cut dresses.

Becomes involved with a diplomat for the Third Reich. This causes great controversy after the war.	Makes official comeback, introducing the skirt suit and other updated Chanel classics.	Introduces the chain-handled, quilted leather handbag.	Dies of a heart attack on January 10th.
1941	**1954**	**1955**	**1971**

→ Chanel in the 21st century
Karl Lagerfeld twists and turns the symbols of the house of Chanel, such as the use of tweeds and chains. His Spring 2010 collection received unanimous positive reviews from the fashion press, and continues to push the revered house forward.

As head costume designer of MGM during the golden age of Hollywood, Adrian was in a position to influence not only fellow designers but, more importantly, the public at large. Adrian created stunning gowns and elegant daywear that other designers and women adopted, and that had a lasting influence on fashion that continues to this day.

INFLUENCED BY

KEY
● fashion designer
◆ fashion house/brand
■ artistic influence
❖ cultural influence

● Coco Chanel
The French couturier was known for the simplicity and restraint that were also hallmarks of Adrian's work. As Joan Crawford said, 'Adrian said nothing must detract. Everything must be made simple, simple, simple. Just your face must emerge.' Just as Chanel had concluded that a suit would allow women the greatest ease while looking stylish, Adrian created suits that defined the new woman of the 1940s. Both designers relied on white collars to reflect light onto the face and neutral colours to extend the usability of the garment, with a few well-appointed embellishments for style.

● Marcel Rochas
Similar to Adrian, Rochas enjoyed working in black and white, and believed that strong shoulders were one of the most important components of women's dress.

● Madeleine Vionnet
Vionnet had a direct influence on the sexy bias-cut dresses that Adrian created for actresses, such as Jean Harlow and Norma Shearer, and that made appearances throughout his career.

ADRIAN
American
(1903 Connecticut)

Born Adolph Adrian Greenburg on March 3rd in Naugatuck, Connecticut.	After a year studying at New York's Parsons School of Design, Adrian goes to Paris. There, he meets Irving Berlin, who asks him to create costumes for The Music Box Revue on New York's Broadway. The designer decides to combine his father's first name with his own middle name to become Gilbert Adrian, and later just Adrian.	Meets lifelong mentor Robert Kall, a theatrical art director. Irving Berlin introduces him to Natacha Rambova, who hires him to create costumes for her husband Rudolph Valentino's next two films.
CHRONOLOGY **1903**	**1920–21**	**1922**

INSPIRED

● Jean Paul Gaultier
Gaultier is often inspired by fashion from the 1940s, exemplified by Adrian, and utilizes padded shoulders and graphic construction (right) to convey his interest in gender roles and feminine power.

● Claude Montana
Montana helped to define the big-shoulder look of the 1980s (right) that Adrian had perfected 40 years earlier. Also like Adrian, Montana's aesthetic was closely associated with an architectural use of fabric.

● Giorgio Armani
Armani has based his career on the perfection of the suit, creating feminine silhouettes out of a traditionally male garment. The suit for women was made popular in the 1940s by designers such as Adrian.

Adrian is best known for his work with Hollywood actresses and the silhouettes of the late 1930s and 1940s that included long lithesome gowns, broad shoulders and a fitted waist. During his time in Hollywood, Adrian developed a design philosophy that stayed with him for the remainder of his career. The Adrian style was based on a delicate balance of texture, graphic lines, subtle fabrications, neutral colour palettes and architectural constructions. *New York Times* journalist Virginia Pope said of his work for retail, 'There is something heroic about Adrian's styles. They are statuesque. One might call it architectural dressmaking.'

CAMOUFLAGE AND METAPHOR
For his retail design work, Adrian used many of the skills of camouflage that he had acquired in working with actresses who did not necessarily have perfect figures. He used

several styling and design techniques to allow Norma Shearer to seem like she had slim hips and long legs, Joan Crawford to appear well proportioned, and to take best advantage of Greta Garbo's stunning bone structure. Adrian also made great use of symbolism and metaphor in fashion, such as dressing Jean Harlow in virginal white to underscore her sultry sexuality.

AMERICAN IDENTITY
From World War II onward, Adrian joined fellow American designer Claire McCardell in rejecting the influence of Paris to develop a uniquely American look. Adrian used symbols that are often associated with American identity, such as quilts, images of the Amish, Pilgrims, farmers, the Wild West and the fabric gingham. Adrian was also sensitive to the change in women's status during the war, and created suits

← **Adrian's ideal**
This ensemble in green moiré shows off Greta Garbo's broad shoulders with a halter dress and a trench-style evening coat. Adrian is taking advantage of Garbo's propensity to dress boyishly without a great deal of frippery. A simple skullcap hat frames her beautiful features and straight hair.

■ **Greta Garbo**
More than any other actress Adrian worked with, Garbo was the ideal in her figure and stylish simplicity. Throughout his career, Garbo's thin figure, statuesque shoulders and long lean legs would inspire Adrian's creations.

Begins working with Cecil B. DeMille, firmly establishing his talents and ability to create stunning one-of-a-kind pieces that help the actresses become stars.

1926

◆ **Viktor & Rolf**
Although Adrian may have been inspired by the soft drapery of Greece, many of his dresses are so carefully constructed that they often appear stiff and controlled. Viktor & Rolf's artistically self-conscious Autumn 2009 collection displayed hard, stiff fabric that was meant to look as if it had been sculpted into soft Grecian forms.

'What I am trying to create for the screen are ultra modern clothes which will be adaptable to the street.'

Adrian

→ Framing the face

The multicoloured plaid bow and jacket collar frame actress Eleanor Powell's face, while the shape of the collar and bow helps to broaden her shoulders. The use of the same plaid on the waistcoat minimizes the waist, all for a more pleasing silhouette.

INFLUENCED BY

KEY
- ● fashion designer
- ◆ fashion house/brand
- ■ artistic influence
- ❖ cultural influence

■ Greek and Roman symbols
Adrian used Greek and Roman symbolism throughout his career in the form of draping, Greek key patterns (right) and the military masks that appeared on vases and artwork.

■ Pola Stout
The Polish textile artist created several of Adrian's best-known retail pieces. The two designers would work together, either to create a programmed stripe or pattern specific to an Adrian design, or Adrian would adapt his creation to her textile.

ADRIAN CONTINUED

	Begins work at MGM as head of design, sketching and interpreting the costumes for more than 200 films there.	Meets Woody Feurt, a department store merchandise manager. Feurt eventually becomes Adrian's business partner in 1942.	The dress he creates for Joan Crawford in the film Letty Lynton is copied in department stores and sells more than 50,000 copies in New York's Macy's alone.	Designs an influential fashion show segment within the film The Women. Starring Norma Shearer, Rosalind Russell and Joan Crawford, it is one of Adrian's best-known films.
CHRONOLOGY	1928	1929	1932	1939

INSPIRED

● Ralph Lauren
Lauren came into prominence by utilizing and reinterpreting recognizable American iconography, such as the Wild West, Ivy League culture and the golden age of Hollywood. Such inspirations can be closely identified with Adrian's own interests. Both designers have reinterpreted the usage of common fabrics to create elegant fashion statements. In Lauren's Autumn 2008 collection, the homage to Adrian can be seen in the alternative use of buffalo plaid, which is normally used for lumberjack shirts.

→ 1940s glamour
In Ralph Lauren's Autumn 2008 collection, the designer references early 20th-century glamour and the love of feathers in hats, but mimics Adrian's ability to frame the face with a dramatic collar on a plaid jacket.

for women that were not only practical and wearable for their new responsibilities, but also suggested a sense of patriotism and common goals. The wearing of a suit complied with the fabric restrictions of the war, but also signalled a purpose to women's activities. When Christian Dior later introduced his New Look in 1947, Adrian was deeply disappointed at the constrictive armholes, nipped waist, padded hips and full skirts. He said in a magazine interview, 'I do not like padded hips. To try and make women pad their hips in this day and age is a little like selling armour to a man.'

Adrian's initial concept of a strong female with broad shoulders and narrow hips was mined by designers of the 1980s, because of its ability to hide figure flaws and suggest a sense of professional responsibility, and continues to influence the work of many contemporary designers.

❖ **Military dress**

Adrian's career as a retail designer coincided with WWII, and helped to define the American look that would separate the United States from Paris's style rule at that time. Military embellishments came in many forms, from tassels and ropes to frogs and epaulets, and helped women feel more patriotic.

Leaves MGM because of a dispute over the costumes of Greta Garbo. Opens his own boutique in Beverly Hills.	*Suffers a heart attack and retires to his ranch in Brazil.*	*Dies on September 13th.*
1942	**1952**	**1959**

● **Alexandre Herchcovitch**

The Brazilian designer's Autumn 2009 collection relied on prominent shoulders as well as other identifiable Adrian styles, such as military symbolism and a studied contrast of masculine and feminine shapes and details.

● **Zac Posen**

Inspired by 1940s silhouettes, Posen's Autumn 2009 collection featured several Adrian-esque design solutions, such as broad shoulders with a nipped waist and textile patterns arranged to highlight the hourglass figure.

← **Hollywood heroine**

In the 1946 film *Humoresque*, Adrian's designs for Joan Crawford emphasize a powerful wartime image of strength of purpose, leadership and power, while never forgetting that she is a woman to whom a man can come home. Adrian helped to cement Crawford as a glamour queen by creating simplified ensembles that hid any figure flaws.

Christian Dior's designs are so iconic that any piece with a cinched waist, sloping shoulders and a full skirt is compared to Dior's 1947 New Look. Desiring to create clothing that would make women feel like women again after the privations of World War II, Dior created architectural feats of beauty that emphasized the essence of being female and defined the 1950s silhouette.

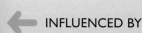

INFLUENCED BY

KEY
- ● fashion designer
- ◆ fashion house/brand
- ■ artistic influence
- ❖ cultural influence

■ Jean Cocteau
Dior was greatly inspired by the surrealist writer and artist, realizing that Cocteau's work in theatre and dance would have a major impact on society and other artists.

● Paul Poiret
Poiret was a larger-than-life designer who considered himself an artist rather than just a dressmaker. Dior saw parallels between the work of Poiret and that of Jean Cocteau and other artists, and for the first time considered that he might like to be a couturier.

■ 19th-century dress
Dior was inspired by the grandness and ostentatious displays of the 19th century, and often cited his fashionable mother as an early muse. The fitted silhouette of the 19th century inspired him to create evening ensembles with full skirts and fitted waists (left).

CHRISTIAN DIOR
French
(1905 Granville)

CHRONOLOGY	1905	1923–26	1928	1930–31
	Born January 21st in Granville, Normandy.	Attends École Libre des Sciences Politiques in Paris. He would like to be an architect, but his family wants him to be a diplomat.	Persuades his father to fund an art gallery, which he opens in Paris with friend Jacques Bonjean. Galerie Jacques Bonjean sells work by all the coolest artists of the time, including Pablo Picasso and Georges Braque.	His mother and brother pass away from illness. To escape the pain, he travels to Russia, where he falls in love with the shapes and colours.

INSPIRED

● John Galliano
Named design director of Dior in 1996, Galliano's first collection coincided with the 50th anniversary of the house, and saluted Dior's craftsmanship and sculptural solutions. Galliano has continued to mine the Dior archives and iconic image, invigorating the luxury brand and creating trends for looks from the late 1940s and early 1950s.

● Alexander McQueen
In a statement about luxury and excess, McQueen created a monumental collection for Autumn 2009 that used symbols and silhouettes from Dior, among other fashion giants.

➜ Très chic
John Galliano's Autumn 2009 collection for the house of Dior reminds us of the power of the image of Dior, yet brings that image into the 21st century by using fabrics that are traditionally associated with lingerie. The model becomes quintessentially French, as a confectionery coquette wrapped in gauzy fabrications.

In the immediate post–World War II era of 1947, Dior was lucky to be in the right place at the right time, and to be observant enough to realize that women wanted to look feminine. The Western world had suffered extreme degradation throughout the war, and seen depravity in humankind that everyone would have preferred to forget.

POSTWAR CONFORMITY

Throughout Europe and the United States, the postwar period was marked by the desire for security, homogeneity and conformity. Traditional family structures were encouraged, requiring that men be the primary breadwinners once more. Women were encouraged to become loving wives and mothers, and to help stimulate the war-torn economy by buying at an unprecedented rate. Dior's collections were emblematic of this shift in society, creating a

■ Architecture
Dior originally wanted to pursue a career in architecture, but his parents persuaded him to try to be a diplomat. Dior never lost his admiration for the structure and form of architecture, even when he became a world-famous couturier.

Closes his art gallery because of financial difficulties.	*Begins drawing fashion sketches, and sells his first hat design to the milliner Madame Agnes.*
1932	**1933**

● Marc Bohan
Bohan took over from Yves Saint Laurent as designer for the house of Dior from 1960 to 1989. Known for close adherence to the Dior legacy, he created collections for older clients who had originally been attracted to the house.

← The New Look
This ensemble from Dior's famous Spring 1947 Corolle collection – the New Look – is called the bar suit, and has been one of the most referenced pieces since its introduction. The jacket redefines the 19th-century emphasis on the waist, sloping shoulders and luxurious full skirt, yet it is completely modern in its interpretation, suggesting neither costume nor excessive ornament.

→ Botanical influence

This Dior ensemble from the early 1950s displays one of the designer's favourite themes: the flower or anything botanical. Dior saw the flower as the perfect metaphor for the delicate but arresting beauty of a lovely woman.

← INFLUENCED BY

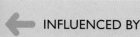

KEY

● fashion designer
◆ fashion house/brand
■ artistic influence
❖ cultural influence

■ Gardening and flowers

Dior acquired a love of gardening from his mother, providing him with a peaceful pastime between collections. The famous Corolle (ring of petals) collection of 1947 – the New Look – was inspired by the blossoming flower. Dior said of the collection: 'I designed clothes for flower-like women.' His favourite flower was lily of the valley (left), and he had sprigs of the flower tucked into the hems of the collection's dresses for luck. In Spring 1954, he created the Muguet (lily of the valley) collection.

CHRISTIAN DIOR CONTINUED

CHRONOLOGY	With help from Michel de Brunhoff, editor of French Vogue, Dior freelances for numerous couturiers, including Elsa Schiaparelli and Cristóbal Balenciaga.	Joins Robert Piguet as design assistant, and learns about clothing construction.	After a brief period in the army at the outbreak of WWII, Dior goes to live with his family in Provence. Returns to Paris to work for Lucien Lelong, eventually becoming primary designer. Starts designing 19th-century-style costumes for actress Odette Joyeux.	Negotiates with cotton manufacturer Marcel Boussac to open his own couture house.
	1935–38	**1938**	**1939–46**	**1946**

→ INSPIRED

● Gareth Pugh
For his Autumn 2008 collection (right), Pugh featured several pieces that abstracted the famous Dior silhouette to create a commentary on the connections of feminism and vulnerability.

● Thierry Mugler
Mugler has adopted many of the heavily constructed and architectural techniques that are associated with Dior, forcing the figure to conform to the dress.

● Vivienne Westwood
In her Spring 1988 collection, Westwood cleverly took symbols of Dior constructions and manipulated them to create a feminist statement. In her Autumn 1995 collection, she paid homage to a famous menswear-inspired Dior jacket.

● Jacques Fath
A contemporary of Dior, Fath created similar silhouettes, featuring nipped waists, full skirts and soft shoulders.

silhouette that was reminiscent of the idealized 19th-century Victorian era. Even if a woman could not afford an actual couture garment, many women could afford to wear copies of Dior's creations.

BELOVED COUTURIER

Dior was already 42 in 1947 when he launched his first collection, and was an unlikely candidate to set the fashion world on fire. He was shy and sensitive, and had not shown a great deal of ambition up until that point. It was not until the mid-1930s that he had begun to shift his artistic inclinations towards fashion, but after working for Lucien Lelong in the early 1940s, he came to have stronger opinions about women's dress. For the 10 short years that he worked under his own name, Dior established himself as one of the most beloved couturiers of all time.

DESIGN PROCESS

Dior's collections always started with fabric appointments and consultations with the three women – Mitza Bricard, Raymonde Zehnacker and Marguerite Carré – who helped him carry out his ideas. He was not as interested in the colour or texture as he was in the body of the fabric. Once the fabric was chosen, the dress was made up on the model.

A collection would consist of 175 outfits with coats to go with them. He first made tiny sketches, editing and expanding on those that he liked. Carré would then take the sketches to the seamstresses to be made into muslin toiles (test garments). Even the seemingly nonformfitting pieces of Dior's creations featured layers of heavy boning, padding and the use of corsets to achieve the desired wasp waist and silhouette. Dior would sit with a gold-tipped cane and

'I must admit that clothes are my whole life. Ultimately everything I know, see or hear, every part of my life, turns around the clothes which I create. They haunt me perpetually, until they are ready to pass from the world of my dreams into the world of practical use.'

Christian Dior

↑ **Trend creation**

After his revolutionary return to the fitted waist in 1947, Dior again changed fashion in 1955 when he introduced the popular A line. The biggest controversy was the raising of the hemline, predicting the changing trends from season to season that are taken for granted today.

● **Lucien Lelong**
Dior worked for Lelong before opening his own couture house, and carried many of Lelong's business practices into his own company.

● **Edward Molyneux**
Molyneux was a proponent of clean, uncomplicated, tailored looks for women. Dior sought advice and approval from Molyneux throughout his career.

● **Cristóbal Balenciaga**
Although Balenciaga dismissed Dior for creating uncomfortable clothing without consideration for wearability or comfort, Dior referred to Balenciaga as 'the master', and often strove to emulate the clean, architectural quality of Balenciaga's work.

Introduces the Corolle collection. Carmel Snow, editor of Harper's Bazaar, tells Dior, 'It's quite a revolution, dear Christian. Your dresses have such a new look. They're quite wonderful, you know.' Dior's New Look is a sensation.	*Designs prolifically, producing 70 collections in 10 years.*	*Dies of a heart attack on October 24th. Design assistant Yves Saint Laurent is named his successor.*
1947	**1947–57**	**1957**

● **Yves Saint Laurent**
Saint Laurent said, 'Working with Christian Dior was a miracle for me. My admiration knew no bounds. He has created a fashion house that was unique by surrounding himself with exceptional people. He was an extraordinary master, who taught me the fundamentals of my art. I owe a large part of my life to him, and no matter what happens, I will never forget the years spent by his side.' Dior laid the foundation for a love of couture and dramatic dressing that would influence Saint Laurent for the rest of his career. Although Saint Laurent was keen to separate himself from the master couturier's shadow, he eventually found his way back to creating alluring and romantic showpieces, like his mentor.

discuss the toiles, assign fabric to the surviving ones and select which model was to wear what dress.

WORKS OF SCULPTURAL ART

Dior's amazing use of shape, proportion and construction are what creates such an aura of mystique and true beauty. The clothing is architectural and structural, and renders the female form almost into a work of sculptural art. In today's culture, women would refuse to be contorted into such uncomfortable shapes as the Dior dresses commanded. However, for all the emphasis on domesticity and perceived setbacks that women received post–World War II, it is hard not to notice the cool strength that exudes from the models in magazines. Regardless of how uncomfortable a dress may have been, women would have been assured that they looked like the flowers that inspired Dior's imaginative creations.

Claire McCardell came to embody the overall definition of American fashion, from her personal determination to her emphasis on wearability and comfort. Her philosophies of practical design have become so ubiquitous among designers that it is sometimes hard to remember her many contributions to the fashion industry.

 INFLUENCED BY

KEY
- ● fashion designer
- ◆ fashion house/brand
- ■ artistic influence
- ❖ cultural influence

■ **Neoclassical and Greek dress**
As many designers before McCardell recognized, such as Paul Poiret and Madeleine Vionnet, an empire waistline and well-placed swags of fabric are flattering to any body type.

● **Madame Grès**
McCardell was inspired by the simplicity and restraint of Grès's elegant eveningwear.

● **Madeleine Vionnet**
First exposed to the work of Vionnet during her education in Paris, McCardell was fascinated by the use of the bias cut. In 1938, McCardell created the ground-breaking monastic dress (left) – an untailored, bias-cut shift dress that could be belted to suit the wearer – that was clearly inspired by the work of Vionnet in its simplicity and use of bias. Both designers eschewed rigid undergarments, and preferred to let the body's natural shape dictate the silhouette of the garment.

CLAIRE McCARDELL
American
(1905 Maryland)

CHRONOLOGY	1905	1926–28	1929–38
	Born May 24th in Frederick, Maryland.	Enrolls at Parsons School of Design in New York. Encounters the designs of Madeleine Vionnet during a study programme in Paris.	Hired by independent ready-to-wear designer Robert Turk, she follows him to work at Townley Frocks, taking over as head designer on his death. Introduces many innovations, including interchangeable separates and the unconstructed bathing suit. Her monastic dress is a big success, but unauthorized copies create financial troubles that overwhelm Townley Frocks and they are forced to close.

 INSPIRED

● **Bill Blass**
Blass was clearly inspired by McCardell's American look of uncomplicated, wearable, yet sophisticated dressing. He also used bold patterns and textures.

● **Halston**
Halston adopted many of the same ideas as McCardell, creating comfortable, easily packed knit dressing, and looks that provided professional elegance for a burgeoning movement of working women.

● **Issey Miyake**
A genius in his own right, Miyake also designed clothing that was practical, wearable and comfortable, with original silhouettes. An inveterate experimenter, Miyake created new classics in every collection, much like McCardell.

● **Rudi Gernreich**
Gernreich was inspired by the practicality and affordability of McCardell's collections. As an innovator who recognized the impracticality of Paris design for Americans, Gernreich adopted many of the same dictates that McCardell had already forged.

It is said that Claire McCardell often referred to the process of designing clothes as an exercise in problem solving, and stated that a successful garment was one that fulfilled her requirements of functionality and performance. This statement defines a monumentally important facet of McCardell's design philosophy. Designing in the truest sense of the word has a connection to architectural, product or industrial design. However, many fashion designers are stylists, or primarily focused on the social, political and emotional aspects of clothing. McCardell's philosophy was to create functional, useful garments that also had aesthetic principles applied to them.

McCardell's emphasis always started with functionality, from her use of fabrics and construction techniques to her focus on interchangeable separates. She routinely used herself as a source of inspiration, since she was an active career women with two stepchildren and a sporty lifestyle. McCardell's clothing played an important role in many women's lives during the defining years of World War II and the subsequent baby boom of the 1950s.

CREATOR OF AMERICAN FASHION

For all her emphasis on practicality, McCardell was initially met with scepticism and apprehension by many of the designers and manufacturers that she worked for. Before the war, McCardell experienced a great deal of frustration at the American fashion industry's insistence that all fashion must come from Paris. She believed that the fabrics and silhouettes did not meet the needs of women in the United States, and often attempted to interject her own design contributions, frequently with disappointing results. Even before the wartime restrictions on fabrics and

Wearable elegance
This 1946 summer dress by Claire McCardell is as elegant and chic as it is comfortable to wear. The dolman sleeves afford ease of movement, the belt is adjustable, the shirring around the hips helps to accommodate multiple body shapes, and the crisp cotton fabric is both breathable and beautiful.

→ Modern swimsuit
We take for granted that swimwear is functional, but before McCardell, swimwear often had boning and strict construction. McCardell revolutionized swimwear, as seen in this 1946 swimsuit, by simplifying the construction, applying drape and dressmaker details for beauty, and elevating the side seam to lengthen the appearance of the leg.

INFLUENCED BY

KEY
- ● fashion designer
- ◆ fashion house/brand
- ■ artistic influence
- ❖ cultural influence

❖ World dress
In her early days of design, McCardell often went to Paris to copy garments from the fashion shows, as was the practice of the day. Although she eschewed Paris's influence in her own work, she was greatly inspired by her travels to Budapest and Vienna, and her research into North African and Asian dress.

❖ Sports
As an avid skier, horse rider and hiker, McCardell utilized closers, such as metal buckles and hooks and eyes, from sportsgear that she used. She also created stylish hoods based on preventing discomfort from the cold while skiing.

CLAIRE McCARDELL CONTINUED

	Works for Hattie Carnegie. Wins first prize for costume design at the 1939 New York World's Fair.	Townley Frocks reopens, and McCardell returns as head designer on the condition that she be able to design under her own name.	Her leotard designs are featured on the cover of Life magazine.	Becomes a partner in Townley Frocks.	Frank Perls Gallery in Beverly Hills, California, holds a 20-year retrospective of her designs.
CHRONOLOGY	**1938–40**	**1940**	**1943**	**1952**	**1953**

INSPIRED

● Isabel Toledo
As a designer who does not seem to be constricted by trends, Toledo focuses on designs that provide women with maximum comfort and timeless stylishness (right). Another similarity to McCardell is her use of herself as a source of inspiration in terms of need and usability.

● Mary Quant
During a trip to the United States, Quant was impressed with McCardell's ability to create affordable, well-made and stylish clothing for a variety of age groups and customers. Quant was also influenced by many of McCardell's ready-to-wear innovations and her reliance on knit dressing.

● Isaac Mizrahi
Mizrahi's work is characterized by elegant but practical everyday wear. His collections for discount retailer Target best epitomize the influence of McCardell, with Mizrahi saying that 'good design should be for everyone'.

construction, McCardell was focusing on durable cottons, wool jersey and other fabrics made in the United States. Her clothing was affordable, easy to care for, comfortable and durable, making her popular with women everywhere.

When World War II pulled women into the workforce, McCardell became all the more important and influential. In 1945, Lord & Taylor department store heavily promoted Claire McCardell and the American look, which may be a primary reason that she is given the accolade of creator of American fashion. Interestingly, McCardell rejected the dominant male-suit-inspired look associated with the war years. Rather, predating Christian Dior's New Look of 1947, McCardell kept shoulders soft, with a fitted waist and soft skirt, allowing women to feel feminine.

FIVE INTERCHANGEABLE SEPARATES

Claire McCardell created a bevy of pieces that she often revisited and perfected, referring to the signature touches that she used repeatedly as 'McCardellisms'. In 1934, in response to her own travelling needs, McCardell introduced a system of five interchangeable separates that were easy to pack, durable and offered a multitude of looks.

She liked to use spaghetti straps and sashes that were adjustable for different body types and sizes. McCardell never put fasteners on the back of garments, citing the frustration for single women of being unable to dress by themselves. She instead preferred brass hooks and eyes that were easier to open and close, but proved to be sturdier than complicated loops and buttons.

'I like comfort in the rain, in the sun; comfort for active sports, comfort for sitting still and looking pretty.'

Claire McCardell

■ 19th-century dress

Although she was a supremely practical designer, McCardell could also be somewhat of a romantic, and was clearly inspired by the soft shapes and femininity of the 19th century.

❖ Menswear

Three younger brothers and an active lifestyle pulled McCardell's attention towards standard menswear finishes, such as flat felled seams (right), and the ease of movement that was not present in womenswear.

● Coco Chanel

Chanel inspired McCardell to focus on relaxed clothing that borrowed elements from menswear, and on knit dressing for ease and practicality.

Becomes third-ever fashion designer to be featured on the cover of Time *magazine.*

Dies March 22nd, and is posthumously inducted into the Coty Hall of Fame.

1955 | **1958**

● Donna Karan

Echoing McCardell's system of five interchangeable separates, Karan introduced her own seven easy pieces. Karan also focused on the needs of working mothers. Her use of monochromatic knits and soft woven fabrics allowed women to pack a mix-and-match wardrobe for a business trip, and overcame many of the shortcomings of existing professional wear for women. Like McCardell, Karan rejected large shoulder pads, opting for a softer but still powerful feminine look.

LEISURE CLOTHES

Another vital contribution to fashion was her emphasis on relaxed leisure and sports clothes. In 1937, McCardell introduced the unconstructed bathing suit that had no interior boning, extra construction or padding, since the designer felt that the swimsuit must 'be for swimming'. She developed adjustable and interchangeable pieces, such as skirts, halters, leotards and cover-ups. Her cotton dresses often included elastic in the bodice for easier fit, with flat felled seams for durability. For wives and mothers, she introduced the supremely practical popover dress and the self-aproned kitchen dinner dress that allowed women to cook and clean but not necessarily look like they did.

Claire McCardell continues to be cited by contemporary designers as a major influence in creating practical, wearable, yet supremely elegant designs.

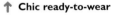

↑ Chic ready-to-wear

McCardell popularized casual clothing for women, suggesting that comfort, practicality and a sense of chic did not have to be separate considerations. This 1952 ensemble displays deep patch pockets that are equally functional and decorative. McCardell loved espadrille sandals, which she discovered on her travels to Europe.

← Favourite looks

Claire McCardell loved bare shoulders, and often opted for wide belts to give her customer the greatest number of options and camouflage. In his Spring 2008 collection for Donna Karan, Peter Speliopoulos references both, along with McCardell's love of the sandal.

For all his trademark simplicity and slow development of ideas, Halston helped to cement American fashion in the world market. Appearing at a point when the American look needed to be refined, Halston took the best from American and European designers before him, and created a distinct philosophy that influenced the fashion industry for many years to come.

 INFLUENCED BY

KEY
● fashion designer
◆ fashion house/brand
■ artistic influence
❖ cultural influence

● Charles James
Halston hired the retired couturier as a technical consultant, and also helped to sponsor a retrospective of James's work at New York's Pratt Institute. Halston referred to James as the Leonardo da Vinci of fashion, because James was more interested in the construction technique than what was seen on the surface.

● Mainbocher
Mainbocher was known for the chic and uncomplicated gowns he designed, most notably for Wallis Simpson. Halston's Spring 1973 collection was a homage to Mainbocher.

● Claire McCardell
Halston created the savage bathing suit in the 1970s (right); it was essentially McCardell's diaper suit with a lower décolletage. He also saw the ingenuity in McCardell's use of spaghetti straps, adjustable waist and bias-cut fabric. He created his own version of McCardell's five interchangeable pieces, all in wool jersey, for working women to pack easily.

HALSTON
American
(1932 Iowa)

	Born Roy Halston Frowick on April 23rd in Des Moines, Iowa.	Moves to Chicago, where he attends night classes at the Art Institute, and by day works in a department store. Begins an affair with Andre Basil, a hairdresser in the prestigious salon of the Ambassador Hotel. Basil displays Halston's hat designs in his salon.	Moves to New York to design hats for milliner Lilly Daché, then for Bergdorf Goodman department store. He garners enough attention to have his name displayed (now just Halston), and acquires a following of actresses and socialites, notably Jacqueline Kennedy.
CHRONOLOGY	**1932**	**1952**	**1958–59**

 INSPIRED

● Marco Zanini
Zanini designed the Autumn 2008 collection for the newly revived Halston label. The young designer dutifully mined the Halston archives, but ultimately did not create any excitement.

● Dries Van Noten
Van Noten's latest collections, especially Spring 2009 (right), feature charmeuse tunic pieces that might have appeared on Halston's catwalk.

● Marc Jacobs
Jacobs's Autumn 2007 collection reinterpreted the Halston aesthetic, featuring knit dressing in long, lean silhouettes. Matt jersey dresses and sheet sequin pieces were also notable Halston influences.

● Doo-Ri Chung
The young Korean–American designer has made a name for herself by creating beautifully draped, matt jersey dresses that hearken back to Halston's experiments with Charles James as a collaborator.

Halston has become a hallmark of the American fashion industry largely because of the time period in which he came into prominence. Apart from designers such as Claire McCardell and Bonnie Cashin, the United States largely lacked the refinement or panache that would propel American design onto the world stage.

SIMPLICITY AND SOPHISTICATION
Halston created clothing that had the casual simplicity and wearability of McCardell, combined with the sophistication of European designers such as Yves Saint Laurent and Hubert de Givenchy, but transformed into something uniquely his own.

In 1973, Halston remarked, 'The American look in fashion is coming to the fore. The modern way of life is American and it has to work for the world market. All of a sudden the American designer, if he has an original point of view and a product, has an opportunity he never had.'

The philosophy of clothing that Halston promoted was that of simplicity and ease, because he felt that the unadorned was more graceful and ultimately more wearable. Halston became all the more important because his design ideas functioned so perfectly for a growing workforce of women. After the post–World War II era of the 1950s, women began demanding equal rights and saw the full blossoming of the sexual revolution. Women wanted to look sexy and attractive, yet professional and comfortable, and Halston was there with the answers.

In the 1970s, when the wearing of trousers by women was still being debated, Halston said, 'They [trousers] give women freedom they have never had before and she is not about to give them up.'

← **Halston the milliner**
Halston, pictured here with Italian film star Virna Lisi in 1964, got his start in millinery. Having no formal training, hats presented less of a challenge in their construction. Halston's clever and fresh perspective shows through, regardless of what he was creating.

• **Yves Saint Laurent**
Like the French couturier, Halston embraced the changes that were happening in society, and created clothing for the new young woman. Halston said, 'Saint Laurent is the most avant-garde designer in the world.'

• **Madeleine Vionnet**
Rather than visiting Parisian fashion shows, Halston was said to pore over magazines from the 1930s that featured Vionnet's work, preferring the understated elegance of her bias-cut dresses.

Bergdorf Goodman offers him the opportunity to create clothing under his own label in the store. The arrangement lasts only a year.

Creates Halston Ltd, initially to sell hats, but introduces a clothing line later in the year.

Opens his own boutique, selling ready-to-wear and custom-made garments. Launches Halston Originals to sell his ready-to-wear collection to high-end department stores.

1966   **1968**   **1972**

• **Stephen Burrows**
Burrows came into prominence when Halston was well established. Burrows is known for his clean use of draped fabrics, similar to Halston's aesthetic, but with a distinctive lettuce-edge hem. Halston encouraged Burrows to open his own shop in New York, named Stephen Burrows' World.

• **Giorgio Sant'Angelo**
Like his contemporary Halston, Sant'Angelo showed flowing caftans and knit dressing that featured little if no fastenings, and were inspired by the new woman of the time period.

• **Donna Karan**
Over many seasons, Karan has explored the Halston look in the form of softly draped dresses, formfitted knit dressing and clean, uncomplicated outerwear and suits.

THE EFFECT OF BIAS

Halston was known for his soft, luxurious fabrics, his use of bias – that is, cutting diagonally across the fabric, rather than straight along the grain (the direction of the threads in a woven fabric) – and his quest for the fewest seams and closures, feeling that they were too intrusive to the silhouette. Halston correctly perceived that fabric and cut allowed women to feel sensual and evocative, and therefore confident and sexy: 'I just think bias is more sexy. I keep cutting straight-grained clothes and they all look too familiar somehow. The bias gives you the plus. At night I think you want to be turned on and there is nothing more of a turn-on than a fabric which hits the body the way bias does. It adds another dimension of softness.'

→ **Smartly suited**
This 1972 jumpsuit is a wonderful example of Halston's sensitivity to smart, well-put-together looks for women who were in the early stages of defining a more independent spirit. Halston loved trousers on women, and was one of the first designers in the United States to promote them as a suitable option.

'To me, this [designing] is the most interesting part; to invent new cuts and new points of view in fashion. And how that happens isn't that a light bulb goes on and, click! You have it. You have to pull it out of yourself – and pull and pull and pull until it comes. As Martha [Graham, the dancer] says, "It's like giving birth to a cube."'

Halston

 ## INFLUENCED BY

KEY
- ● fashion designer
- ◆ fashion house/brand
- ■ artistic influence
- ❖ cultural influence

● Cristóbal Balenciaga
Halston said, 'Balenciaga was really the great one. You would see his collection and say "I don't believe it!" What this man has done. He has done clothes for everybody in the world market.'

■ Elsa Peretti
Model-turned-accessories designer, Peretti created the Halston perfume bottle, bags, jewellery and mesh bras. The two designers worked so well together that their names are inextricably linked.

● Hubert de Givenchy
Givenchy is famous for the unfussy elegance epitomized by his muse Audrey Hepburn. Halston's celebrity muse was Liza Minnelli, whom he dressed in effortless yet sophisticated dresses, pyjamas and suits (right).

HALSTON CONTINUED

CHRONOLOGY	1973–74	1984	1986	1990	1991
	Norton Simon Industries purchases all of Halston's companies, his trademark and his exclusive design services. Halston wins the Coty American Fashion Critics' Award for the fifth time.	Halston is fired as chief designer because of his erratic and destructive behaviour, caused by drug abuse.	Revlon buys Halston's companies.	Dies of complications caused by AIDS on March 26th.	Halston retrospective held at New York's Fashion Institute of Technology.

 ## INSPIRED

● Calvin Klein
Klein picked up the baton that Halston dropped in the late 1970s and early 1980s, continuing the message of simplicity and wearability in soft neutrals and pastels. Both designers created clothing for the working woman, and used luxurious and expensive fabrications that imbued the wearer with sexiness and confidence. Both eschewed trends in order to stay consistent with their philosophy of dressing, and to provide a reliable source of clothing. Klein also learned from Halston's licensing mistakes, allowing Klein to create a financial empire of which he was in complete control.

➔ Grace revisited
Calvin Klein's Autumn 2002 collection featured black charmeuse dresses that took advantage of the grace afforded by cutting fabric on the bias. Klein adds cut-work details, in a contemporary twist on Halston's long-sleeved, jewel-necked dresses in silk jersey or cashmere of the 1970s.

LICENSING HIS IMAGE

Halston is also notable as a designer because he was at the forefront of the corporate takeover of the fashion industry. Halston was one of the first designers to license his name for fashion-related items that he did not produce. This is a standard practice today, and indeed funds most fashion houses, so that the actual clothing is used only as a promotional tool.

Halston licensed his name to a variety of price points, allowing the mass market to share in the glamorous image of the designer. Halston was ultimately a victim of corporate business, having sold his name and company in its entirety for a hefty profit. When his drug use and accumulated exhaustion caused erratic behaviour, Halston was fired from his own label.

Pastel dream
This 1975 pastel confection, pictured on legendary model Naomi Simms, is both luxurious and poised, with a reference to modern dance in the silhouette, ease of movement and fabrication. Halston designed costumes for modern dance pioneer Martha Graham, and the experience reinforced his understanding of movement in clothing.

Mary Quant is a pivotal designer in fashion history, who helped set an example for many women in an era of new definitions of youth and femininity. Essential ideas, such as ease of movement, affordability and youthful playfulness, that Mary Quant helped to translate for a generation of women have a lasting influence today.

INFLUENCED BY

KEY
● fashion designer
◆ fashion house/brand
■ artistic influence
❖ cultural influence

● **Claire McCardell**
Quant identified with the focus on physical activity and the sense of lightheartedness and fluid fit in McCardell's work. She was also impressed with the American clothing industry's mastery of the mass market in terms of fit and affordability.

● **Coco Chanel**
Chanel was an independent woman who created clothing that defined the era in which she lived. The two designers shared an affinity for wearable clothing that emphasized youth and movement. Quant also recognized the importance of a collar, particularly a white one, to change the look of an outfit.

● **André Courrèges**
Although they had a bitter rivalry over who invented the miniskirt, there is no doubt that they would have had some type of influence on each other, as they both sought to define a new approach to dress for women.

● **Pierre Cardin**
The futurist designer was expelled from the Chambre Syndicale, the governing body of the French fashion industry, for focusing on ready-to-wear – a focus that Quant would have agreed with. Cardin was also experimental and innovative, and was caught up in the same youth movement as Quant.

MARY QUANT
British
(1934 London)

	Born February 11th in Blackheath, London.	Opens store named Bazaar in Chelsea, London, with future husband Alexander Plunket Greene and accountant Archie McNair.	Has success with white plastic collars that can be attached to dresses or sweaters for a new look. Starts to create her own clothing after receiving attention for the 'madhouse pyjamas' she designed for the opening of Bazaar.	Opens a second Bazaar store in nearby Knightsbridge, because of the overwhelming popularity of the store in Chelsea.
CHRONOLOGY	**1934**	**1955**	**1956**	**1957**

INSPIRED

● **Betsey Johnson**
Johnson adopted Quant's playfulness and focus on youth, while never forgetting affordability. Johnson's shop and design headquarters in SoHo in New York bear a great deal of resemblance to Quant's Bazaar.

● **Rudi Gernreich**
Gernreich was greatly affected by what was happening in the London youthquake movement. He showed his collections in a boutique at the beginning of his career, and like Quant, always strove for affordability.

● **Miuccia Prada**
Quant is quoted as saying, 'Vulgarity is the life blood of fashion' – an idea similar to Prada's philosophy as she explores ideal beauty. This Autumn 2002 piece (left) for Prada's Miu Miu label uses unusual colour combinations as well as synthetic fabrics to create a silhouette and look that are reminiscent of Quant's 1960s innovations.

Mary Quant helped to define what it meant to be a woman during one of the crucial philosophical and social shifts of the 20th century. In 1955, a young Quant did not feel that the selection of clothing being offered to women her age was acceptable. Not only was it not affordable, but it also did not allow for the range of activity and comfort that she herself required. In her 1966 autobiography *Quant by Quant*, she said, 'The young were tired of wearing essentially the same thing as their mothers.' Her answer was to open a store called Bazaar, decorated with brightly coloured pop art references, that quickly attracted young women.

IN TUNE WITH THE TIMES
Although she had no formal training, Quant started designing the clothing for Bazaar after she discovered that there were no other designers who shared her newly found focus: 'We were in at the beginning of a tremendous renaissance in fashion. The clothes I made happened to fit in exactly with the teenage trend, with pop records and espresso bars and jazz clubs.'

MINISKIRTS AND GO-GO BOOTS
There is disagreement over whether Mary Quant or André Courrèges first developed the miniskirt, that iconic symbol of the 1960s. Whatever the case, the primary difference between the two designers was price point, with Quant striving to keep her prices within the range of the average 'shop girl'. Mary Quant developed the white plastic, calf-length go-go boots and little plastic collars that could be worn with a variety of sweaters or dresses to brighten and change the look of an outfit. She used bright optic prints, created balloon skirts with built-in trousers that resembled

← The Quant look

Mary Quant, pictured center with models in 1967, is emblematic of her work as much as the actual clothing. Quant preferred flat shoes, opaque tights, short skirts, boxy fit and short cropped hair, a look that is synonymous with the era when she was most prominent.

↓ Graphic reinterpretation

Anna Sui is very fond of the 1960s – a fun, carefree time centred on youth. This Spring 1996 look is a perfect example of the revivalism that was so popular in the 1990s. The dress is updated in fit to show a more womanly figure.

❖ Youthquake

Quant was influenced by the youthquake movement booming in London – a youthful exuberance and unique style from groups such as teddy boys and mods, as reflected in pop music.

❖ Women's rights

Domestic roles were changing as young women began rejecting ideas of conformity and respectability. Quant was inspired by these ideas, and sought to provide clothing with a new focus on youth.

■ Pop art

Quant admired the graphic qualities of artists such as Andy Warhol and Roy Lichtenstein, as well as the psychedelic prints and motifs inspired by the popularity of psychotropic drugs.

Begins to export to the United States with great success. Launches the Ginger Group, a lower-priced line for mass production.	*Invents the miniskirt (also claimed by André Courrèges).*	*Creates the 'paint-box' make-up set in which all make-up colours are consolidated on one palette. Receives OBE (Officer of the Order of the British Empire).*	*Launches her wildly popular hot pants. At the zenith of their popularity, they could even be worn at formal occasions under high-slit skirts.*	*Resigns as design director from Mary Quant Ltd. The company continues to enjoy success in Japan, particularly with cosmetic products.*
1962–63	**1965**	**1966**	**1969**	**2000**

● Marc Jacobs

Jacobs has often mined the 1960s time period during his career, producing many cute A-line dresses with graphic details that are reminiscent of Quant.

● Diane von Furstenberg

Von Furstenberg designs many dresses that use graphic black and white colour blocking, as well as the short minidresses popularized by Quant.

● Emma Cook

Cook has shown a number of designs that are a clear homage to Quant, from pieces with graphic colour blocking to A-line minidresses.

● Anna Sui

Sui is similar to Quant in her interest in the aesthetic symbols of the 1960s, along with her association with a young trendy customer. Both designers have in common the desire for affordable clothing for the young.

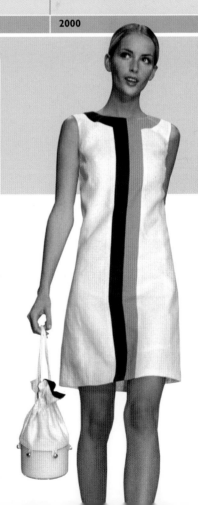

short pantaloons, and made pinafore dresses in bright colours. Her colourfully patterned opaque tights were quint-essential of the new youthful look, as well as her shoes and boots with a low flat heel. Mary Quant herself modelled the archetypal 1960s Vidal Sassoon bowl haircut that quickly became synonymous with her clothing.

After opening her second store, Quant decided to go wholesale to keep prices down. When she began exporting to the United States in 1963, she was an instant sensation. To keep up with demand, she began mass-producing clothing under the label Ginger Group. Mary Quant was a pivotal influence to all female designers as an entrepreneur and an essential contributor to the youthquake movement.

'Good designers must catch the spirit of the day and interpret it in clothes before other designers begin to twitch at the nerve ends… I just happened to start when that "something in the air" was coming to a boil.'

Mary Quant

Giorgio Armani revolutionized a type of uniform that men have been wearing since the dawn of the 19th century: the suit. The suit for men, and perhaps more importantly for women, has changed monumentally to reflect the latest developments in gender politics in our society.

 INFLUENCED BY

KEY
- ● fashion designer
- ◆ fashion house/brand
- ■ artistic influence
- ❖ cultural influence

● **Claire McCardell**
McCardell has had an impact on all designers who have invested in a soft, unconstructed silhouette. She has particularly influenced Armani's use of softly draped halter dresses, hardware, large belts and soft-shouldered jackets, which are featured prominently in many of his collections.

● **Cristóbal Balenciaga**
Balenciaga created architecture on the form, and was opposed to fashion becoming too complicated or hard to wear. The two designers also share a philosophy that it is a bad business move to deviate from what the customer is used to, a theory that has served Armani well.

● **Coco Chanel**
One of the first designers to incorporate men's clothing into womenswear, as well as promote a lithesome physique, Chanel has had an enormous impact on Armani as a designer, as seen in his Autumn 2009 collection (left).

GIORGIO ARMANI
Italian
(1934 Piacenza)

	Born July 11th in Piacenza in northern Italy.	Works as assistant photographer, window dresser and then head buyer at La Rinascente department store in Milan.	Begins working for Nino Cerruti as menswear designer, creating knits and shirts for the Hitman line, and later advancing into suits.	Begins freelancing for several companies while continuing to consult at Hitman.	Creates his own company, Giorgio Armani S.p.A., with partner Sergio Galeotti. Continues to freelance.
CHRONOLOGY	**1934**	**1957–63**	**1964**	**1970–74**	**1975**

→ **INSPIRED**

● **Bruno Pieters**
In his Autumn 2008 collection (right), Pieters examined the connection between menswear and feminine dressing – something that Armani has done throughout his career.

● **Ralph Lauren**
Lauren has expanded beyond his early strictly thematic collections to encapsulate an understated elegance that often borrows aesthetic styling from Armani.

● **Jil Sander**
Sander often included soft, unlined business attire that allowed the fabrics to mould to the feminine form, in the same way that Armani had introduced in the 1970s.

● **Donna Karan**
Karan was undoubtedly influenced by the innovations of Armani as she strove to redefine professional women's attire.

First and foremost, Giorgio Armani's impact on fashion will always be associated with the softer, unconstructed suit that has now become ubiquitous in professional wear. His innovations are placed equally in menswear and womenswear, allowing a relaxed elegance and sophistication in both.

RELAXING AND SOFTENING THE SUIT
In a world overwhelmed by large shoulders and dark colours for men, Armani used the subtle colours of brown and taupe, and blue and cream, while relaxing the shoulders and softening the silhouette. For women, Armani created a refined soft suit that suggested a quiet strength: 'I have always had a rather carefree, easy-going woman in mind, but not one who is brazenly so; a woman who wants to dress, but not overstate who she is, or what part she plays in the world. A woman above all and at all costs. A woman who knows how to live alongside a man with the sense of equality she deserves.'

TAILORING FOR WOMEN
Armani's clothes were able to make women feel comfortable and unrestricted by their clothing, yet also feminine and soft. Armani realized that the new professional woman was not interested in being a man, but instead wanted to be equal to him: 'My style changed [women's] way of presenting themselves. I sensed women wanted to be a little different. My fluidity gave them a way of interpreting their bodies in a more personal, individual way.'

His younger sister and her friends were perfect examples, as they borrowed men's clothing and tried to adapt it to their own bodies. Armani used tailoring not only to soften the fit of the jacket to suit a woman's figure, but also to

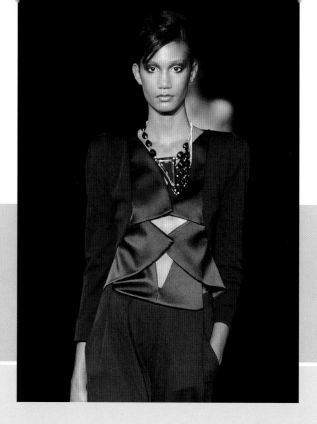

→ Chic tuxedo

Armani's Spring 2010 collection featured several feminine interpretations of the famous Yves Saint Laurent tuxedo. Saint Laurent was the first designer to use menswear details as a metaphor for power and strength in women.

INFLUENCED BY

KEY
- ● fashion designer
- ◆ fashion house/brand
- ■ artistic influence
- ❖ cultural influence

● Halston

Halston made a name for himself with his soft-shouldered and largely unconstructed pieces, allowing Armani room to create his own innovations with the soft suit.

● Yves Saint Laurent

One of the French couturier's signature looks is Le Smoking tuxedo suit for women. Saint Laurent often incorporated men's dress details into womenswear, starting in the 1970s, and Armani has done the same thing in the 1980s and beyond.

GIORGIO ARMANI CONTINUED

CHRONOLOGY	1976	1978	1979	1980	1981	1982
	Shows his first menswear collection, followed by a women's collection.	Launches Giorgio Armani Le Collezioni, a less expensive menswear collection.	Launches Le Collezioni for women.	Richard Gere wears Armani in the movie American Gigolo. Armani enters into a licensing agreement with L'Oréal to create Armani fragrances.	Launches Armani Junior, Emporio Armani and Armani Jeans.	Featured on the cover of Time magazine, the first fashion designer since Christian Dior.

INSPIRED

● Joseph Abboud

Abboud is known as a menswear designer, but has translated his menswear into a soft feminine silhouette using menswear fabrics (right), much in the way that Armani premiered.

● Louis Dell'Olio

Dell'Olio used softened tailoring and silhouettes from Armani, combining them with his experience working at Anne Klein, to create clothing for professional women in the 1980s (right).

● Calvin Klein

Klein expanded his collections from hard-line suits to include beaded soft dress pieces, as well as taking Armani's lead in creating soft suiting.

address the drape of a garment that traditionally has always helped to construct the figure architecturally: 'The jacket should be running down the body without sticking to it; a second skin.'

Apart from his innovations with suits, Armani offers a subtle and sophisticated choice for eveningwear, with clean, uncluttered silhouettes, refined beading and embroideries, and a colour palette that lends itself to understated elegance.

INTERNATIONAL REPUTATION

In Armani's extensive career, he has established a loyal following, most notably in the entertainment industry. As actress, director and producer Jodie Foster says, 'I suppose I wear Armani because it suits who I am, someone who cares for comfort, fit, subtle fabrics. I don't need to be the flashiest person in the room, just the most confident.'

He has supplied clothing for countless Hollywood blockbusters, from *American Gigolo*, which firmly established Armani in the United States, to *The Untouchables*, *Gattaca*, *Joe Versus the Volcano* and many more. Many actors and actresses wear his clothing on the red carpet, helping to cement Armani's reputation on an international scale.

Armani is consistent, never swerving to accommodate a new trend, colour palette or silhouette. Women and men turn to Armani time and again because of how well his formula works: 'I think, more than anything else, of the ladies that I like to dress. I have stepped away from doing something that is a surprise, that gives a "wow" effect, and taken more into consideration the fact that I have to dress my clients in such a way that they feel good.'

'I thought there must be a way of refining the freedom that I saw everywhere. I had to reject convention, but I did not want to discard everything that was good in the past. I had to find a new way of inventing and thinking about clothing for a new era.'

Giorgio Armani

● Paul Poiret
Although a comparison to the flamboyant and theatrical Poiret seems unlikely, in fact Armani often creates clothing that has an elegance and mysticism reminiscent of Poiret's work inspired by the Ballets Russes.

● Jean Patou
Patou became famous for incorporating activewear inspirations into daywear for women in the 1930s. Patou softened the shoulders and promoted physical health with his clothing, much like Armani.

● Mariano Fortuny
The two Italian designers share a desire for opulent simplicity, as well as shapes in clothing that are largely unchanged because they work so well.

Designs clothes for the television series Miami Vice.	New York's Metropolitan Museum of Art holds an exhibition, 'Giorgio Armani: Images of Man'.	Launches A/X Armani Exchange, a chain of boutiques geared to urbanwear.	New York's Guggenheim Museum holds a 25th-anniversary Armani retrospective.
1984	**1990**	**1991**	**2000**

● Alberta Ferretti
Ferretti often uses a neutral colour palette, as well as beading and sheer luxurious fabrics, that call to mind the work of Armani.

← Sheer femininity
Sheer suits in the Spring 2010 Alberta Ferretti collection utilize Armani-like fit, but push the sense of femininity further with the use of ethereal layers of sheer fabrics. The jacket, which has its basis in a men's suit jacket, employs soft drape on the front for a feminine finish.

↑ Stunning textiles
Giorgio Armani shows a wonderful sense of restraint in his Autumn 2009 eveningwear, with the colours and textiles conveying a feeling of luxury and sophistication. Here, the velvet skirt and silk chiffon scarf have subtle jewel tones that create a play of shadow and light.

There are many fashion designers who are household names because of the longevity of their careers, their licensing deals or their innate ability to understand the times and how women want to dress. Yves Saint Laurent's career encompassed all these elements and combined them with originality, helping to define the changing ideas of women from the 1950s through the 1980s.

INFLUENCED BY

KEY
- ● fashion designer
- ◆ fashion house/brand
- ■ artistic influence
- ❖ cultural influence

❖ **Youth culture**
The association of multiculturalism and women's rights to the youth movement of the 1960s and 1970s was ingrained in all Saint Laurent's collections of that time. Saint Laurent brought legitimacy to ready-to-wear by creating his hugely popular Rive Gauche collections, thus helping to shift the primary focus of fashion.

■ **Theatre**
Having considered theatre design before couture, Saint Laurent never forgot his love of the theatre, winning several citations and awards for his costume work. Theatricality and the stage found their way into his couture collections throughout his career. (Right: Yves Saint Laurent adjusts Roland Petit's costume during a performance of *Les Chants de Maldoror* in 1962.)

YVES SAINT LAURENT
French
(1936 Oran, Algeria)

CHRONOLOGY	1936	1954	1957–58	1959
	Born August 1st in Oran in French Algeria.	Wins first prize in an International Wool Secretariat competition for young fashion designers. Michel de Brunhoff, editor of French Vogue, introduces him to Christian Dior, who hires him.	Named successor of the house of Dior after Dior's death. Presents his first Dior collection, Ligne Trapèze, to much acclaim.	Designs his first theatre costumes and scenery for choreographer Roland Petit's Cyrano de Bergerac. Designs for many theatre productions over the following years.

INSPIRED

● **Tom Ford**
From 2000 to 2004, Ford served as creative director at the house of Yves Saint Laurent with much success. Ford used Saint Laurent's love of colour, romance and drama, such as in this Autumn 2003 piece (right), but received harsh criticism from Saint Laurent himself.

● **Alber Elbaz for Lanvin**
Elbaz created his Spring 2009 collection with a playfulness and adroit use of fabric and colour that are reminiscent of the iconic Saint Laurent.

● **Marc Jacobs for Louis Vuitton**
Jacobs's Spring 2009 collection for Louis Vuitton paid homage to Saint Laurent and the theatricality of the 1980s. Jacobs has often cited Saint Laurent as an inspiration, because the noted designer helped to define fashion in Jacobs's formative design years.

That Yves Saint Laurent is one of the most influential designers of the 20th century is indisputable, and in large part this is because he was able to adapt his style to accommodate the changes in fashion created by developments in society.

THREE CAREER PHASES
Yves Saint Laurent had three distinct phases in his career that correspond to the decades in which he actively designed. First, as assistant and heir to Christian Dior's legacy in the 1950s, Saint Laurent was the shy and introverted artist who wanted to be accepted.

Second, in the 1960s and early 1970s, Saint Laurent met his business and romantic partner, Pierre Bergé. Bergé, along with the new emphasis on youth, the sexual revolution and antiwar movement, emboldened Saint Laurent to become a rebel in the fashion world, abandoning the couture traditions in favour of the more affordable ready-to-wear.

As his empire grew, Saint Laurent entered the third phase of his career in the 1980s, in which he retreated to his first love of the fantasy of theatre. The easiest way to combine fantasy and clothing is through couture, so Saint Laurent left the harsh realities of a saleable ready-to-wear business to assistants. Saint Laurent said in 1983, 'I maintain that the designer who cannot call himself a couturier, who has never mastered the subtlest intricacies of the actual putting together of his creations, is like a sculptor who hands over his designs to some artisan to work out. This sort of truncated method of working is akin to an interrupted act of love – the result inescapably impoverished and flawed.'

← Smart beauty

Later in Yves Saint Laurent's career, he became known for creating dramatic and artfully crafted work, as seen in this Spring 1992 ensemble, that provided his incredibly loyal customers with what they needed, while also inspiring other designers in their level of skill.

↓ Ode to Mondrian

Saint Laurent literally brought his love of modern art to fashion in 1965, with the creation of the Mondrian dress. Shown here at the retrospective couture show in 2002, the dress was groundbreaking because of its fashionable interpretation.

■ Art

An avid collector with partner Pierre Bergé, Saint Laurent intertwined art in some of his most important collections. From his famous Mondrian dress to pop art, art was a primary influence for Saint Laurent.

Presents a controversial couture collection inspired by street fashion. On being drafted into the French military, he is replaced at Dior by Marc Bohan.	*Starts his own house with partner Pierre Bergé. His first collection under his own YSL label is a great success.*	*His Autumn collection, Ligne Mondrian, is heralded as a masterpiece.*
1960	**1961–62**	**1965**

● Christian Lacroix

Echoing Saint Laurent, Lacroix's overarching style has been one of rich colour, embellishments and theatricality, from his work at the house of Patou to his own eponymous couture collections.

● Nicolas Ghesquière for Balenciaga

Ghesquière's Autumn 2009 collection (left) utilized draped charmeuse with a mix of prints and hard tailoring that call to mind many of the experimental constructions that appeared on the Saint Laurent catwalk.

ARTISTIC INSPIRATIONS

Yves Saint Laurent had originally wanted to become a theatre and costume designer, before succumbing to fate in the world of fashion design. Throughout his career, he designed costumes and stage sets for ballets, plays and operas. Later in life, he was honoured with many retrospectives – for example, an exhibition of his set designs and theatre costumes at the Galerie Proscenium in Paris in 1974, and an exhibition of his theatre designs at the Musée des Arts Décoratifs in 1986. He also received numerous awards, including a fashion Oscar as the greatest couturier for his lifetime's work, presented to him at the Paris Opéra in 1985.

Yves Saint Laurent and Pierre Bergé were avid collectors of modern and contemporary art, with several seminal examples within their collection. Saint Laurent's fashion collections of the 1960s through the 1980s were often inspired by artists such as Vincent van Gogh, Pablo Picasso, Georges Braque, Henri Matisse, Piet Mondrian, Andy Warhol and others.

LOVE OF THE EXOTIC

Another primary theme in Saint Laurent's work was multiculturalism, or the love of the exotic. Having grown up in French Algeria, he had a different perspective from that of a native Parisian. His experiences, along with an emphasis on non-Western ideas in the 1960s and 1970s, helped to inform several of his most memorable collections and broadened the view of the fashion world. Yves Saint Laurent was the first major fashion house to use black and Asian models in its fashion shows.

'I belong to a world devoted to elegance. I grew up in another time much attached to tradition, yet at the same time, I wanted to change all that. I felt myself drawn to the past, while the future drove me ahead. I feel divided, and I think I always will be, for I am familiar with one world, yet am aware of the presence of another.'

Yves Saint Laurent

INFLUENCED BY

KEY
- ● fashion designer
- ◆ fashion house/brand
- ■ artistic influence
- ❖ cultural influence

● Christian Dior
As Dior's assistant, there is no doubt that the young Saint Laurent was influenced by Dior's sense of drama, romance and deep respect for the couture traditions.

❖ North Africa
Having grown up in French Algeria, Saint Laurent was continuously inspired by the area's mystery and exoticism, and the silhouettes of regional dress.

● Coco Chanel
In his 1994 collections (left), Saint Laurent paid homage to the late Chanel, using her signature colours of black and white, as well as the Chanel bow and striped shirt. Chanel had a great respect for Saint Laurent's work; in fact, she approached him to take over her company in the late 1950s. They each understood the changes in womenswear, and the need for comfortable yet elegant clothing. Both also adapted menswear for women, and developed signature looks that appeared each season.

YVES SAINT LAURENT CONTINUED

	The Autumn collection features his first tuxedos for women. Opens the first Rive Gauche ready-to-wear boutique in Paris.	His Spring collection draws influence from African art. He dresses Catherine Deneuve in the film Belle de Jour.	Introduces the safari look in his Spring collection.	Retrospective of his work is held at the Metropolitan Museum of Art's Costume Institute in New York.	Palace of Fine Arts in Beijing, China, hosts a retrospective of his work. Awarded the French Légion d'honneur.
CHRONOLOGY	**1966**	**1967**	**1968**	**1983**	**1985**

INSPIRED

● Stefano Pilati
Creative director of the house of Yves Saint Laurent since 2004, Pilati plays with the iconic images and impressions of the YSL label, while venturing onto his own path of architectural silhouettes. Within each collection, there is almost always a reference to iconic YSL pieces, such as Le Smoking or the safari jacket, but he is never slavishly referential. As Pilati said at his Autumn 2008 show, 'I don't think you want to go out advertising a brand anymore. You just want to feel proud walking down the street.' This is perhaps his greatest similarity to Saint Laurent, who struggled in his early career to forsake the shadow of Christian Dior.

➜ Le Smoking
Stefano Pilati's Autumn 2009 collection for the house of Yves Saint Laurent is a clear reference to the YSL staple, Le Smoking. The reason the dinner jacket for women continues to be so popular is the wonderful balance between matt and shine, structure and softness, and (with a plunging neckline) masculine and feminine.

TUXEDOS FOR WOMEN

The embrace of the sexual revolution by Yves Saint Laurent was essential to his wide success. Today, trousers for women are ubiquitous in both a personal and professional setting. It is hard to believe, therefore, that in the 1960s and 1970s, they were not largely accepted for women's dress.

Yves Saint Laurent was the first major couture house to introduce trousers for women, in the iconic Le Smoking suit based on a man's dinner jacket. Saint Laurent was able to show that women could look feminine and appealing while wearing a man's suit, as he stated in 1969: 'I have been strongly influenced by photographs of Marlene Dietrich in a man's suit. A woman who dresses like a man – in tuxedo, or blazer – has to be infinitely more feminine in order to wear clothes which were not meant for her. She must be pretty and refined down to the smallest detail.'

• Elsa Schiaparelli
Schiaparelli was the first designer to identify with artists and their work. Her sense of the theatrical and her love of art made a clear impression on Saint Laurent.

• Cristóbal Balenciaga
Balenciaga was a notable influence on any Parisian fashion designer of the era, because of his exquisite craftsmanship and use of experimental shapes and fabrics, as emulated by Saint Laurent.

Stages an extravagant fashion show at the final match of the football World Cup in Paris.	Officially retires.	Dies on June 1st of brain cancer.
1998	**2002**	**2008**

• Ralph Lauren
In 1994, Saint Laurent successfully won a lawsuit against the American designer for Lauren's blatant copy of Le Smoking tuxedo suit.

• Zac Posen
A celebrity favourite for the red carpet, Posen has clearly been inspired by the stellar dramatic looks that populated Saint Laurent's couture collections.

← Feminine mobster
This suit was inspired by the 1930s revival that took place during the 1970s. Films such as *The Godfather* and *Bonnie and Clyde* celebrated the romantic notions of gangster or mob life. The beautiful fit of the suit leaves no doubt that it is for a woman.

Azzedine Alaïa has made a career of living outside the rules of fashion, yet continues to be an incredibly important designer whose work is often referenced in the collections of others. Having helped to define body-conscious dressing in the 1980s, Alaïa's work has evolved to connect the past and the future of design.

 INFLUENCED BY

KEY
● fashion designer
◆ fashion house/brand
■ artistic influence
❖ cultural influence

● **Madeleine Vionnet**	● **Cristóbal Balenciaga**	● **Issey Miyake**	● **Charles James**
Alaïa was featured in a book about Vionnet, deconstructing her techniques. He expressed an overwhelming admiration for her work. Within his own career, he has chosen to focus on craft and technique, much as Vionnet did.	Like Alaïa, Balenciaga focused primarily on technique and the advancement of the technologies of dressmaking. In addition, Balenciaga also had an estranged relationship with the fashion press.	Miyake has emphasized the interconnection of fabric and body, and developed numerous innovations in the craft of fashion with his techniques and philosophies, just as Alaïa has done.	James was known to ignore deadlines and shipping orders, because of his own requirements of handcrafted work or his desire to innovate construction, like Alaïa. The difference between the two designers is that James was said to have a difficult personality, whereas Alaïa is warm and affectionate.

AZZEDINE ALAÏA
Tunisian
(1940 Jemmal)

Alaïa has claimed of his exact birth date: 'Having tried hard, I forgot it.'	Briefly studies sculpture before becoming a dressmaker's assistant.	Moves to Paris and works at the house of Dior for just five days, then in the tailoring department at Guy Laroche.	Becomes private dressmaker and personal assistant to the Comtesse de Blegiers, before opening his own dress shop.	Several of his pieces are featured in Elle magazine. He continues to have a loyal following among women who love his construction abilities.
CHRONOLOGY **1940**	**1955**	**1957**	**1960–65**	**1979**

 INSPIRED

● **Julien Macdonald**	● **Bryan Bradley for Tuleh**	● **Martin Grant**		● **Charlotte Ronson**
Macdonald borrowed many style details that are reminiscent of Alaïa's brand of sexy power to create the silhouettes of his Spring 2010 collection.	Bradley created some kicky, short swing skirts and open neckline jackets that are reminiscent of Alaïa.	The Australian designer incorporated an Alaïa signature of a knit hood with a slinky and sexy dress in his Autumn 2009 collection.		In her Autumn 2009 collection (left), several looks reference Alaïa's use of shearling and leather, short skirts and the enlarged houndstooth that he made popular in the 1980s

Azzedine Alaïa has the eternal moniker 'king of cling' attached to his name because of his body-hugging dresses made of stretchy viscose knits that defined the fashion of the 1980s. To wear Alaïa's clothing, a woman would have to have a well-toned physique and the confidence to show it off. If those requirements are present, the outcome is devastating, which is why so many models and actresses are associated with Alaïa's name.

For many of Alaïa's clients, the dresses are made specifically for them, so that the fit is perfect. Alaïa has many loyal followers among models who have otherwise been characterized as prima donnas – Naomi Campbell, for example, who is said to call Alaïa 'Papa'. Some models, including Stephanie Seymour, Linda Evangelista and Claudia Schiffer, have worked for Alaïa for free during times when his career has ebbed. Cathy Horyn of the *New York Times* has such respect for Alaïa that she visits his studio and home in Paris to chat or have a bite to eat. Their conversations and her admiration for his work are evident in the many articles and blog entries that she has published.

FEMININE STRENGTH AND POWER
The influence of Alaïa's work is ultimately not about the models who wear his clothing or the powerful members of the fashion press. It is about the pieces he has created that have helped to define feminine strength and power. Azzedine Alaïa has unintentionally helped to define the third wave of feminism, in which women take command of the objectification of their bodies, and turn it around as a form of control and potent sexuality.

There have actually been a great number of pieces introduced by the Tunisian designer that do not show a great deal

King of cling

This outfit from Spring 1991, among others, has helped to cement Alaïa's nickname of 'king of cling'. Playing on a graphic variation of the masculine houndstooth, the full-length gloves, bra and miniskirt are combined for an ultra-feminine presentation.

→ A View to a Kill

Alaïa dressed Grace Jones for the 1985 James Bond film *A View to a Kill*, most notably this devastating look that takes full advantage of her striking height, figure and presence.

INFLUENCED BY

KEY
- ● fashion designer
- ◆ fashion house/brand
- ■ artistic influence
- ❖ cultural influence

● **Christian Dior**
Dior designed clothing that redefined the shape of women and became iconic in the 20th century. Alaïa will always be associated with the 1980s, just as Dior is with the 1950s.

AZZEDINE ALAÏA CONTINUED

	Launches a ready-to-wear collection, but refuses to participate in Paris Fashion Week.	Designs clothes for Grace Jones in the James Bond film A View to a Kill.	Retrospective of his work is held at the Groninger Museum in the Netherlands.	Enters a partnership with the house of Prada, on condition that an archive of his work be set up and that he be allowed to work in his usual way. Retrospective of his work is held at New York's Guggenheim Gallery, showing his pieces on clear plastic mannequins to emphasize the sculptural qualities.
CHRONOLOGY	1981	1985	1998	2000

INSPIRED

● **Giles Deacon**
In Spring 2008, Deacon created several pieces that showed a reference to Alaïa tailoring, particularly a sexy swimsuit that was reminiscent of Alaïa shorts.

● **Yigal Azrouël**
Azrouël has shown several silhouettes that reference the work of Alaïa, such as the short tight dresses in his Spring 2010 collection (left).

● **Isabel Toledo**
Toledo has chosen to ignore the traditional fashion week timeline to devote herself to the pursuit of her craft and technique. She works within a studio that is also her home, as Alaïa does, always in pursuit of innovation but at her own pace.

of skin nor are particularly revealing, yet in each piece what remains is the undercurrent of allure and provocation. Alaïa clearly loves women, and wants to create clothing that makes them not only beautiful but also confident: 'I really love it when a woman wears a new dress and someone falls in love with her the same day!'

STUBBORN PERFECTIONIST
Alaïa stubbornly refuses to adhere to any seasonal timeline constructed by the fashion industry. He shows garments when he chooses, making editors and buyers come to Paris solely for him. This has created a lot of problems for Alaïa within his career. He has not been featured in *Vogue* magazine, despite his influence on the fashion industry, because he does not operate on big budgets, nor does he court the fashion press.

Alaïa insists on creating each sample garment himself, and refuses all but the most minimal staff. This has often affected his delivery dates to stores, because he refuses to rush production or development. Not only is he a perfectionist about construction and finishing, but he is also one of the few designers to believe that quality of life is more important than work. Alaïa is devoted to his work, but he does not let it overtake him.

BRIDGING THE OLD AND THE NEW
Alaïa tinkers and experiments with many couture techniques that he has adapted for a more contemporary aesthetic. His innovations in construction and fabrications are routinely seen on the catwalks of other designers, yet he is unaffected by trends, preferring to work according to his own philosophies of fashion. Although Alaïa has a real appreciation and

'What drives me to continue is the pleasure to keep on learning. In other words, perfection is never achieved so you need to go on working.'

Azzedine Alaïa

→ Model attraction
Alaïa has a great deal of influence on models such as Daria Werbowy, pictured here in 2007. Alaïa's clothing shows everything on the female figure to the best advantage while also being relaxed and comfortable.

❖ Africa
Alaïa often references his native North Africa in fabrication or silhouette, infusing French fashion with new details and ideas. (Left: Sculpture of North African women.)

● Yves Saint Laurent
Saint Laurent was born in Algeria and, like Alaïa, references of his childhood in North Africa can often be seen in his work. The two designers also helped to define powerful femininity in their own time.

■ Contemporary art
Alaïa commissioned artist Julian Schnabel to create the interior of Alaïa's boutiques. As the artist said, 'When you are in fashion you have to always be aware of everything.'

Presents his first couture collection, to great excitement.

After not being invited to an exhibition at New York's Metropolitan Museum of Art about the relationship between designers and models, Alaïa asks the models that he designs dresses for not to wear his creations to the opening. Many models, such as Naomi Campbell, refuse to go at all.

New first lady Michelle Obama wears an Alaïa dress to a NATO summit dinner in Germany, in contrast to the tradition of wearing American designers.

2003   **2008**   **2009**

● Hervé Léger
Léger was known for his body-conscious clothing that had a similar aesthetic to Alaïa's work. The French designer used materials traditionally reserved for undergarments, and designed tight-fitting, sexy dresses in bold, bright colours. He also created stripes by using strips of heavy knit that would pull in the figure for a flattering look.

● Frida Giannini for Gucci
Giannini has a reputation for sexy, provocative clothing, and what better designer to look at than Alaïa.

love of couture, along with an admiration for past designers' work, he has never been tempted to model his own work on the creations of others: 'When I see beautiful clothes, I want to keep them, preserve them… Clothes, like architecture and art, reflect an era.' Alaïa understands that we cannot continue to look backward in the pursuit of a look for the 21st century.

Alaïa's work is easily recognizable, yet it continues to expand in scope. Ultimately, it is this balance that helps him bridge the old and the new, advancing the definitions of image, feminism, materials and techniques, but with a healthy respect for the past.

← All the right places
Hervé Léger has followed in Azzedine Alaïa's footsteps, becoming known for his thick strips of elasticized fabric that suck in or push out the figure in all the right places, such as this Spring 1995 look.

In the mid-1980s, Donna Karan simplified women's clothing to seven interchangeable pieces that would function from day to evening and in any situation. Using her own needs as a guide, she eradicated any unnecessary or annoying parts of the clothing, and designed a new uniform for women everywhere.

INFLUENCED BY

KEY
- ● fashion designer
- ◆ fashion house/brand
- ■ artistic influence
- ❖ cultural influence

● Anne Klein
Karan's formative training came from Klein's no-nonsense approach to women's clothing. Karan said, 'Anne Klein was a woman who understood women. I was in awe of her, she was such an innovator.'

● Claire McCardell
Like Karan, McCardell believed that women wanted comfortable, easy clothing that solved their problems, not created new ones. McCardell also introduced a system of interchangeable pieces.

● Mariano Fortuny
In her Autumn 1997 collection as well as at the 1997 Biennale di Firenze international contemporary art exhibition, Karan used cut velvet in colours and shapes that suggested the mastery of Fortuny.

● Tom Ford for Gucci
Karan's Autumn 2003 collection featured jersey dresses with cutouts and attached jewellery, reminiscent of Tom Ford for Gucci.

● Yohji Yamamoto
In addition to Karan's shared fondness for black, the Japanese designer has clearly influenced her in the approach to fabric and its proximity to the body.

DONNA KARAN
American
(1948 New York)

Born Donna Faske on October 2nd in Queens, New York. Her mother is a showroom model; her father and stepfather are tailors.	Attends New York's Parsons School of Design, but leaves to work for Anne Klein.	Promoted to associate designer and then head designer after Anne Klein's death.	Leaves Anne Klein and begins her own company, Donna Karan New York.	Launches DKNY, a diffusion line aimed at younger women. DKNY is designed by Jane Chung, who was with Karan at Anne Klein.

CHRONOLOGY	1948	1968	1971–74	1984	1989

INSPIRED

● Isaac Mizrahi
Mizrahi was a student at Parsons School of Design when Karan served as a critic. She taught Mizrahi and other students the importance of drape and construction in terms of wearability.

● Narciso Rodriguez
Rodriguez states: 'Donna was my idol as a teenager. I had one dream, to go to Parsons and work for Donna Karan… I mean, she was it for me.'

● Douglas Hannant
The young designer has clearly been inspired by the work of Karan, from the ease and comfort of his silhouettes to the use of fur as a sleeve detail in his Spring 2010 collection (left).

● Adrienne Vittadini
Although Vittadini began her career in the 1970s, her style and philosophy have changed to suit the same woman that Karan appeals to.

Donna Karan's greatest innovations and her most significant contribution to fashion occurred mid-career when she began her own company in 1984. Her primary goal was to create clothing that could truly function for a working mother such as herself: 'You know, there is so much stuff out there, I wanted to simplify – simplify life, simplify how to dress, be able to travel, do things, be in the world… Why should a woman ask, "Excuse me what shoe do I wear with this? What clothes do I wear with this?" They want the full picture.'

SEVEN EASY PIECES
The result was Karan's seven easy pieces that she refined and expanded upon for the rest of the 1980s and early 1990s. The seven pieces were meant to take women from day to evening, without feeling uncomfortable or ill at ease. She designed for professional women, who did not have a

lot of time to construct a wardrobe and might not have the perfect size-10 figure. Karan used herself as a model, because she was a size 12 or 14, at the time with a young child, and running a business: 'I've always known that my insecurities were other people's too. I'm just like everybody else.'

Karan relied on a largely knit wardrobe that used tailoring to hide potentially problematic areas of the figure on many women, such as the belly or hips. Jackets were always long enough to cover the backside, hung from the shoulders and could either be belted or worn loose to allow for elegant camouflage. Having been annoyed one too many times by her shirt tails popping out of her waistband, Karan created body suits that used a shirt top with a unitard bottom.

Karan also introduced monochromatic dressing for the ease of matching. Each season saw a new set of monochromatic colours, but always matching previous seasons. Karan

← New career woman
This Autumn 1986 outfit is a prime example of the significant contribution that Donna Karan has made to professional wear for women. The design of the garment helped women to feel confident despite imperfect figures, while also allowing for comfort during an active and industrious day.

'For me designing is a personal expression of who I am – a woman, a mother, friend and businessperson – the many roles women everywhere are trying to balance.'

Donna Karan

● Madeleine Vionnet
Vionnet has had a clear influence on Karan's work, from the use of drape to her views on the interaction of body and fabric.

● Halston
Karan said, 'Halston understood comfort clothes, and real ease, in a simple, sexy kind of way. Halston had expressed the possibilities of jersey.'

Resigns as CEO of her company, but remains creative director. Peter Speliopoulos takes over designing the Donna Karan collection.

Sells Donna Karan International to luxury goods company LMVH.

1997   **2001**

● Isabel Toledo
Toledo is known to use her own clothing needs, as well as her figure, to test clothing before introducing it to the public. Karan defined her business in the mid-1980s with this same philosophy.

● Stella McCartney
Much in the same way that Karan helped to define the women of her generation, McCartney exemplifies a new idea of comfort in women's fashion, combined with a sense of ethical activism.

● Peter Speliopoulos
After working for Karan from 1993 to 1997, Speliopoulos left to work for the house of Cerruti, but returned to Karan in 2002. He has endeavoured to create clothing that takes Karan's principal philosophies into the 21st century, helping women to continue defining themselves through their clothing.

incorporated her monochromatic approach into her accessories, working with famed jeweller Robert Lee Morris to create a series of accessories that perfectly matched, so that women would not even have to think about coordinating the finishing touches of their wardrobe.

→ Continuing tradition
The Spring 2010 collection that Peter Speliopoulos designed for Donna Karan continues the tradition of creating feminine clothing that can be worn by multiple body types, and appeals to the independent, stylish woman.

INNOVATIVE DESIGN SOLUTIONS

Donna Karan has been hailed by both the fashion press and loyal customers alike for her innovative design solutions that helped to empower women in the business world: 'I allow people to do their own thing. I help to facilitate what they want. Some people know what they want, some people don't. Another thing to me is that I wanted to show that it is not about age, it's a state of being. It's about somebody who's secure with their own self and their own body. It's about helping that process along.'

Miuccia Prada became a major force in trendsetting in the 1990s, and has continued into the 21st century. She has managed to keep her brand at the forefront of fashion because of her forceful desire for change and re-examinations of everything from craft, femininity, beauty and maturity to the ultimate question of what clothing means in the contemporary context.

INFLUENCED BY

KEY
● fashion designer
◆ fashion house/brand
■ artistic influence
❖ cultural influence

● **Yves Saint Laurent**
Much has been made of Prada's distribution of communist propaganda in the late 1960s dressed in Yves Saint Laurent. Beyond wearing his clothing, Prada's Spring 2007 collection was clearly influenced by Saint Laurent, who created luxury for the young intellectuals of Paris in the 1960s and 1970s, a clientele not dissimilar to that of Prada.

● **Karl Lagerfeld**
Lagerfeld has said that there is no beauty without some strangeness in the proportions, a philosophy that might also describe Prada's approach to beauty.

● **Ossie Clark**
Prada's Spring 2008 collection was inspired by the art nouveau revival of the 1970s (left) and light ethereal prints, both reminiscent of Ossie Clark.

MIUCCIA PRADA
Italian
(1949 Milan)

Maria Bianchi born May 10th in Milan in northern Italy; she later becomes professionally known as Miuccia Prada. She is the granddaughter of Mario Prada, who cofounded the Prada luxury goods company with his brother in 1913.	*After earning a doctorate in political science and then studying mime, she takes over the family business, but with great hesitation.*	*Opens a shop in Milan that is reflective of a more contemporary aesthetic.*	*Launches a footwear collection.*
CHRONOLOGY 1949	1978	1983	1984

INSPIRED

● **Behnaz Sarafpour**
In Sarafpour's Spring 2008 and Spring 2010 collections, the influence of Prada can be seen in the use of allover lace and in some of the silhouettes and details.

● **Christopher Bailey for Burberry**
In both his men's and women's collections, Prada's influence can be seen in Bailey's colour palette, shapes and silhouettes, and even the jewellery he used in Autumn 2008.

➜ **Loving lace**
The young New York designer Behnaz Sarafpour has always been fond of lace, and in her Spring 2010 collection uses it in much the same way as Prada a year earlier. She is also referencing men's clothing with the henley opening (the short buttoned opening at the neck of the dress), just as Prada referenced menswear with button-down shirts under her lace dresses.

Miuccia Prada has made a name for herself as an iconoclast, yet one who has helped to move the fashion industry in new directions through the almost constant trends that her collections set. She approaches fashion with an objective viewpoint; although she has a family heritage in the fashion luxury business, she also has a doctorate in political science and a rich history of individualistic life decisions.

BALANCING CREATIVITY AND FUNCTION
Prada's detached viewpoint of women's clothing is helped along by a nontraditional fashion education; for her, the collections must make sense as a functioning yet expressive idea, not always defined by convention. She has said, 'I follow my instinct, and even if a question arises whether what I am doing makes perfect sense to me or others, in reality the important thing is that I truly believe in it.'

← **Overcoming prejudice**
It is said that the reason that Miuccia Prada created almost an entire collection out of lace for Autumn 2008 was that she has always disliked the material. While that seems implausible, Prada has made a name for herself as someone who embraces what she is afraid of or dislikes in order to understand it.

● **Emmanuelle Khanh**
Early in Prada's career, she garnered attention for her formfitting, 1960s-inspired dresses that gave rise to the term 'ugly chic'. Khanh's work of the late 1960s and early 1970s display many similar proportions and details.

◆ **Biba**
The iconic London fashion store of the 1960s and 1970s was famous for a 1920s-inspired look that translated into a perpetual doll-like vision of femininity. Prada often integrates that idea into the Miu Miu diffusion collection, and draws liberally upon the Biba aesthetic.

Introduces the iconic Prada backpack made of waterproof nylon.	Launches the first Prada collection to be largely disliked by fashion critics, who consider it ugly and drab.	Launches diffusion line Miu Miu (her nickname), and then menswear.
1985	**1989**	**1992**

● **Vera Wang**
Wang often uses a rich colour palette and surface decoration, both first popularized by Prada.

● **Hannah MacGibbon for Chloé**
MacGibbon put cropped, Prada-style satin shorts on the catwalk for her Spring 2009 collection.

Her impact is so pronounced within the fashion industry because her perceptive understanding of functional clothing and business practices dictates that her designs must fill the needs of others: 'You have to balance creativity with an understanding of what happens around you and the reality is that selling is the only way to prove that what you are doing makes sense to people.'

UGLY CHIC

Prada's work clearly makes sense to a lot of people, and has come to be part of a larger reevaluation of idealized beauty for women. In her early career, Miuccia Prada was criticized for ungainly proportions, drab colours and unflattering silhouettes, and the term 'ugly chic' was coined for her work. Yet for many women, the shapes and colours made perfect sense, and the brand became associated with

➔ Inventive combinations

Miuccia Prada first had an eye for beautiful clothing as a customer, well before she ever started designing. In her Spring 2010 collection, Prada utilizes classic Balenciaga shirred (gathered) construction in the jacket, and pairs it with tiny shorts and girlish ponytails in her typical combination of high-brow and low-brow.

 INFLUENCED BY

KEY
- ● fashion designer
- ◆ fashion house/brand
- ■ artistic influence
- ❖ cultural influence

● **Rei Kawakubo**
Like Kawakubo, Prada has continually tried to redefine the ideal of beauty, and discourages the notion that femininity must be contingent on coquetry.

● **Cristóbal Balenciaga**
Prada has a penchant for the crisp, hard tailoring that Balenciaga perfected. Influences of the master are seen throughout many of Prada's collections.

MIUCCIA PRADA CONTINUED

CHRONOLOGY	1994	1996	1998	1999–2006
	Holds her first fashion show in New York. Opens a London boutique designed by architect Rem Koolhaas.	*Opens a large boutique in Manhattan in New York, designed by Koolhaas. By the late 1990s, the house of Prada has 40 store locations, 20 of which are in Japan.*	*Launches Prada Sport, and opens a men's store in Los Angeles.*	*House of Prada buys stakes in Helmut Lang and Fendi, takes over Jil Sander and buys controlling stock in Azzedine Alaïa. By 2006, all these holdings are sold off except Alaïa.*

 INSPIRED

● **Tomas Maier for Bottega Veneta**
Maier's Pre-Autumn 2009 show was all about easy elegance in muted purples and wines – a favourite palette of Prada's. The accessories of long gloves, opaque tights and clunky heels were also in tune with Prada.

● **Phillip Lim**
In his Spring 2010 collection, Lim incorporated military looks that had made Prada famous in the 1990s.

● **Phoebe Philo for Céline**
Philo's debut 2010 resort collection for Céline (left) borrowed from the military inspiration that Prada popularized in the 1990s.

forward-thinking intellectualism and luxury that was not based on sex.

Prada began asking the question: What was more appealing, the woman and her brain or the body of the woman? Prada suggested that clothing could imply the interesting and complex nature of the feminine spirit, a spirit that was often hidden from view: 'I don't like things that are too obvious and so I always try to introduce something that is wrong or different. Beauty in itself is too easy.' The result of her collections is to allow women to be feminine and alluring, yet not have to revert to a masculine form to suggest intelligence or autonomy.

PUSHING THE BOUNDARIES

With an absence of fashion training, Miuccia Prada often seems to approach the design process with a 'Why not?' attitude, assuming that anything is possible: 'My research for the new pushes me to invent every time a different process… Designing if you want to push boundaries is not easy. I like to embrace the complexity and choose one theme through which I try to express it.'

She therefore holds no process sacred, and is drawn to what interests her. Each season, Prada introduces collections that vary in their mood, construction or focus on textiles, colours or prints, yet that have a consistent aesthetic and always reflect an abstract understanding of women in our times. As Prada says, '[My work is] to express, in a simple banal object, a great complexity about women, aesthetics, and current times.'

← **Muted femininity**
Prada's Autumn 2010 collection emphasized healthy feminine proportions as well as revisiting Prada looks from the 1990s. The textiles were reminiscent of the time period in colour and pattern, from a preference for muted browns, greens and blues to the use of a scratchy plaid print.

● **Jil Sander**
Prada has been greatly influenced by the starkness, simplicity, and functionalism of the German designer's clothing – it is no random accident that Sander's company was once acquired by the Prada Group.

An exhibition in Seoul, Korea, 'Waist Down: Skirts by Miuccia Prada', features Prada's favourite item of clothing in a range of motions.

2009

◆ **Proenza Schouler**
Proenza Schouler's Autumn 2006 collection featured the richly coloured textural fabrics and geometric shapes that were part of the trends started by Prada.

'I like irony in my work, it's very much about sometimes what I like, but it's also about analysing why people like something and I try to find an ironic way of looking at it, like from the outside.'

Miuccia Prada

Claude Montana helped to define the 1980s woman, not by making her a fierce warrior, but by combining the archetypes and traditional symbols of masculinity and femininity to create a new silhouette. Monumentally influential during his time, Montana has often been referenced by contemporary designers, who remember his unique and powerful style.

 INFLUENCED BY

KEY
● fashion designer
◆ fashion house/brand
■ artistic influence
❖ cultural influence

● Madame Grès
Grès was known for her solid foundations that yielded soft drape, her manipulation of fabric and her emphasis on body-conscious construction, which can all be seen in Montana's work. Montana has said that Grès is one of the designers he most admires.

● Cristóbal Balenciaga
Balenciaga treated fabric architecturally, using shapes and construction that were both flattering and comfortable. In the many collections of Montana's in which the emphasis was not placed on the shoulders, Balenciaga's influence can be seen in the architectural treatment of fabric, as well as the luxurious austerity present in both designers' work.

● Christian Dior
Dior wanted to allow women to feel beautiful after the hardships of WWII. Montana used the same emphasis on form to create feminine silhouettes after the women's movement of the 1960s and 1970s.

● Yves Saint Laurent
Like Montana, Saint Laurent was known for his rich use of colour, as well as his early work that borrowed from menswear to imbue women with strength.

CLAUDE MONTANA
French
(1949 Paris)

CHRONOLOGY	1949	1971	1972	1973	1979–81	1983–86
	Born June 29th in Paris to a German mother and Spanish father.	Travels to London and designs papier-mâché jewellery encrusted with rhinestones.	Returns to Paris and designs leather biker clothing for Mac Douglas leather company.	Designs ready-to-wear leather clothing with Michelle Costas.	Creates an eponymous clothing collection for women. Follows with a menswear collection, Montana Hommes.	Opens two Montana boutiques. Launches a fragrance company.

 INSPIRED

● Stefano Pilati for Yves Saint Laurent
In his Autumn 2009 and Spring 2010 collections, Pilati showed leather, exaggerated shoulders and metal that looked as if they were inspired by the work of Montana.

● Riccardo Tisci for Givenchy
Tisci is often inspired by 1980s designers, with Montana's influence seen in many of his shows, such as the exaggerated shoulders of the Spring 2009 Givenchy couture collection (left).

● Zac Posen
The American designer created an Autumn 2009 collection that was equal parts Montana and Oscar de la Renta. Montana's influence can be seen in the architectural treatment of fabric, as well as the large shoulders.

◆ Proenza Schouler
The Spring 2009 collection featured the Montana silhouette and also paid homage to the model Jerry Hall, who was closely associated with Montana in the 1980s.

Claude Montana had a relatively short career as a designer, but was so influential in his look, philosophy and aesthetic that his contributions are referenced repeatedly. In the 1980s he was vilified by feminists, who felt that a return to high glamour, waist cinching and high heels was a step backward for all women. Having only recently staked out ground in a world dominated by men, many feminists believed that flat shoes, trousers and practical notions of dress were the way to be respected and succeed in a professional setting. Most women, however, wanted to find a balance between fitting into a 'man's world' and retaining their feminine character.

STRONG SHAPES
Montana emphasized strong shoulders throughout most of his career, along with large, dramatic collars. Although doing this suggested a masculine physique, large shoulders also promoted the much more feminine characteristic of a small waist. Montana often used a peplum (a short skirt or ruffle attached at the waistline) on cinched-waist jackets or full skirts to emphasize feminine shape. He rejected the use of corsets, understanding that modern women were interested in an idealized figure without discomfort.

Montana's favourite fabric was leather, which held the shapes he wanted to create and was also supple and soft for comfort. In addition, the use of leather suggested an undercurrent of sexuality and a sense of cool aloofness that worked well with women's changing image of themselves.

Montana's clothing also emphasized the need for physical fitness and self-control. The look of Montana's ideal woman was one of polished severity that suggested power and strength, and rejected the blurred lines or fleshy sexiness of the 1970s slick disco era. His models were often icy blondes,

← 1940s glamour

Montana's satin jacket ensemble from his Autumn 1991 collection for the house of Lanvin references the air of sophistication and glamour most often seen in Adrian's film costume designs of the 1940s. The hood and soft drape of the jacket are wonderfully flattering, as well as the shoulder pads that make the waist seem smaller.

'I hate doing the same thing over and over again, otherwise I wouldn't do this anymore.'

Claude Montana

● Adrian

Adrian often used large shoulders to emphasize a small waist, minimize larger hips and frame the face, just as Montana did after him.

● Pierre Cardin

Cardin was an early champion of the large shoulder, and helped to popularize its benefits to the figure. He also designed clothing that created an architectural geometry, which Montana learned from.

● Coco Chanel

Chanel is the quintessential French icon that so many designers reference as a source of chic. Montana was often inspired by Chanel, from the cut of a pair of trousers to the more literal striped fisherman's sweater that she popularized in the 1920s.

Works for the house of Lanvin. Launches State of Claude Montana, his own diffusion line.	Forced to close his company and declare bankruptcy.	Launches Montana Blu, a lower-priced line, but it fails to create enough revenue and is eventually closed.
1990–92	**1997**	**1999**

● Alexander McQueen

McQueen was undoubtedly influenced by the big names of the 1980s, not least Montana, whose soft architectural forms help to suggest the idealized silhouette that could be seen on McQueen's catwalk.

● Jonathan Saunders

For his Autumn 2009 collection, the British designer opened the show with several pieces that traced their roots back to the work of Montana in the use of exposed zips, bold colours, black legs and an emphasis on the shoulder.

● Marc Jacobs

Jacobs offered homage to Montana in his Autumn 2008 collection, with the large shoulders and asymmetric fez hats that had appeared on Montana's catwalk.

and his carefully orchestrated fashion shows required models who almost sneered at the audience.

COLOUR AND GRAPHIC DETAILS

Claude Montana eventually abandoned the strong shoulder, because it became an object of jokes and a symbol of the excess of the 1980s. He attempted to shift his philosophies of fit and balance into a 1990s perspective. Throughout that decade, Montana produced clothing that helped to camouflage a less-than-perfect figure, by emphasizing colour and graphic details. Unfortunately, his style so defined the 1980s that he was unable to create a new look that appealed to the changing aesthetic. In recent years, young designers who remember the 1980s have borrowed from his significant contributions, creating the translation that Montana himself was unable to accomplish.

→ Ode to a memory

Marc Jacobs is often influenced by his memories of fashion from when he was younger. Montana perfectly embodied the style and sophistication that in the 1980s seemed so new and exciting. For the Autumn 2008 Louis Vuitton show, Jacobs tapped into his excitement from seeing Montana's clothing at the height of their importance.

Jean Paul Gaultier wanted to create a new idea of fashion that directed questions at the establishment. What resulted was a designer who helped to define our present understanding of multiculturalism and sexual equality, and paved the way for a host of designers to follow in his iconoclastic footsteps.

INFLUENCED BY

KEY
- ● fashion designer
- ◆ fashion house/brand
- ■ artistic influence
- ❖ cultural influence

● Marcel Rochas
Gaultier was introduced to the world of couture by the 1944 film *Falbalas* about a fictional couturier, with all clothes provided by Rochas. The teenager watched the film and studied the costumes to understand the world of couture.

● Christian Dior
Gaultier was entranced by the technical prowess of Dior. Gaultier also believes that Dior was important because he provided change before women knew they wanted it, and was supremely successful.

● Pierre Cardin
Gaultier got his first job with Cardin in 1970. Cardin was committed to following his own agenda in fashion and being open to all possibilities, which taught a young Gaultier lessons he would never forget.

● Jacques Esterel
A now little-known designer, in the 1950s and 1960s Esterel earned the title 'court jester' for some of his outlandish ideas, such as a plaid skirt for men, trousers with zips back and front, and his ventures into the entertainment industry, all of which Gaultier has done in his own career.

JEAN PAUL GAULTIER
French
(1952 Arcueil)

CHRONOLOGY	1952	1970–71	1971–73	1974–75	1976
	Born April 24th in Arcueil.	Works as an assistant to Pierre Cardin and then for eccentric designer Jacques Esterel on the menswear line.	Works at the house of Patou.	Returns to work as a stylist at Cardin in the Philippines, and supervises the manufacture of a ready-to-wear range for the American market.	Unveils his first collection, with school friends Francis Menuge and Donard Potard. After two collections, they are in debt for $12,000.

INSPIRED

● John Galliano
Galliano, who came of age in the 1980s, was inspired by the diversity of thought and groundbreaking philosophical viewpoints that Gaultier was showing in his collections.

◆ Wunderkind
In the Wunderkind Spring 2009 collection (right), designer Wolfgang Joop sent out looks with a wild amalgam of prints, textures and inspirations – hallmarks of Gaultier.

● Dries Van Noten
Van Noten is well known for his interest in ethnic dress and his free mixing of prints, both of which have often appeared on the Gaultier catwalk.

● Martin Margiela
Like Gaultier, Margiela is an iconoclastic designer who is sometimes so far ahead of fashion that he is criticized, only to be copied the next season.

Jean Paul Gaultier is a multimillion-pound couturier, but a couturier who does not take himself so seriously that he loses touch with what is happening in real life. Gaultier is known for his philosophical and political fashion that centres on the controversial issues of humanity, such as equality, acceptance and our place in the world. Gaultier uses camp humour and extreme aesthetics to cause a reevaluation of ethnicity, gender bias, sexual orientation and beauty.

We take Gaultier's messages seriously because of the level of craftsmanship and sophistication with which he delivers them: 'I use the rules and tradition… to renew them in today's spirit… but the problem is that some of these traditions have not evolved or been transformed to correspond to our current world… I use and respect tradition, but try and find new elements which will make it younger.'

OPEN TO DIFFERENCE

Jean Paul Gaultier approaches the idea of idealized beauty in many ways, either by using models that he sees on the street or models that are older, overweight or different ethnicities, or by pushing the level of aesthetics to points that can be perceived as tacky or obscene. Gaultier says, 'I want to be open to difference. I like very different types of people, different types of beauty, different types of living.'

By pushing visual ideas of nudity, S&M or gender mixing, Gaultier begins the process of normalizing the unexplored. When Gaultier dresses men in skirts or corsets, he is asking why it is unacceptable for men to wear women's clothes, yet acceptable for women to wear men's clothing. He also plays with gay iconography to emphasize the question of male strength versus feminine fragility.

French homage

Gaultier has made the blue-and-white striped shirt his style signature, and has always been fascinated by masculine symbols of gay culture, such as the sailor. Both shirt and sailor regularly appear in Gaultier's perfume advertisements. On his 30th anniversary show in 2006, Gaultier paid homage to himself with the creation of this fun evening dress.

➜ Menacing bride

The conical breast is a Gaultier signature that was made famous in the 1980s by Madonna. In his Spring 2008 collection, Gaultier adds points to a bride's corset – a garment that has historically been seen as a symbol of submission – to transform it into a symbol of danger.

 INFLUENCED BY

KEY
- ● fashion designer
- ◆ fashion house/brand
- ■ artistic influence
- ❖ cultural influence

❖ **Marie Garribe**
Gaultier visited his maternal grandmother, Marie Garribe, every weekend when growing up, and has said, 'From her I learned the importance of physical appearances as it relates to the interior life – the importance of the attitudes, gestures, movement and how everything is connected.'

● **Vivienne Westwood**
The two designers have played with innerwear as outerwear, and pushed the boundaries of sexual reference and good taste. Both are interested in female power, seeing the corset as protective armour rather than a symbol of submission.

JEAN PAUL GAULTIER CONTINUED

	Berthe Moline promises financial backing for a third show, in return for Gaultier designing a collection for them. They withdraw 10 days before the show.	*Signs a licensing deal with Japanese manufacturer Kashiyama to finance a thematic collection based on James Bond, propelling Gaultier to worldwide notice.*	*Receives additional backing from Italian companies Gibo and Equator, and begins to open boutiques around the world.*	*Designs the costumes for Madonna's Blond Ambition tour, including the famous conical bra.*
CHRONOLOGY	**1977**	**1978**	**1981**	**1990**

➜ **INSPIRED**

◆ **A.F. Vandevorst**
For Autumn 2008, the Dutch duo used facets of Gaultier's established style to create a collection of innerwear as outerwear, featuring garters, bras and girdles.

● **Xuly Bët**
Bët has a similar aesthetic to Gaultier's, pulling in a wide variety of nontraditional fabrications and displaying a focus on multiculturalism and ethnicity.

● **Alexander McQueen**
Both designers have used the traditions of haute couture to execute their alternative view of design. Although their work promotes unconventional and often unsettling ideas, their collections cannot be ignored or treated like an amateur joke. Gaultier provided rich inspiration for McQueen, who enjoyed addressing issues of beauty, equality, sexuality and the inherent strength of women by combining a rich cross-section of inspirations. Both designers have achieved respect within the fashion industry by routinely putting forth work that, although controversial, is a unique and personal voice. In the early 1980s, Gaultier was assigned the title of 'enfant terrible' for his iconoclastic aesthetic, and McQueen inherited this title.

PERCEPTIONS OF STRENGTH AND BEAUTY

Gaultier uses female nudity and sexuality, and traditional feminine symbols, to emphasize the dichotomy between perceptions of strength and beauty and the reality. An example would be the famous corset with large conical breasts that Gaultier created for Madonna's Blond Ambition tour. By using such comical shapes to signify the breasts, Gaultier is commenting on the objectification of and focus on a female entertainer's body.

In his Spring 1998 couture show, Gaultier dressed a female model in an all-white suit with integrated panniers. The panniers – hoops used to hold out women's skirts at the sides, a feature of 18th-century fashion – called attention to the natural shape of a woman of childbearing age; these symbols of feminine subjection and maternal duty were contrasted with the three-piece suit, a symbol of masculine power and independence. The choice of white suggested virginity, purity or innocence, but also a new beginning or blank slate.

FASCINATION WITH WORLD CULTURES

Jean Paul Gaultier is also fascinated by different cultures and ways of dress. He has shown collections that are inspired by China, Mongolia, Spain, Mexico and many other locations, while also causing controversy with his collections that draw from Hasidic Jewish dress or play with Catholic symbols.

However, as much as he loves the cultures and ideas of the world, Jean Paul Gaultier is also enthralled with his own country, France. From his own uniform of the blue-and-white Gallic shirt to beautiful dresses inspired by the Belle Époque, Paris appears often in his work.

→ Saintly endeavour

Gaultier has never shied away from touchy subjects, such as religion, politics or sexual orientation. In his Spring 2007 collection, he used iconography of the Catholic religion to examine the dichotomy of the madonna/whore stereotype.

● Yves Saint Laurent

About the iconic designer, Gaultier said, '[S]eeing the scandal YSL caused in the 70s was important, because he captured everything that I love – glamour and sexual aggressiveness and even political shock. It was all the things that ever made me dream about being a part of the world of fashion. What he did definitely influenced me later and also made me realize the point in fashion: that if you are too far in advance it appears as a provocation.'

● Sonia Rykiel

Gaultier has said, 'In the 70s Rykiel was like Saint Laurent for me. She did revolutionary things, but quietly. When they are good, women in fashion are better than men because they really have something to say.'

Launches his first fragrance packaged in a plain tin can, with the bottle resembling Elsa Schiaparelli's torso bottle for her Shocking perfume, but wearing his signature corset.	Creates JPG by Gaultier diffusion line, launches men's fragrance Le Mâle and presents first couture collection.	Sells 35% of his eponymous collection to Hermès, and becomes creative director of Hermès.
1993	**1994–97**	**2003**

← East meets West

In the tradition of Gaultier's controversial collections, Alexander McQueen's Autumn 2003 show looked at the difference in gender politics between the Western world and specifically Japan. The model wears a hat that looks like the Japanese flag. The Japanese kimono usually hides the female form, but McQueen's kimono-style top reveals the form, as is the Western custom.

'Clothes must have something to say if they are to be strong. They are a reflection of everything that is happening, all around in society. Success is about choosing the right moment so that people say "yes that is it", even if they did not realize it before.'

Jean Paul Gaultier

Through her romantic, spare and spiritual collections, Ann Demeulemeester has become an important voice in describing how women perceive themselves in the 21st century. She has set an example for many younger designers with her definitions of modern feminism as well as her independent business success.

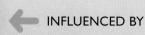

INFLUENCED BY

KEY
● fashion designer
◆ fashion house/brand
■ artistic influence
❖ cultural influence

● **Rei Kawakubo**
Kawakubo has been an important aesthetic influence on Demeulemeester. Perhaps more importantly, Kawakubo is a wonderful example of a private businesswoman who has remained independent, as well as sponsoring up-and-coming younger designers.

● **Yohji Yamamoto**
The Japanese designer's penchant for black is now legendary, but the primary influence of Yamamoto is his planar approach to fabric on the body, as seen in Demeulemeester's Spring 2010 collection (right). Yamamoto and Demeulemeester also share a vision of what contemporary women are all about.

● **Martin Margiela**
Early in his career, Margiela worked within a darkly romantic aesthetic that, for him, created the larger trend of deconstructionism. Many of those early style impulses were influential for Demeulemeester.

ANN DEMEULEMEESTER
Belgian
(1959 Waregem)

	Born December 29th in Waregem.	Studies fashion design at the Royal Academy of Fine Arts in Antwerp. She is one of six graduates who go on to become known as the Antwerp Six – avant-garde designers who put Antwerp at the cutting edge of fashion.	Founds the company BVBA «32».	Shows at Paris Fashion Week for the first time.	Integrates menswear into her Paris shows. Sets up a company that supports young talent, such as Haider Ackermann.
CHRONOLOGY	**1959**	**1978–81**	**1985**	**1992**	**1996**

INSPIRED

● **Alexander McQueen**
At the beginning of his career, McQueen was particularly interested in the gothic romanticism that is so prevalent in Demeulemeester's work.

● **Rick Owens**
Owens seems to be influenced by Demeulemeester's silhouette preference. He also uses black or white within most of his collections, and his work has an overall mood of romanticism.

● **Olivier Theyskens**
Theyskens began his career by dressing Madonna in a black leather gown that seemed very similar to many ideas that have appeared within Demeulemeester's collections.

● **Haider Ackermann**
Ackermann has benefited from guidance and sponsorship from Demeulemeester, and approaches the silhouette of the figure in a way similar to that of his mentor.

● **Veronique Branquinho**
The two Dutch designers have a similar approach to feminine dressing, and often rely on the colour black and long, lean silhouettes.

Like so many designers from Belgium and Japan, Ann Demeulemeester is not concerned with following trends or forcefully changing her philosophy or aesthetic each season. Instead, she approaches fashion as a new discovery, and as a development of the soul or spirit that she feels is so important to the contemporary woman: 'Fashion has a reason "to be" because in fashion you can find new expressions of human beings. Beauty is constantly redefined; it is the joy that you feel when you discover it.'

INTELLECTUAL AND INTROVERTED
Demeulemeester takes an intellectual approach to design, focusing on the ephemeral and transitory spirit of women, much in the same way as Japanese designer Yohji Yamamoto. Her colour palette of choice is black and white, which for her suggest shadow and shape, and are the most poetic and strongest colours. Her philosophy of design is quiet, introverted and deeply personal: 'With every collection I turn myself inside out and bare my soul. I want to make it the most beautiful, to mean something to someone.'

SHAPE AND FORM
Demeulemeester insists that she is not making clothing that should be considered art, although her clothing has been displayed in several international exhibition venues. She makes clothing to be worn, used and lived in, and tries on every garment to make sure that it really 'works'.

Since her emphasis is on practicality, she opts for a 'less is more' idea of clothing, placing the emphasis on shape and form rather than extraneous decorative additions: 'In my opinion there are "architects" and "decorators" and that applies to fashion too. You can design forms, but you can

'Those that think my clothes are androgynous also still believe that women should look like Barbie dolls. That's precisely the problem, the deep-rooted assumptions about what is feminine. I am more inspired by the balance between men and women. A confrontation of masculine and feminine elements, even in a single silhouette; it is the unobvious that fascinates me.'

Ann Demeulemeester

■ Patti Smith
Smith is Demeulemeester's 'soul sister', affecting the designer through her poetry and singing. Smith has influenced several collections as well as appeared on the catwalk; she has also provided soundtracks for Demeulemeester's fashion shows, and wears the designer's clothing in every public appearance.

● Helmut Lang
Lang did a great deal of work with sheer layers, expressing a philosophy that was centred in feminine strength and sexuality. Like Demeulemeester, he was also known for his androgynous looks.

● Madeleine Vionnet
Vionnet draped fabric on the body in ways that expressed the movement and spirit of the woman she was dressing. Demeulemeester has undoubtedly been influenced by both Vionnet's craftsmanship and her philosophy.

Opens a store in Antwerp.	*Her work is featured in several exhibitions in venues such as New York's Metropolitan Museum of Art and the Flanders Fashion Institute in Antwerp.*	*Because of its popularity, she begins showing her menswear collection separately from the women's to allow for a greater selection.*	*Opens stores in Tokyo, Hong Kong and Seoul.*
1999	**1999–2004**	**2005**	**2006–07**

● Sophia Kokosalaki
In common with Demeulemeester, Kokosalaki's work often combines a rock 'n' roll sensibility with a soft and feminine silhouette.

◆ A.F. Vandevorst
Although An Vandevorst (who forms one half of Dutch design duo A.F. Vandevorst, along with Filip Arickx) served as Dries Van Noten's assistant for many years, the influence of Demeulemeester's style sensibility can be seen on the couple's catwalk.

also decorate existing forms. There are people who are more concerned with the former, and others the latter. I think I am more of an architect than a decorator.'

Much of her simple and wearable clothing has been labelled as androgynous. When Demeulemeester's clothing is examined, however, what can be construed as genderless is actually a much more current view of femininity that heralds what women are and will become, rather than what they were.

↑ Breaking new frontiers
In the Autumn 2008 collection, Demeulemeester alludes to her friend Patti Smith and references the 19th-century American frontier, creating a romantic metaphor of women's increasing power and influence in society. The look is an alternative to the refined feminism or sexual provocation that is so important in the collections of many of her contemporaries.

→ Kindred spirit
The look of A.F. Vandevorst's Autumn 2009 collection shares the philosophy of Demeulemeester, if not the exact style references. The clothing is dark, not clingy or sexy, and allows the wearer to be defined by everything but her body.

Marc Jacobs is one of the few designers to whom the fashion press, buyers and diffusion markets pay close attention for the direction and focus of each season. With the innate ability to tap into the mood and style of a generation, Jacobs delivers what people want to wear, and has become one of the most influential designers of our age.

 INFLUENCED BY

KEY
● fashion designer
◆ fashion house/brand
■ artistic influence
❖ cultural influence

● **Halston**
Halston represents the essence of New York chic, which Jacobs emulated in the use of long, languid shapes in his Autumn 2007 collections.

● **André Courrèges**
In Autumn 2003 for Marc Jacobs as well as Louis Vuitton Spring 2000, Jacobs referenced the short, crisp looks that Courrèges was famous for in the 1960s.

● **Elsa Schiaparelli**
The influence of the 1930s designer can be seen in the whimsy and sense of humour that Jacobs routinely infuses into his shows.

■ **Contemporary art**
Jacobs is an avid art collector. The philosophical or aesthetic concepts that he is attracted to in art are often expressed in his catwalk collections, such as the use of colour, humour or irony that are frequently found in pop art (left).

MARC JACOBS
American
(1963 New York)

	Born April 9th in New York.	Attends New York's Parsons School of Design.	While still in school, Jacobs sells a collection of handknit sweaters. Upon graduation, he begins designing for Ruben Thomas, Inc.	Starts designing collections under his own name, with a favourable response from the fashion press and buyers.	Becomes vice president and design director of Perry Ellis, with business partner Robert Duffy serving as president.
CHRONOLOGY	**1963**	**1981–84**	**1984**	**1986**	**1989**

 INSPIRED

◆ **Proenza Schouler**
Lazaro Hernandez and Jack McCollough are young designers who have been influenced by Jacobs's infatuation with the 1970s and 1980s, and also share Jacobs's ability to define their generation's sense of style and aesthetic. All three designers have experimented with alternative fabrications, ignoring the traditional concepts of seasonally correct fabric. Jacobs showed sheer trousers and blouses in Spring 2008; Proenza Schouler followed this trend in Spring 2009 (right).

◆ **Bruce**
Designers Nicole Noselli and Daphne Gutierrez understand and decode the type of New York downtown chic that is omnipresent in all Marc by Marc Jacobs shows.

● **Christopher Bailey for Burberry**
Bailey has been inspired by Jacobs's use of utilitarian clothing as style basics, adding luxury to create a desirable and fresh approach.

Marc Jacobs is a creative force that extends beyond any traditional limitations, such as market or price point, as he translates and synthesizes style impulses into a fresh perspective. Jacobs has an overwhelming influence on the fashion industry as creative director of Louis Vuitton based in Paris, as well as his eponymous lines Marc Jacobs in New York, Marc by Marc Jacobs, Marc Jacobs Men, Stinky Rat, Little Marc and countless licences, all of which are sold internationally.

PULLING TOGETHER STYLE IMPULSES
Jacobs's harshest critics have accused him of copying, styling and generally not being original. However, the fact remains that a simple copyist could not set the tone for an entire season by pulling together style impulses, mood, colour and silhouette in a consistently fresh way that is heralded by the fashion press and consumers alike. Jacobs combines esoteric,

intellectual and philosophical concepts from art, design and culture, and translates them in an original way into something that is approachable for women. As influential *New York Times* style columnist Cathy Horyn says, '[In Jacobs's work] you see a fashion that increasingly has its own identity… what Jacobs has really done is not to exclude any method or idea that might be vital to him.'

In the Loïc Prigent documentary *Marc Jacobs & Louis Vuitton*, Jacobs has a rather blithe attitude towards elucidating his concept or philosophy of creation and design, as evidenced of his explanation that he 'just likes things fucked up'. At the same time, it is clear that a primary focus of his work is to make clothing wearable and approachable to all women: 'I like to think that the clothes have a life after the show is over. I love it when I see strangers wearing my clothes…'

← **Playful luxury**

Marc Jacobs's Autumn 2010 collection for Louis Vuitton placed an emphasis on feminine curves and softness. This look is emblematic of Jacobs's blending of style influences, matching a generous boyfriend sweater with a full circle skirt in exquisite French fabric for a playful look at luxury.

• Yves Saint Laurent

In the Autumn 2009 Louis Vuitton collection, Jacobs connects to the sense of sexual frivolity that Saint Laurent perfected in the 1980s. Jacobs displays an ironic slant and perhaps a sense of enduring optimism by using over-the-top symbols of the 1980s at a time of economic recession.

• Coco Chanel

The famous tweed coat of Chanel made appearances throughout Jacobs's collections in Spring 2008, as well as the ladylike jewellery that the French couturier made famous.

Introduces the infamous grunge collection that leads Perry Ellis to fire him and cancel production. With partner Robert Duffy, Jacobs launches the licensing and design company Marc Jacobs International, designing both women's and men's clothing under his own name.

1992–94

• Behnaz Sarafpour

Like Jacobs, Sarafpour pulls together an amalgamation of historically referenced looks to create a new and contemporary look.

• Miuccia Prada

Similar to Jacobs, Prada uses fabric, colour and shape to add emphasis and meaning to the deeper philosophical commentaries on image and sexuality.

GENERATIONAL SENSE OF COOL

Marc Jacobs, a member of the X generation, has always been influenced by growing up in New York in the 1970s, as well as his love of the dance clubs, parties and nightlife of the 1980s, and his mature appreciation of art and design. Music is always an important component of his creativity, from bands such as Sonic Youth to classical music such as Pachelbel's *Canon*. Jacobs is said to listen to the same music repeatedly throughout the design process. An early example of music's influence on Jacobs's work is the Spring 1993 grunge collection that he created for Perry Ellis. Although the collection ultimately got him dismissed from his post as design director, Jacobs established himself as a translator of a generational sense of cool.

Marc Jacobs seems to travel through fashion phases, focusing on an idea or a set of style problems that he needs

→ High-glam neon

Marc Jacobs's eponymous Autumn 2009 collection is a celebration of 1980s high glam and the neon colours so often seen on fashion catwalks during that decade, such as those of Claude Montana. Jacobs infuses the entire collection with a sense of the sinister through the hair, make-up and styling, perhaps as an acknowledgement of our love/hate relationship with the decade.

INFLUENCED BY

KEY

- ● fashion designer
- ◆ fashion house/brand
- ■ artistic influence
- ❖ cultural influence

● Rei Kawakubo
Kawakubo's influence can be seen in Jacobs's Autumn 2006 collection for Louis Vuitton, as well as the Autumn 2006 and Spring 2008 Marc Jacobs collections, in the abstraction of form, silhouette and relationship of clothing to the body.

● Claude Montana
The strong shoulders and bold shapes that were signature styles of Montana's work from the 1980s were present in both the Louis Vuitton and Marc Jacobs collections for Autumn 2008.

MARC JACOBS CONTINUED

CHRONOLOGY	1997	2001	2006	2006–07
	Appointed artistic director of luxury brand Louis Vuitton. Opens his first freestanding Marc Jacobs store in New York's SoHo.	Launches Marc by Marc Jacobs for men and women, a diffusion line that features younger looks inspired by the Village in New York.	Launches Stinky Rat, a diffusion menswear collection that focuses on themed T-shirts and accessories.	Opens first freestanding European stores in Paris and then London.

→ INSPIRED

● Derek Lam
Lam combines sporty silhouettes with luxury fabrications, a trend that Jacobs helped to popularize.

● Phillip Lim
Like Jacobs, Lim often uses multiple vintage references that are not always consistent from season to season, choosing instead to examine new style ideas with a fresh perspective. Lim's Autumn 2009 collection (right) referenced the propensity for 'peacock males' to wear fur vests in the 1960s, as had Jacobs the year before.

→ Downtown girl

Derek Lam courts the same downtown girl who wears Marc Jacobs. Lam's customers like fashion-forward details, as seen in the form of the neckline and the unexpected combination of a casual black belt with a hot pink cocktail dress in this piece from Lam's 2010 resort collection.

to solve before moving on. There are some designers who approach the process of design with a consistent aesthetic, but Marc Jacobs has no problem moving from one idea to the next. Jacobs also blends several different style snapshots into one collection. Throughout his career, he has approached historical references from a 1960s, 1970s or 1980s point of view, sometimes combining them with a quintessential New York or Parisian chic, only to shift completely to a Japanese focus on abstraction and philosophy.

Like many of his generation, Jacobs has a sentimental view of the style symbols that he grew up with, since the look of the times is important in conveying a larger mood or feeling. Jacobs's interpretations of these fleeting impressions of an entire generation become universal and therefore essential to the design dialogue of our century.

→ Easy elegance

The models for Marc Jacobs's Autumn 2010 show wore only light make-up and had slightly mussed hair to suggest the ease that he felt to be sorely lacking in contemporary fashion. This luxurious cut fur ensemble in an easy shape resembles tweed, which Jacobs says is new precisely because it 'isn't trying too hard to be new'. According to Jacobs, the fashion industry's constant striving for newness has made newness lose its impact.

❖ Pop culture

Everything from films, music, style and literature to high-school marching bands and Japanese anime (left) has influenced Jacobs, which helps him to translate a generational aesthetic.

Enters rehab for substance abuse. Filmmaker Loïc Prigent makes a documentary of Jacobs creating his collections.	*Awarded the Chevalier de l'Ordre des Arts et des Lettres for his contributions to the French cultural inheritance.*
2007	**2010**

• Antonio Marras for Kenzo

Marras has experimented with cultural references in conjunction with silhouette shapes. The young designer's ideal customer is a savvy, downtown girl who has a bit of edge and is influenced by wearability as well as a rougher, cooler vibe. This same girl undoubtedly shops at Marc Jacobs.

'I like romantic allusions to the past: what the babysitter wore, what the art teacher wore, what I wore during my experimental days in fashion when I was going to the Mudd Club and wanted to be a New Wave kid or a punk kid but was really a poseur. It's the awkwardness of posing and feeling like I was in, but I never was in. Awkwardness gives me great comfort.'

Marc Jacobs

Stella McCartney has become influential on the international fashion scene as a designer who is helping to define a generation of women who are seeking a new level of comfort and ease in their clothing, while also choosing to be socially and environmentally responsible.

INFLUENCED BY

KEY
● fashion designer
◆ fashion house/brand
■ artistic influence
❖ cultural influence

● Katharine Hamnett
Hamnett was known for creating politically charged fashion statements. McCartney has taken this philosophy as her own, pulling the attention of her audience towards issues that she feels most strongly about.

● Marc Jacobs
Jacobs effortlessly uses pop and youth culture to create clothing that seems fresh and innovative. McCartney and Jacobs also share a love for 1970s and 1980s style, which often appears on their catwalks.

● Claude Montana
Montana seems to have lent his love of bold colour and geometric shapes to McCartney, who would undoubtedly have grown up with Montana as an aesthetic influence.

● Miuccia Prada
Prada understands that her clothing cannot exist without actually being liked and used by the customer. Prada serves as an example to McCartney of how to balance innovation with marketability.

● Tom Ford
Ford served as a mentor and friend to McCartney when she joined Gucci Group to form her eponymous line. His beliefs on commercial fashion have clearly influenced McCartney's own ideas.

STELLA McCARTNEY
British
(1971 London)

Born September 13th in London. Her father is Paul McCartney, formerly of the band the Beatles.	Begins an internship at Christian Lacroix and later apprentices with Savile Row tailor Edward Sexton.	Graduates from Central Saint Martins. London boutique Tokio buys her graduate collection.	Appointed creative director of the house of Chloé.	Gucci Group offers McCartney her own label.	Launches her first fragrance, Stella.
CHRONOLOGY 1971	1986	1995	1997	2001	2003

INSPIRED

◆ Preen
The young British design duo has been influenced by McCartney's penchant for tailored but loose jackets and feminine tops (right). Bright colours are also consistently featured on both companies' catwalks.

● Vanessa Bruno
Bruno has a similar aesthetic to McCartney, with girlish and flirty clothing that looks comfortable and easy to wear.

● John Patrick for Organic
Organic, sustainable fabric and production are at the forefront of Patrick's concerns. He is also often influenced by similar time periods as McCartney.

● Richard Chai
In his Spring 2010 collection, Chai showed several pieces that were similar to McCartney's soft tailored jackets and roomy, comfortable pants.

Stella McCartney is a forward-thinking designer, not just because of her cute, street-savvy clothing that appeals to her sophisticated young customer but also because she is one of the first designers to use environmentalism and animal rights as a branding tool. This appeals to those who are concerned about a responsible and sustainable future, allowing McCartney's customers to feel good about doing the 'right thing', and starting the dialogue of what the fashion industry must acknowledge in the 21st century.

ENVIRONMENTAL CONCERNS
Stella McCartney uses no leather or fur, and is an outspoken vegetarian. Her website features quotes about environmental concerns, plus tips on energy and resource conservation; she has a beauty line that is organic; and she has been recognized with several awards for her melding of fashion and environmentalism. Yet in such a newly defined arena of fashion, McCartney often sounds defensive when speaking about her branding strategy: 'I am a fashion designer. I'm not an environmentalist. So the main thing that I need to do is create, hopefully exquisitely beautiful clothes; desirable objects for my customers. That's my job first and foremost. If I can make you notice that it happens to be out of bio-degradable fake suede, if I can make you notice that it hasn't killed any cows or goats or unborn baby lambs, then I am doing my job. I don't want to do a scratchy oatmeal-coloured thing; that defeats the object.'

SUSTAINABLE DESIGN
What has made McCartney so successful is her consistent attempt to create clothing that is about the aesthetic qualities first, with the added benefit of sustainable design

← Flirty feminism

Stella McCartney's Spring 2010 collection perfectly illustrates her understanding of her customer, who is both flirtatious and feminine, while also taking for granted her influence and responsibility in the working world. No longer worried about sending mixed messages, the McCartney woman is confident in her image and body.

● Donna Karan

Karan is a source of inspiration for many female designers, including McCartney, not only as an independent entrepreneur, but also in the confidence to use themselves as sources of inspiration.

● Ossie Clark

As a child of the 1970s and 1980s, and the daughter of environmentally aware parents, McCartney grew up surrounded by clothing from designers such as Ossie Clark. His dreamy use of prints and loose silhouettes can be seen in interpretations on McCartney's catwalk (right).

2004	2005	2006	2007	2008	2009
Signs an agreement with Adidas to create stylish activewear.	Designs a sell-out collection for fashion retailer H&M.	Launches Stella in Two, which splits the two major notes of peony and amber in the original fragrance Stella. This allows women to combine the two scents as desired.	Launches organic skincare line CARE, in collaboration with Yves Saint Laurent Beauté.	Launches a lingerie collection, and a limited-edition travel collection with LeSport Sac.	Designs a collection of environmentally friendly childrenswear for clothing retailer Gap.

● Phoebe Philo

Philo worked with McCartney at the house of Chloé, and then took over as design director after McCartney left to form her own line. The two designers share a love of soft tailoring.

◆ Proenza Schouler

The American design duo's Spring 2009 collection featured the soft tailoring and one-piece jumpsuits that have become characteristic of McCartney's style.

● Antonio Berardi

The young English designer's Spring 2010 collection combined soft tailoring in drapey fabrics with lingerie looks that seem to have been influenced by McCartney.

second. McCartney has rejected the idea that, in order to be environmentally friendly, clothing must be drab or lack trendy ingenuity: 'I am in the fashion business but I feel when I design I'm in the business of trying to figure out what people want and why they need it.' McCartney designs clothing that is flirtatious and sexy, but also comfortable; something to move, relax and live in: 'Wearable – it's almost a dirty word in fashion, wearable, but that's what I do. And yeah, it can get a bit boring, but I can push it each season into something more relevant for that season.'

→ Trend watching

The look that Antonio Berardi followed in his Spring 2010 collection, along with many others, has been developed and honed by Stella McCartney and is a testament to her influence on fashion.

'As a female designer it's really empowering to see the way women have more ownership of how they dress now.'

Stella McCartney

CHAPTER 3
ARTISANS

Clothing appeals to our most basic senses: sight, sound and most notably touch. Designers use the medium of cloth to create unique forms – works of art that have the potential to transform us, shape us and affect us through our senses. The designers in this chapter are primarily concerned with the development of craft in order to achieve new heights of cut, drape, shape and technique.

CRAFT OF CONSTRUCTION

The primary focus of the early artisan designers was the craft of construction and the formal qualities of dress. Many of them were interested in creating or accessing innovative fabrics that would allow them greater variety in shape, colour or texture. Others focused primarily on cutting or draping techniques to define a new silhouette that advanced fashion in a new direction.

In an effort to formalize the level of technique required to be called a couturier, the Chambre Syndicale de la Haute Couture was created in France in 1868. To be considered a couturier, all pieces needed to be fit a minimum of three times to an individual client, with a minimum of 35 employees (today it is down to 15), and at least two shows a year in the atelier for the different seasons.

ARTISTIC MEDIUM

For the first half of the 20th century, any innovation in clothing came from the couturiers. The artisan couturiers, such as Madeleine Vionnet, Cristóbal Balenciaga and Madame Grès, were among the few who actually participated in the entire process of creation, from designing on paper, fabricating and draping to cutting, sewing and finishing the garments. Most of the other couturiers employed cutters and seamstresses to craft the dresses they had envisioned. The artisan couturiers used fabric like an artistic medium, just as a sculptor uses marble or a painter oils on canvas.

Designers such as Christian Lacroix believe that the traditional practices and skill sets of couture, which are quickly disappearing, are essential to the progression of design. As the economy and society changes, couture may fall out of favour, but the passion for quality, technical innovation and mastery continues to find new forms in the 21st century.

MANIPULATION OF FABRIC

Some of the artisan designers, such as Mariano Fortuny, Issey Miyake, Yohji Yamamoto, Romeo Gigli, Dries Van Noten and Francisco Costa, have been interested in the manipulation of fabric, such as surface design, colour or prints, to appeal to the haptic relationship that we have with clothing – that is, our response to the feel of cloth on the skin. There is a greater focus on the emotional qualities of clothing through sensuality, romanticism and exoticism.

Part of an artisan designer's branding strategy is to suggest the artist's hand in the creation of the piece, which many customers find appealing. Modern-day artisan designers incorporate craft into their work in many of the same ways that the great artisan couturiers did before them, but have adapted the philosophy of couture to a contemporary context by involving technology and modern production practices.

Fortuny did not want to be a part of the fashion world, and only really saw clothing as the best way to use his fabrications. However, his influence on fashion is overwhelming, not only in his work as an artisan, but also in his innovations and philosophies in a pivotal era of fashion history.

INFLUENCED BY

KEY
- ● fashion designer
- ◆ fashion house/brand
- ■ artistic influence
- ❖ cultural influence

❖ North Africa
The primary subject for his father's paintings was scenes from North Africa, so Fortuny was steeped in the romance of the region at an early age, and this continued to influence his work.

❖ Venice
The Italian city was filled with an ancient mysticism that inspired Fortuny to paint, etch and photograph Venice, as well as create several textile designs.

■ Renaissance
Many of the prints on Fortuny's textiles were taken from Renaissance images. Michelangelo was one of his favourite and most admired artists.

■ Greek dress
Fortuny was influenced by ancient Greek dress. The Charioteer of Delphi statue, also known as the Delphos (right), was the primary source of inspiration for Fortuny's famous Delphos dresses.

MARIANO FORTUNY
Spanish
(1871 Granada)

Born Mariano Fortuny y Madrazo on May 11th. His father, Mariano Fortuny y Marsal, is a well-known painter.	*Studies art in Paris, then moves to Venice. Visits Bayreuth in Germany, where he discovers the works of Richard Wagner, theatre design and eventually clothing.*	*Begins working on textiles, experimenting with different techniques. He registers more than 20 patents that deal with the manufacturing of fabric, as well as engineering, industrial design and stage lighting.*	*Acquires the Palazzo Orfei and names it Palazzo Fortuny, opening his first boutique there. Introduces the Delphos gown.*

CHRONOLOGY	**1871**	**1875–92**	**1901–34**	**1905–09**

INSPIRED

● Madeleine Vionnet
The two designers were equally attracted to the practicality and design perfection of ancient Greek dress. Fortuny's work in textiles would undoubtedly have influenced Vionnet.

● Paul Poiret
Poiret greatly admired Fortuny's work, and displayed Fortuny's textiles and dresses in his own boutique.

● Madame Grès
Grès used Greek-inspired drapery in her clothing, and displayed a love for pleating and manipulation of fabric, all of which was influenced by Fortuny.

● Romeo Gigli
Gigli's love of rich colours, tactile fabrications, glass-bead embellishments and the neoclassical silhouette is clearly influenced by the work of Fortuny.

● Issey Miyake
Miyake has a similar approach to Fortuny in his experimentations with textiles, as well as a rejection of trends. His Pleats Please brand owes a great deal to Fortuny's inventions.

Mariano Fortuny was representative of the artistic philosophies at the turn of the 20th century. Many artists and designers were inspired by the Arts and Crafts movement of the 19th century, and by the musical pieces, operas and writings of Richard Wagner, who created the philosophy of *gesamtkunstwerk*, or total artwork. Wagner's original idea centred on a synthesis of performing arts. Designers – such as the artists' collective Wiener Werkstätte in Vienna, Fortuny in Italy, Paul Poiret in France, the Mackintosh Four in Glasgow and Frank Lloyd Wright in the United States – interpreted these ideas as a total environment of living, including architecture, interiors, textiles and clothing.

Fortuny considered himself to be first and foremost a painter, having come from a family of painters. However, he was also an inventor, engineer, photographer, textile artist and interior designer. He was a gifted copyist, and was adept at mimicking the styles of well-established painters. This obviously had a large impact on Fortuny's ability to mine the vast array of influences that came to life in his beautiful textiles.

DELPHOS DRESSES

Fortuny was familiar with Greek art and dress, and appreciated a wide variety of cultures that gave him the ideas for his clothing. His Delphos dresses were variations on ancient Greek clothing and drapery, and the shawls and coats that went with them were based on North African tunics, Byzantine cloaks and Indian saris, among others. Fortuny's pieces were extremely popular with actresses, dancers and the intelligensia of Europe in the golden years before and after World War I. Isadora Duncan, Eleanora Duse, Sarah Bernhardt, Dorothy and Lillian Gish, and the famous hostess known as La Casati all wore Fortuny.

'I have been interested in many things, but have always considered painting to be my profession.'

Mariano Fortuny

■ **Aesthetic movement**
Fortuny was influenced by the aesthetic movement of the late 19th century, which emphasized the value of beauty over all other things, and displayed a keen interest in the art of Japan. It was also associated with the dress reform (or rational dress) movement that advocated the adoption of more comfortable clothing, in particular the modification of women's restrictive undergarments.

■ **Richard Wagner**
Wagner was an influential composer at the end of the 19th century, who through his writings and music created the philosophy of 'total artwork' – artwork that is a synthesis of many art forms, as espoused by Fortuny.

■ **Arts and Crafts**
Led by William Morris, the Arts and Crafts movement rejected the barriers between the different arts, believing that each art form informed the others, and that an intimate knowledge of raw materials was essential to innovation – beliefs that Fortuny shared.

Opens a textile factory. Transfers his collections to a dealer, who promotes them to actresses and society.

Closes factory briefly because of financial problems. American interior designer Elsie McNeill Lee reshapes the business to make it into an international success.

Fascists take over Italy. Unable to access quality fabrics, Fortuny closes down.

Dies May 2nd at Palazzo Fortuny. McNeill Lee takes over the textile factory, which continues production to the present day.

| 1919–20 | 1933 | 1938 | 1949 |

● **Alberta Ferretti**
Ferretti uses Greek dress as a primary style direction, and has become known for her rich colour choices that are often strikingly similar to Fortuny's.

● **Mary McFadden**
McFadden used pleating and embellished velvets – as originally made famous by Fortuny – to create her signature look in the 1970s and 1980s.

BEAUTY AND COMFORT

Fortuny's work was an essential part of the equation that shifted women's dress away from clothing that imposed a shape on the figure, to the figure dictating the shape of the clothes. The fabrics undulated on the women's bodies, creating a dramatic, exotic and seductive look, as well as being comfortable and practical. Since strict undergarments such as stays or corsets were not needed, Fortuny pieces were often worn not in public, but while receiving or lounging in one's own home.

Today, actresses and models continue to appear in Fortuny's work on the red carpet. His influence can be seen in the approach of designers to their craft, as well as his rich, sensitive colour palette, beautiful textiles and interpretations of historic and ethnic dress.

← **Grecian influence**
Alberta Ferretti plays with the pleating and rich colours that were so prevalent in Fortuny's work. Her Spring 2010 collection continued her appreciation of the timeless beauty of Greek dress, and the qualities that create a consistently stylish silhouette that is preeminently wearable.

Madeleine Vionnet's influence on contemporary design is profound, and can be seen on the catwalk every season. The technique of the bias drape that she perfected, as well as her examination of the connections between fabric, body and movement, ensure that she remains eternally modern and central to fashion design.

INFLUENCED BY

KEY
- ● fashion designer
- ◆ fashion house/brand
- ■ artistic influence
- ❖ cultural influence

◆ **Callot Soeurs**
Vionnet had copied the French sisters' work while she was in London, and was again exposed to their designs at the 1900 Paris World's Fair, before starting to work for them in 1901. One of the sisters, Madame Gerber, did not know how to cut or sew, but improvised fabric draped in muslin on a live model. This inspired Vionnet, who made the toiles that Madame Gerber draped: '[I]t was in this field that I rendered her service, because carried by her creative genius, she didn't burden herself with the practical side of things. In this field, my duties were comparable, in architecture, to a building site director.'

❖ **Japanese kimono**
From the 1900 Paris World's Fair and her time at Callot Soeurs, Vionnet was introduced to the work of visiting Japanese dancer Sada Yacco (left). Throughout her career, Vionnet played with the basic concept of the sleeve and the wrapping techniques of the kimono.

MADELEINE VIONNET
French
(1876 Chilleurs-aux-Bois)

	Born June 22nd at Chilleurs-aux-Bois in the Loiret, north-central France.	Apprentices to seamstress Madame Bourgeuil.	Moves to London to study tailoring and English. There, she works for Kate Reilly, who copies Paris fashion.	Begins working for Callot Soeurs in Paris, learning exacting standards of craftsmanship and construction.	Hired by Jacques Doucet to make his company 'a young fashion house'.	Opens her own house at the urging of private clients.
CHRONOLOGY	**1876**	**1888**	**1895**	**1901**	**1906**	**1912**

INSPIRED

● **Issey Miyake**
Miyake first saw a Vionnet creation early in his career, and it had a profound influence on his aesthetic. As if outlining his own philosophy, Miyake said, 'Vionnet's clothes are based on the dynamics of movement, and they never stray from this fundamental ideology.'

● **Isabel Toledo**
Toledo constructs garments in a similar way to Vionnet, exemplified by her virtuosity with alternative seams, use of geometric forms and ability to create wearable, flattering clothing (left).

● **Claire McCardell**
McCardell first discovered Vionnet when she studied in Paris. Finding the dresses in secondhand shops, she would carefully dissect them to study the methods of construction. McCardell's own fame was sealed when she created the bias-cut monastic dress, which she freely admitted was inspired by Vionnet.

Although Madeleine Vionnet is most well known for her use of the bias cut – that is, cutting diagonally across the fabric in order to produce garments with greater stretch and a more fluid drape – she was not the inventor of the technique. She was first introduced to the process by Madame Gerber at Callot Soeurs, in the form of small pieces within a gown. Vionnet altered the technique by utilizing it for the entire dress, which radically transformed the shape and style of fashion.

DRESSMAKER AND CREATOR
Vionnet defined herself as 'just a dressmaker, but I was also a creator, which is rare'. Her skills, perfected over years of work as a dressmaker in others' salons, allowed her to define clothing in her own unique way and transform 20th-century fashion.

Having come of age during one of the most exciting and innovative times in Paris, Vionnet adopted several of the philosophical ideas of artists and intellectuals around her. Vionnet was a modernist, desiring clothing that discarded excessive ornament and allowed greater movement and comfort for a new type of woman. Like her modernist counterparts, and based on influences from Greek and Roman dress, Vionnet felt that clothing must conform to the body rather than the body be forced into shape by clothing. Women who wore Vionnet's gowns were forced to abandon the corset and instead keep themselves athletically trim.

TECHNICAL INNOVATOR
Vionnet was a master at manipulating fabric, bending and shaping it to do as she wished, but with no interior construction to force it into place. Indeed, there are several stories

Grace in black and white

Madeleine Vionnet was able to create graceful, innovative and stunningly attractive pieces, regardless of the time period, style or silhouette. These 1930 dresses, one in black velvet trimmed in white ermine and the other with a white crepe bodice and panne velvet skirt, are testaments to Vionnet's sense of the dramatically elegant.

→ **Balanced beauty**

This 1934 dress is a wonderful example of how significant Vionnet's contributions to fashion really are. Vionnet achieved the perfect balance of detail and simplicity to create a modern sense of clothing that learned from the advances that came before, but interpreted them in a beautiful and unique way.

 INFLUENCED BY

KEY
● fashion designer
◆ fashion house/brand
■ artistic influence
❖ cultural influence

● **John Redfern**
The British couturier, who had ateliers in Paris and New York, was most well known for his innovative use of jersey knit to create a costume with a then unusual slim silhouette for the actress Lillie Langtry in 1879. This would have influenced Vionnet in her experiments with alternative techniques and shapes.

■ **Isadora Duncan**
The dancer performed in Paris in 1906. She was inspired by Greek dress, and helped to develop modern dance. Duncan was also a proponent of doing away with any undergarments for ease of movement, which greatly affected Vionnet.

MADELEINE VIONNET CONTINUED

Closes her house during the war, and designs for private clients in Rome.	*Reopens her atelier, and wins a lawsuit against a dressmaker who has counterfeited her dresses. Vionnet announces that all gowns must have her signature, an assigned number and a copy of her thumbprint to authenticate a true Vionnet piece. She carefully documents each piece.*	*Opens a new store in Paris. Georges de Feure, architect of the Galeries Lafayette department store, remodels the interior. Featuring frescoes of Greek-style figures wearing Vionnet gowns, it becomes known as the 'temple of fashion'.*
CHRONOLOGY **1914**	**1918–19**	**1923**

→ **INSPIRED**

● **Halston**
Halston discovered Vionnet in magazines from the 1930s, and recognized the great effect of bias-cut fabric on the figure. Halston went on to utilize Vionnet's simplicity, as well as her famous developments in the use of bias.

● **Azzedine Alaïa**
In the 1980s, Alaïa created stunning gowns for the striking Grace Jones. An avid draper himself, many of Alaïa's pieces incorporated several of Vionnet's techniques.

● **Doo-Ri Chung**
Chung made her name with softly draped jersey dresses and alternative seaming details (left) that are clearly influenced by Vionnet.

● **Donna Karan**
Starting from Spring 2007, Karan has regularly shown bias-cut and loosely draped pieces in delicate lightweight fabrics that call to mind the French couturier.

about clients being left helpless if they did not remember the exact pattern of folding, twisting or arranging that was required. A true mathematician, Vionnet worked in geometric forms that, when either set on the bias or combined with other pieces, collapsed against the figure for an altogether flattering and feminine look.

Vionnet worked on small quarter-sized wooden mannequins on which she arranged fabrics and experimented with construction. She would cut, pin and drape the muslin, and then a quick sketch would be made. The miniature muslins were then translated by the seamstresses into full-sized versions and tried on models.

Beyond the technique of bias, Vionnet created hundreds of gowns constructed using every angle of cutting the fabric and a variety of silhouettes. The different methods she used to create seams helped the clothes to wrap around the figure in a flattering way, visually minimizing the width of the waist or expanding the width of the shoulders.

ENDURING INFLUENCE

What is so amazing about much of Vionnet's work is that it continues to look so contemporary more than 70 years after she retired in 1939. With her focused and recognizable aesthetic, and her expansive body of designs, Vionnet has influenced the work of hundreds of modern-day designers. The sense of balance, form and proportion in her garments is breathtaking, and the technical wizardry she achieved makes Vionnet one of the most important designers in the history of fashion.

'The important thing is to learn about how to be true to yourself in your life and your work; to be completely sincere. This really involves imposing your character, but you must find the means to do this within yourself – and you must be patient. You must surpass yourself to reach your goals.'

Madeleine Vionnet

● Jacques Doucet
Although she did not care for the ornate way Doucet designed, Vionnet did adopt much of his surface decoration in her own creations.

● Jeanne Paquin
Paquin was a pioneering female couturier who promoted simplified modern clothing for women. Vionnet admired her restraint and delicacy.

■ Greek and Roman dress
Having first been exposed to ancient Greek and Roman costume at the 1900 Paris World's Fair, Vionnet continued her interest during WWI, when she studied sculptures in Rome. The strong influence surfaced throughout her career, in everything from her logo to her dress designs.

■ 19th-century dress
In 1934, the emphasis of fashion shifted to romanticism, and Vionnet responded by creating full-length circle skirts and sleeves that display an amalgamation of 19th-century influences.

With the advent of WWII, Vionnet decides to retire. Her financial backers will not support design assistant Madeleine Chapsal taking over, so the house closes. Awarded the French Légion d'honneur.	*Begins giving draping classes at fashion schools.*	*Dies March 2nd.*
1939	**1945**	**1975**

● Sophia Kokosalaki
The Greek designer worked for the resurrected house of Vionnet for one year in 2006–07, producing two collections – the first collections for the house since Vionnet retired in 1939. For Autumn 2007, Kokosalaki was not overly reverential, deciding to bring the house into the contemporary era. She created several pieces that employed the techniques of Vionnet, but interpreted them into a sleeve or collar. She also used silhouettes from the archives, but utilized new types of fabric to bring new life to the design. Although the designs quickly sold out, Kokosalaki opted to leave Vionnet, because of differing opinions with the owners of Vionnet over the best direction for the house.

← Similar philosophy
This dress for Sophia Kokosalaki's Spring 2009 collection suggests a philosophy similar to Vionnet's, in which the fabric is allowed to swathe the figure, as well as an experimental attitude regarding construction and final outcome. Kokosalaki also follows Vionnet's lead in letting the fabric and drape become the centre of attention, rather than any surface ornamentation.

→ Simplicity belied
Although Vionnet's pieces often have the appearance of being relatively simple, in fact the opposite is true. This 1935 bias-cut dress hangs gracefully and comfortably on the figure in an apparently simple way, but is actually cut and draped ingeniously to highlight the figure's best features.

A Balenciaga gown cost considerably more than that of any other couturier of the time, ignored trends or fads and was never advertised, but Balenciaga commanded attention, respect and deep loyalty. The aura of a Balenciaga creation was of startling simplicity, innovative and well-made construction, and an elegance that continues to inspire.

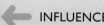 **INFLUENCED BY**

KEY
● fashion designer
◆ fashion house/brand
■ artistic influence
❖ cultural influence

❖ **World dress**
Balenciaga was inspired by his travels to the rest of Europe, including Austria, England, Italy and Switzerland, as well as the United States. He was also influenced by non-Western dress, adapting elements of the kabuki coat (right) in 1955 and the Indian sari in 1963–65. He would have been exposed to Asian imports, because so much comes into Europe through the port of San Sebastián.

❖ **Religious art and ecclesiastical dress**
Balenciaga was deeply religious and spent many hours in cathedrals and churches, where he would no doubt have seen religious-themed paintings and sculptures. He was inspired by ecclesiastical garments, with their propensity for black, deep red and hushed tones.

CRISTÓBAL BALENCIAGA
Spanish
(1895 Guetaria)

	Born January 21st in Guetaria in the Basque region of Spain. His mother teaches dressmaking.	Apprentices as a tailor in fashionable seaside resort San Sebastián.	Opens couture house in San Sebastián, frequented by royalty and the aristocracy. He later sets up additional houses in Madrid and Barcelona.	After the outbreak of the Spanish Civil War, Balenciaga leaves Spain, going to London and then Paris. He establishes a couture house in Paris, with fellow Spaniards financier Nicolás Bizcarrondo and hat designer Vladzio d'Attainville.
CHRONOLOGY	**1895**	**1908**	**1919**	**1937**

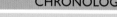 **INSPIRED**

● **André Courrèges**
A former assistant, Courrèges was influenced by Balenciaga's structural and architectural forms, and used these elements to create clothing that was emblematic of the space age and advancing technology (left).

● **Christian Dior**
His greatest competitor had a great deal of respect for Balenciaga, saying, 'Where Balenciaga leads, we follow.'

● **Emanuel Ungaro**
Ungaro said, 'Balenciaga is an extraordinary person. He has very strong dimensions. He is generous and so clever and so human. I worked very very hard there, but was happy to work there with him.'

● **Francisco Costa**
Like Balenciaga, Costa experiments with shape, simplicity and structure, and uses alternative fabrications to create truly modern clothing.

Despite the fact that Cristóbal Balenciaga was rarely photographed, never spoke in public because he was intensely shy, and distanced himself from his clients as well as the press, he was often referred to in the fashion world as 'the master'. Balenciaga was known not only for his meticulous attention to detail, cut and construction, but also for his sense of experimentation with fabric, drape and proportion. He ignored trends and, in fact, often went against them, because they might not have suited his customer. Balenciaga instead chose to experiment and perfect his own ideas, providing clothing that was timeless in elegance, sophistication and beauty.

Balenciaga was reputed to have said that the task of the couturier was to be an architect, sculptor, painter, musician and philosopher, all rolled up into one, and to be able to deal with the different problems of planning, form, colour, harmony and proportion.

FABRIC COLLABORATIONS

Balenciaga was involved in the entire process of producing a garment, from sketching, cutting and sewing to the display and presentation of the collections. He often collaborated with fabric houses to create new fabrics utilizing alternative content, resulting in a new texture or finish. The most notable of these fabric collaborations was the creation of silk gazar in 1958, with the textile firm Abraham.

Balenciaga's interest in Lurex and plastic fibres led to his working with the firm Marescot, creating a stiffened lace that glistened slightly because of a fine thread of clear plastic interwoven in the lace. Fabric was the most important component of his collections. Balenciaga refused the French government's offer of a subsidy to use French fabric manufacturers after World War II, because he did not want to be limited in his choices or his control of production.

→ Spanish influence

This 1951 dress is reminiscent of Francisco Goya's paintings of subjects wearing the traditional layered flounces so associated with Spanish dress. The shape of this Balenciaga gown is innovative for the time, with the skirt being cut away at the front with a long back, which Balenciaga popularized.

❖ Spain

Balenciaga was incredibly influenced by his native Spain, drawing upon the country's romance and mystery, but also its sense of solemnity and austerity. Balenciaga left Spain as an adult, but only after the Spanish Civil War made it impossible for him to make a living there. He made many references to the Spanish carnation (left) in his collections, as well as toreadors and flamenco dancers. A clear connection with historical Spanish painters, such as Francisco de Zurbarán, Francisco Goya and Diego Velázquez, can be seen in Balenciaga's use of lace and embroidery, as well as the shape of his garments.

The house of Balenciaga stays open throughout WWII, but reduces the number of pieces from 150 to 40 because of fabric shortages.	*Launches the perfume Le Dix. Later fragrances are La Fuite des Heures and Quadreille.*	*D'Attainville dies and Ramón Esparza takes over designing hats. The young André Courrèges becomes Balenciaga's design assistant.*
1939–45	**1947**	**1948–50**

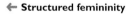

● Hubert de Givenchy

A former assistant, Givenchy was to follow Balenciaga's strategy of delaying shows for fear of copy artists. Givenchy also adopted Balenciaga's sense of simplicity for daywear and romance for eveningwear.

← Structured femininity

Balenciaga effortlessly brings out the best in the feminine figure in this 1948 polka dot dress by shaping, gathering and draping fabric around the model to suggest the ideal figure. The uncommon use of the polka dot for an evening dress suggests youthfulness, and reinforces the mature potential of the feminine form.

'Nothing is so mysterious as simplicity… As always we may expect to see Balenciaga's influence sink deeply, noiselessly, until it pervades the whole world of fashion.'

Carmel Snow, editor of *Harper's Bazaar*

INFLUENCED BY

KEY
- ● fashion designer
- ◆ fashion house/brand
- ■ artistic influence
- ❖ cultural influence

● Madeleine Vionnet
Balenciaga attended Vionnet's shows in his early career, and bought her toiles to copy for his own clients. When Vionnet was elderly and retired, she cited a pink Balenciaga piece as a favourite to wear. From Vionnet, Balenciaga learned the mysteries of the bias cut and the effects of draping, and he undoubtedly picked up the importance of experimentation. The two designers also ignored trends and opted to create clothing that worked for their customers and answered their own aesthetic concepts. (Right: Madeleine Vionnet uses a wooden mannequin to create designs, c.1930.)

● Coco Chanel
Balenciaga was influenced by Chanel's emphasis on ease and comfort for everyday use. Chanel said of him, 'Balenciaga alone is a couturier in the truest sense of the word. Only he is capable of cutting material, assembling a creation, sewing it by hand, and the others are simply fashion designers.'

CRISTÓBAL BALENCIAGA CONTINUED

CHRONOLOGY	1957	1958	1960	1967
	Along with Hubert de Givenchy, Balenciaga presents his collections a month after the other fashion houses for fear of copy artists, forcing foreign buyers to make two trips.	Introduces the high-waisted baby-doll dress, one of the most widely copied silhouettes in the latter half of the 20th century.	British manufacturer T.B. Jones launches three brands of stockings, all named after Balenciaga's perfumes. They help to spread Balenciaga's name, without diminishing it.	On the 30th anniversary of the house, Balenciaga shows his collection at the same time as other Paris designers.

INSPIRED

● Nicolas Ghesquière
Ghesquière was appointed creative director of Balenciaga in 1997 to resurrect the dying house. Ghesquière is now one of the most influential designers in contemporary fashion, combining elements of the heritage of the house with references to his own experiences. The similarities between the two designers are often not obvious. Since Balenciaga ignored trends and catered to an older customer, he is not thought of as cutting edge. In fact, Balenciaga was experimental, as evidenced by his work in fabrics, construction and cut. Ghesquière clearly recognizes this as he uses design ideas that made the house of Balenciaga famous to create cutting-edge ideas of the future.

➜ Feminine armour
As creative director of the house of Balenciaga, Nicolas Ghesquière has explored the archives of the house and identified most with Balenciaga's innovations in shape. For the Spring 2008 collection, Ghesquière also used examples of Balenciaga's floral prints. Florals are not usually seen in Ghesquière's work, but result in a fresh perspective on armoured femininity.

MEETING CUSTOMERS' NEEDS
Balenciaga did not feel that a designer should overwhelm his clients with personal whims or flights of fantasy. He strove to provide clothing that would suit his customers' needs. Balenciaga relied on the tunic, chemise and empire line that would look attractive and feel comfortable to older women, but also appeal to the younger customer. Balenciaga's pieces were particularly popular with Americans, for the simple, practical, wearable lines of the daywear and the extravagant and romantic eveningwear.

MASTER OF CONSTRUCTION
Cristóbal Balenciaga's crucial contribution to the world of fashion was his intense respect for the practices of the couturier. He was a master of construction and shape, filtering his skills to create garments with only the most

← **Sleek grace**

This 1955 collarless wool suit with Persian lamb scarf on the iconic model Dovima is contrasted in its slender strength with the iron gate she leans against. The simplicity of the jacket belies the incredible skill required to allow for such a specific fit.

● Edward Molyneux

Balenciaga admired Molyneux's simplicity and wearability, and his slow development of details and technique over time.

● Elsa Schiaparelli

Balenciaga bought toiles from Schiaparelli, as well as the work of Vionnet, Chanel and Molyneux, to take back to Spain and re-create for his customers. He appreciated Schiaparelli's use of art in clothing.

● Jean Patou

Patou influenced Balenciaga to think about comfort and usability in daytime dressing, in terms of both fabrication and construction.

Closes his house, because fashion is shifting away from couture to ready-to-wear. There are difficulties paying the increasing costs of workers and obtaining fabric on time, and luxury trimmings are no longer popular.

Dies March 24th. The house of Balenciaga lies dormant until it is bought by Groupe Jacques Bogart in 1986.

1968

1972

● Martin Grant

Grant's collections, such as Autumn 2009 (right), have a timeless elegance and focus on subtle yet chic construction, similar to Balenciaga's clean shapes and emphasis on the neck and shoulders.

● Narciso Rodriguez

Balenciaga had a loyal clientele, because he was able to dress them so well. Similarly, Rodriguez's characteristic simplicity, austere seaming and colour palette allow him to compliment a variety of body types and ages.

important seams remaining, as seen in the one-seam jacket of 1961 or any of his gazar dresses from 1958 to the end of his career. Heralding from the old traditions of couture and his native country of Spain, Balenciaga's contribution to fashion ultimately lies in the modern look and wearability of his clothing, providing a rich source of inspiration for contemporary designers.

Madame Grès was equal to the greatest couturiers of the 20th century, but is largely forgotten by the general public. Despite her low profile, work inspired by Madame Grès appears on numerous contemporary catwalks, and her name is spoken with reverence and appreciation by those in the know.

INFLUENCED BY

KEY
- ● fashion designer
- ◆ fashion house/brand
- ■ artistic influence
- ❖ cultural influence

● Jean Patou
Patou was an early proponent of abandoning the 1920s flapper look in favour of the long, lean gowns that came to define the 1930s. Patou was at the height of his career when Grès was considering fashion as a career.

● Adrian
In the early 1930s, Adrian created stunning bias-cut gowns for Hollywood films. Grès seems to have translated the glamour of these films into her own gowns.

◆ Callot Soeurs
The sisters were early proponents of the bias cut and experimental draping that were integral to the work of Grès.

● Madeleine Vionnet
Vionnet is clearly one of the most influential designers to Grès. Whereas Vionnet was mathematical in her approach to draping, Grès was far more experimental. Vionnet did not like a heavy understructure, but supported all detail or cut of fabric by her virtuosity with construction. These techniques and philosophies of fashion allowed Grès to create her own masterpieces.

MADAME GRÈS
French
(1903 Paris)

CHRONOLOGY	1903	1930	1932–34	1939	1941
	Born Germaine Emilie Krebs on November 30th in Paris.	Works for the house of Premet, learning the basics of dressmaking, sketching and cutting.	Begins designing under the names of Alex Couture, Alix Barton and then Alix, selling toiles to other couturiers and then creating her own gowns for private clients.	Exhibits her work at the Exposition Universelle in Paris, winning first prize for haute couture.	Ends her career as Alix, after being forced to escape the Nazi occupation when someone denounces her as a Jew.

INSPIRED

● Doo-Ri Chung
Chung is best known for her jersey dresses that share a close kindred spirit with Grès's work.

● Yohji Yamamoto
Yamamoto created several pieces for his Spring 2005 collection that used the pleating techniques of Grès. Yamamoto has often co-opted the techniques of Western designers and interpreted them for his own aesthetic.

● Claire McCardell
Grès's pleating technique clearly influenced the evening dresses that McCardell created in the 1940s. McCardell also strongly believed in minimal understructure to allow for freedom of movement, a philosophy that Grès had been putting into practice since the 1930s.

→ Modern grace
This dress from Doo-Ri Chung's Spring 2007 collection is one of many examples of the young designer's growing experience in creating beautiful, graceful pieces that bring Madame Grès's influence into contemporary times.

Madame Grès is known primarily for her gowns, with tiny cartridge pleating, that resemble those depicted on Greek statues. However, they were more the result of her intuitive and hands-on draping techniques than any appreciation for classicism: 'These draped dresses, people say it's from Antiquity. But I was never inspired by Antiquity. Before this fabric existed, I never thought of making draped dresses but as soon as I had the fabric, it fell into place by itself.'

INTUITIVE DRAPING

In fact, Madame Grès was responsible for creating a wide variety of gowns that were primarily draped, and all followed the strict traditions of haute couture. Throughout her long career spanning from the early 1930s through the 1980s, she never strayed from these principles, and she created stunning gowns using a variety of techniques and approaches

Fabric abundance
One of Madame Grès's signature techniques was the use of fabric from selvedge to selvedge (that is, the full width of the fabric). The effect in this 1940s gown is a unique form and grace that likens itself to Greek columns and hides any irregularity in the figure.

'The prêt-à-porter designers are always influenced by the couturiers. I feel that prêt-à-porter has indeed given the woman on the street a better neater appearance, but couture is the creative key. It is a grand work – it is truth – it brings something to the world.'

Madame Grès

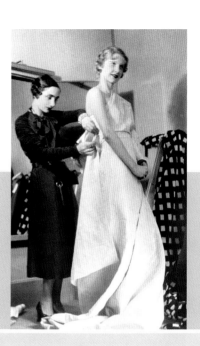

 INFLUENCED BY

KEY
- ● fashion designer
- ◆ fashion house/brand
- ■ artistic influence
- ❖ cultural influence

● Jeanne Lanvin
Lanvin was an early proponent of limiting the interior construction of a gown to accommodate movement and comfort for the wearer, which influenced Grès in her own philosophy of dress.

● Mainbocher
The American couturier was prominent in Paris in the 1930s. He was a proponent of simplicity and unadorned dresses, and may have influenced Grès in that regard.

● Cristóbal Balenciaga
Balenciaga was one of the only couturiers of the time whom Grès openly admired. The two designers were equally obstinate about the importance of couture, and were the only couturiers able to design and create a dress completely by themselves. (Right: Madame Grès dresses a model, 1933.)

MADAME GRÈS CONTINUED

	Begins a new company called Grès, and has to reestablish her reputation.	Nazis force Grès to close her house, because she repeatedly flouts fabric restrictions. Paris is liberated within the year, and Grès introduces a blue, white and red collection, the colours of the French flag.	Takes part in the Théâtre de la Mode, which exhibits French fashion on small wire dolls in sets designed by Christian Berard, Boris Kochno and Jean Cocteau.	Launches first perfume, Cabochard, which translates as 'pig-headed'. Later fragrances are Qui Pro Quo, Grès pour Homme and Alix.
CHRONOLOGY	**1942**	**1944**	**1945**	**1959**

 INSPIRED

◆ Costello Tagliapietra
The New York–based design team claim Grès's work as a major influence, which can be seen in their fluid and draped dresses (right).

● Alber Elbaz for Lanvin
Elbaz often creates pieces that are experimental and freeform in their drape and construction, traits for which Grès was largely unique in her day. He has said that she was a huge inspiration to him, and her look can be seen on the Lanvin catwalk.

➜ Evocative shape
In the 1930s, many designers used the back as the primary erogenous zone of the female figure. In this 1937 gown, Madame Grès asserts her virtuosity with drape by using the back to call attention to the dressmaker details over the backside, creating an evocative shape while never straying into vulgarity.

to dressmaking that demanded incredible virtuosity: 'Clothing follows the evolution of life, this is normal. But you have to keep a sense of shape and materials; you have to love beauty and the female body.'

Madame Grès was initially interested in sculpture and dance as possible career choices, which is very telling when looking at her work. The fabric always flows around the body, highlighting the curves, shapes and uniqueness of the female form. Grès achieved this by intuitive draping, using her hands to the best advantage and letting the fabric tell her what it wanted to do: 'I give the dress I create the line and shape that the fabric itself seeks.' Grès would work either on a mannequin or a live model with a length of fabric that she would gather, tuck, twist or bunch to create a gown.

Rather than keeping with what had brought her the most notoriety early in her career, Madame Grès continued

→ Symbol of defiance
Although this 1946 piece was created after World War II, it is representative of the hardships that the Nazi occupation created for many of Paris's couturiers. The dress is ingeniously simplified, but uses yards of fabric, emblematic of Grès's refusal to pander to the Germans' request for fabric limitations.

● Elsa Schiaparelli
Schiaparelli was a leading couturier of the day, as well as a mother raising a child on her own. The more reserved Grès was influenced by the outspoken Schiaparelli's bold aesthetic, defiant nature and ability to experiment and be playful with her designs.

● Christian Dior
When Dior's New Look collection came out in 1947, Grès changed her look to accommodate the major trends of the day. However, she used her own techniques, accumulated throughout her previous work, to make the silhouette her own.

Becomes president of the Chambre Syndicale de la Haute Couture, the governing body of the French fashion industry.	*A Grès retrospective is held at the Musée du Costume in Paris.*	*Dies November 24th.*	*New York's Metropolitan Museum of Art hosts a Grès retrospective.*
1972	**1981**	**1993**	**1994**

● Isabel Toledo
Toledo has created several pieces that resemble Grès's work. Toledo has certainly been inspired by Grès's independent spirit and the experimental nature of her technique.

● Ralph Rucci
Rucci has said that Grès is a major influence on his work, and his Autumn 1981 collection was homage to her.

● Halston
Halston's Spring 1976 collection featured several off-the-shoulder pieces that resembled Grès's work. His Spring 1980 collection included drawstring shirred (gathered) eveningwear, for which the inspiration was obvious.

throughout her life to refine her experiments with fabric and its relationship to the figure. Despite using numerous yards of fabric to achieve the looks she desired, there was very little if any understructure to the garments. She, like Madeleine Vionnet, wanted women to rely on their natural healthy physical form to allow for the greatest movement and comfort.

STUBBORN ENIGMA

Madame Grès is an enigma whose life was shrouded in mystery, and whose persona defied the typical characteristics of a couturier. She refused to provide an exact birth date, gave confusing information about her family and background, and divulged nothing of her nontraditional married life in which she and her husband never spent more than half a year together. Most notably, she took on several names throughout

her career, from Alix Barton to Alix Grès to Madame Grès, with several variations besides. During the German occupation of Paris in World War II, Alix Grès was one of the only couturiers to stand up to the Nazis, resulting in the forced closure of her house. Her appearance in the 1930s was akin to a dowdy school monitor, and in the latter half of her life was marked by a turban and button-down shirt with a high collar. Not surprisingly, her first and most remembered perfume, Cabochard, means 'pig-headed' in English.

Due to her refusal to give up couture or create licensing agreements or ready-to-wear collections, her house fell into financial ruin, and was sold and eventually disbanded. Although the house has never been resurrected by a young designer, her contribution to the history of fashion is indisputable, and her lasting influence continues to be seen on the catwalks today.

Issey Miyake has been able to do what so many designers hope to achieve and so few have been able to accomplish, which is to meld style, fashion and true wearability in a seemingly effortless way. Miyake has strived throughout his career to create wearable fashion, yet has also been recognized for his artistry, ingenuity and virtuosity.

INFLUENCED BY

KEY
- ● fashion designer
- ◆ fashion house/brand
- ■ artistic influence
- ❖ cultural influence

● Mariano Fortuny
The Italian designer was the first to discover the comfort and ease provided by pleats, for which Miyake has become so famous. Also like Miyake, Fortuny ran a studio that centred on developing techniques with textiles and materials.

● Madame Grès
The French couturier used pleats to sculpt the body in a way that was reminiscent of Greek sculptures. This was undoubtedly influential in Miyake's own education on form and shape.

■ Isamu Noguchi
Although Noguchi was a sculptor and furniture designer, he had a large influence on Miyake as an artist who blended his Japanese culture with his adopted American life. Noguchi was also a humanitarian and supporter of the arts, just like Miyake. (Right: Isamu Noguchi's 1968 sculpture Red Cube in New York.)

ISSEY MIYAKE
Japanese
(1938 Hiroshima)

CHRONOLOGY	1938	1945	1964–65	1966	1968	1969
	Born April 22nd in Hiroshima.	American forces drop atomic bomb on Hiroshima. Miyake loses most of his family.	Graduates with a degree in graphic design from Tokyo's Tama Art University. Moves to Paris to study tailoring and dressmaking.	Apprentices with couturier Guy Laroche.	Becomes an assistant to Hubert de Givenchy.	Moves to New York to work with Geoffrey Beene.

INSPIRED

● Makiko Minagawa
Miyake funded the diffusion line HaaT in 2000, with his textile designer Minagawa at the helm. The emphasis of the collection is the use of traditional craft practices from India and Japan to produce clothing for a contemporary culture. (Left: Traditional woven textiles from Asia.)

● Junya Watanabe
Beyond the obvious shared influence of traditional Japanese dress, Watanabe develops and explores new technologies, just like Miyake.

● Hussein Chalayan
The two designers have the common ancestry of a traumatic childhood, which has influenced their explorations of humanity and the bridging of cultures across time and space.

Issey Miyake has said that his primary focus is the 'importance of imagination and the development of technology in which to make clothing'. This statement belies the enormous impact that the Japanese designer has had on design internationally. He has created wearable, comfortable and practical clothing that has become, for his customers, as ubiquitous as jeans and a T-shirt, yet appears new, innovative and unique.

Miyake has developed several techniques for more efficient production, without having to resort to a weak and watered-down aesthetic. In turn, this has allowed him to negotiate many of the inherent problems and dichotomies between craft practice and technology that face designers.

JAPANESE TRADITIONS
Issey Miyake began his career apprenticing with French couturiers and the quintessential American designer Geoffrey Beene, but returned to his native country to rediscover the rich craft practice and aesthetic of Japan. His basic philosophy can be traced to the traditions of Japanese dress and the kimono. The kimono does not conform to the shape of the body, but instead offers anonymity and ultimately comfort. However, despite his connections to these Eastern ideas, Miyake's clothing has the greatest of ease and approachability, in contrast with that of some other Japanese designers, such as Rei Kawakubo and Yohji Yamamoto.

GROUNDBREAKING TECHNIQUES
Miyake first came to attention in the United States and Europe in the mid-1970s, when he quickly garnered interest and praise from other designers as well as loyal customers. His subsequent groundbreaking design solutions are startling in their simplicity and usability. The Pleats Please brand,

Experiments in pleating
This Autumn 1990 piece is a wonderful example of Miyake's exploration of pleats before he launched his Pleats Please line in 1993. Bright, cheerful and optimistic, the jacket is comfortable, easy to wear and practical, as well as framing the face in an aesthetically pleasing way.

→ **Sensory virtuosity**
Issey Miyake has brought new meanings to the
sensual qualities of fabric by the use of alternative
textures. This piece from Autumn 1994 utilizes
richly textured surface design techniques applied
in a sophisticated and modern way.

INFLUENCED BY

KEY
● fashion designer
◆ fashion house/brand
■ artistic influence
❖ cultural influence

● **Madeleine Vionnet**
Miyake was very influenced by Vionnet's technique and attitude regarding
fashion and clothing, emphasizing the relationship of the cloth to the body
and the ultimate requirements of movement and ease. Miyake has been
quoted as saying that seeing a Vionnet creation early in his career was
a life-altering experience. Her ability to circumvent traditional Western
idioms of shape and cut was integral in allowing Miyake to discover his
own balance between Western and Eastern aesthetics.

ISSEY MIYAKE CONTINUED

	Returns to Japan and forms Miyake Design Studio.	Creates subsidiary company Issey Miyake International Inc. in order to plan and manufacture clothes and related products for domestic and international sales.	Participates in Paris Fashion Week for the first time.	Opens his own store in Tokyo and then Paris.	Wins Japan's prestigious Mainichi Design Award, the first fashion designer to receive it.	Launches menswear collection.
CHRONOLOGY	**1970**	**1971**	**1973**	**1974–75**	**1977**	**1978**

INSPIRED

● **Francisco Costa**
The Brazilian designer has developed
a reputation for creating clean and
precise clothing that is also experimental,
using geometric manipulations of fabric
to define and counteract the figure
underneath. This was first explored
with a Western aesthetic by Miyake.

● **Martin Margiela**
Margiela is keenly interested in the
connection between the body and the
cloth, as well as the designer's hand in
the process. Miyake has been influential
as a designer who adopts the hands-on
process of a couturier, but interprets this
for contemporary society.

● **Rei Kawakubo and Yohji Yamamoto**
These two designers' introduction into the Western
market was paved by the initial forays of Miyake.
The three designers are often grouped together as
overwhelming influences on European and American
fashion design, creating new aesthetic and creative
approaches to wrapping the figure with fabric.

launched in 1993, has become his most profitable venture to
date. The entire collection relies primarily on the staple of
proven silhouettes, but continues to sell. The production
technique is unique in that the garment is cut first and then
pleated, rather than the traditional method of pleating first
and then creating the garment. This innovative technique
reduces manufacturing costs, allowing for a wider variety of
aesthetic solutions and outcomes.

In 1997, Miyake introduced A-POC, which stands for
'A Piece of Cloth'. The clothes are created from a single tube
of knit cloth on which cutting guides are printed; the customer
has to cut out the garment, making decisions about skirt
length, sleeve length and neckline, thereby participating in the
design of the final piece. Miyake's objective in creating A-POC
was to avoid wasting fabric and to encourage individual solutions based on his clothing concepts.

BEHIND THE SCENES
Despite his emphasis on practicality and usefulness, Miyake's
womenswear has been featured in countless exhibitions and
books, and was chosen by renowned fashion photographer
Irving Penn for a monumental photo essay because of its
sculptural and aesthetic qualities.

In 1999, Miyake resigned from actively engaging in the
creation of seasonal collections, leaving that to former assistants Naoki Takizawa and then Dai Fujiwara. Miyake prefers
to be behind the scenes, experimenting and tinkering with
techniques, technologies and concepts. He has also supported
several younger designers in a type of artists' collective or
studio that follows his general philosophy of fashion.

→ Interconnections

The dresses from the Spring 1999 collection are all cut from the same cloth, and for the fashion show were seen still in their connected state. The symbolism of this parade of identical garments out of the same cloth is obvious – we are all more similar than we are different, and if one of us falls, then we all do.

● Geoffrey Beene

Miyake worked with Beene early in his career. Beene was interested in the intersection of geometric shapes and the natural form, an interest that Miyake himself has explored throughout his career.

● Claire McCardell

Miyake admired McCardell's emphasis on wearable clothing. Both designers aspired to create clothing that was so functional as to become ubiquitous.

● Coco Chanel

Chanel developed ideas that worked for her customers, and perfected them throughout her career. This path was also adopted by Miyake, who recognized that truly influential design is rare and requires work to maintain.

Launches Pleats Please brand. Awarded the French Légion d'honneur.	Launches A-POC (A Piece of Cloth) clothing line.	Retires from designing to devote his full-time attention to research.	Design director Makiko Minagawa establishes a new women's line called HaaT.
1993	**1997**	**1999**	**2000**

● Naoki Takizawa

Takizawa became design director of Issey Miyake in 2000 after Miyake officially retired. Takizawa's work emphasized craft and experimental fabric techniques and manipulations. In 2007, he stepped down as chief designer to concentrate on his own collection, which is funded by Miyake.

● Dai Fujiwara

Dai Fujiwara succeeded Naoki Takizawa as design director of the house of Miyake in 2007. He has continued in the tradition of Miyake, experimenting with shapes and their relationship to the body (left).

'I make it, people take the idea and continue it. They are free to do so. To me, design must get into real life. Otherwise it's just couture, it's just extravaganza.'

Issey Miyake

← New interpretations

In his Autumn 2001 collection, Naoki Takizawa carried on the tradition of textile experimentation began by Miyake, allowing the fabric to provide the richness and beauty, and keeping the silhouette simple and therefore eminently wearable.

Along with his fellow Japanese designers, Yohji Yamamoto has helped to redefine clothing and the use of colour, shape and form in relation to the figure. He has also helped to redirect and question the Western ideals of beauty and what it means to be a woman in today's society.

 INFLUENCED BY

KEY
- ● fashion designer
- ◆ fashion house/brand
- ■ artistic influence
- ❖ cultural influence

● Christian Dior
On the surface, Dior's approach to fashion may appear to be in sharp contradiction to Yamamoto's own philosophies. However, Dior allowed strength and aloofness in feminine beauty, both of which are also present in the work of Yamamoto.

● Cristóbal Balenciaga
Balenciaga was known for his precision cutting and draping techniques, as well as his rejection of making women into sex objects. Both his philosophical and technical practices seem to have influenced Yamamoto, who has adopted several of the cutting and draping techniques that the Spanish designer perfected.

● Coco Chanel
Yamamoto has done several homage collections to the iconic French couturier, such as Spring 1998 (left). He undoubtedly admires the strong, independent nature of Chanel, and appreciates her sensible approach to fashion.

YOHJI YAMAMOTO

Japanese
(1943 Tokyo)

CHRONOLOGY	1943	1966	1969	1972
	Born October 3rd in Tokyo. His mother is a seamstress; his father is killed in WWII.	Graduates from Tokyo's Keio University with a law degree.	Graduates from Bunka Fashion College in Tokyo; males account for only 1% of students in the programme. Wins the prestigious So-en and Endo awards, along with a ticket to go to Paris. Tries to sell his drawings there, but when no one wants them, he returns to Japan and works in his mother's dressmaking shop.	Opens his own company.

INSPIRED

● Limi Feu
Yamamoto's daughter was introduced to Paris Fashion Week with her Spring 2008 collection. She shares many of Yamamoto's ideas, such as a heavy reliance on black and asymmetrical shapes, but she is younger and slightly more aggressive in her aesthetic choices than her father.

● Ann Demeulemeester
In addition to a similar use of black as a staple colour in most of their collections, Yamamoto has also influenced Demeulemeester in her philosophies concerning feminine dress and body consciousness.

● Rick Owens
Owens works primarily in black, and often creates silhouettes that have multiple layers, much in the same way as Yamamoto.

→ Space and depth
In her Spring 2010 collection, Yamamoto's daughter Limi Feu carries on the tradition of creating clothing that is not limited to body-confident sexiness. She uses fabric as shapes on the body, creating space and depth around the figure, but with a younger and more adventurous aesthetic than her father.

Yohji Yamamoto is a romantic. When you understand that about his clothing, it is slightly easier to understand his collections. Yamamoto has a fleeting vision of women as quixotic and ephemeral. Women are not meant to be held, and never understood, yet at the same time should be fully appreciated for their intelligence and knowledge. Even the gothic preoccupation with the colour black that appears in most, if not all, of his collections suggests a sense of the unattainable. He has defined his use of black as an 'embracing black' that absorbs all colour and at the same time has the depth of shadow.

FREE FROM CONSTRAINTS
Yamamoto designs for strong women who are ultimately beyond reach, since they are independent and moving at their own pace. Rather than highlighting a woman's overt sexuality, the designer opts to establish a feeling of nobility

Embracing black

Yamamoto's Spring 2007 collection introduced a tragic heroine who in many ways is overcome by the limitations and impositions of both society and biology. There is an obvious reference to the cage crinoline, and an uncharacteristic use of sheer fabric, both of which suggest vulnerability.

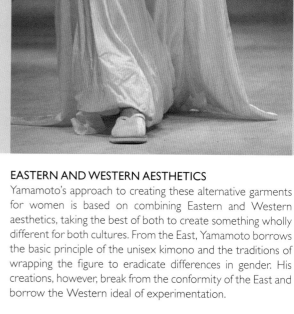

→ Vionnet revisited

Yamamoto's Spring 1998 homage to Madeleine Vionnet is made unique by his interpretation. He adds fabric to the front and back that threatens to overwhelm the model, perhaps as a metaphor for a bride's impending new life.

INFLUENCED BY

KEY
- ● fashion designer
- ◆ fashion house/brand
- ■ artistic influence
- ❖ cultural influence

● Rei Kawakubo
As a strong female Japanese designer, Kawakubo has influenced Yamamoto to think closely about how women interact with their clothing and how men perceive them.

● Madeleine Vionnet
Vionnet has an easy-to-appreciate aesthetic for a Japanese designer who is influenced in the traditions of cut and drape in the kimono. Vionnet designed clothing to hang from the shoulders, a basic principle shared by Yamamoto.

YOHJI YAMAMOTO CONTINUED

	Presents his first collection in Tokyo.	*Debuts in Paris with fellow Japanese designer Rei Kawakubo. Yamamoto sets up his first boutique in Les Halles, a shopping centre in Paris. All the merchandise is imported from Japan.*
CHRONOLOGY	1977	1981

INSPIRED

● Activewear collaborations
Designers such as Stella McCartney, Alexander McQueen and Hussein Chalayan have followed in the footsteps of Yamamoto by entering into creative agreements with activewear companies, taking on the challenge of designing a primarily functional product.

● Olivier Theyskens
Theyskens has a similar romantic view of women as Yamamoto. In Theyskens's early career, he became famous for his use of black leather in eveningwear, which was reminiscent of the Japanese designer.

and intelligence. It would be too simplistic to say that Yamamoto is just being old-fashioned when he covers the body and prefers women with little or no make-up and in flat shoes. Flat shoes are more comfortable and, rather than thinking of them as unattractive, it would be preferable to create flat shoes that are attractive as well as comfortable. Yamamoto is trying, in essence, to free women from the constraints of feeling like they are being judged based on their physical attributes. As he says, 'I think to fit clothes tight on a woman's body is for the amusement of a man.'

Yamamoto takes the most practical aspects of men's design and adapts them for women: 'Men's clothing is more pure in design. It's simpler and has no decoration. Women want that… I always wonder who decided that there should be a difference in the clothes of men and women. Perhaps men decided this.'

EASTERN AND WESTERN AESTHETICS

Yamamoto's approach to creating these alternative garments for women is based on combining Eastern and Western aesthetics, taking the best of both to create something wholly different for both cultures. From the East, Yamamoto borrows the basic principle of the unisex kimono and the traditions of wrapping the figure to eradicate differences in gender. His creations, however, break from the conformity of the East and borrow the Western ideal of experimentation.

WEARABLE, USABLE CLOTHING

Despite his creations being continually likened to pieces of art, Yamamoto insists that he not be considered an artist: 'To create something good, an artist has to take the plunge; he's testing the outer limits beyond which everything falls apart. Art is always a shock because it's pushing up

'There is always an adoration for women in me which resembles the temptation I have for things that have passed me by and so I can only see a woman as someone who passes by; a person who disappears.'

Yohji Yamamoto

↓ **Experiment in luxury**

In his Autumn 2008 collection, Yamamoto examined the idea of luxury by using leather and leaving all the hems unfinished. He also sent out Hermès-style bags, calling attention to the self-conscious display of wealth that is so pervasive in licensing in today's fashion industry.

❖ **Japanese culture**

Yamamoto has based his essential silhouette on traditional Japanese dress, and has been heavily influenced by the Japanese culture of his childhood. (Right: 18th-century silk painting of a Japanese woman wearing traditional kimono.)

● **Issey Miyake**

Like Miyake, Yamamoto feels that clothing for women should ultimately be about daily life and comfort. Miyake paved the way for Yamamoto by introducing a combined aesthetic of Japanese and European dress.

Director Wim Wenders produces a documentary on Yamamoto, called Notebook on Cities and Clothes.	*Presents first haute couture collection in Paris.*	*Debuts Y-3 line in association with Adidas.*	*First solo exhibition at the Musée de la Mode in Paris.*
1989	**2002**	**2003**	**2005**

● **Martin Margiela**

Margiela was significantly influenced in his early career by the work of Yamamoto, who was introducing asymmetry and the obvious hand of the craftsman from a Japanese perspective.

● **Haider Ackermann**

Ackermann's designs exhibit the same planar, asymmetric, geometric drape that is present in Yamamoto's work. He also uses a largely sombre, romantic colour palette.

● **Bernhard Willhelm**

Willhelm often uses shapes on the female figure that are reminiscent of Yamamoto – clean, simple and asymmetrical.

against the acceptable. That's the relationship between artist and the acceptable. That's the relationship between artists and ethics. But in my line of work, there is another factor to be considered: clothes are bought and worn by people every day, so they can't really be considered works of art.'

Indeed, Yamamoto has revolutionized the activewear industry's connection to a more considered design process. His design work with the company Adidas has promoted a new focus on aesthetics, and has opened the door for countless designers to experiment in a potentially lucrative relationship that advances mass-produced design. Ultimately, Yamamoto's aim is to create wearable, usable clothing that helps women change the emphasis from their appearance to their intelligence.

In the 1980s and 1990s, Romeo Gigli provided an important and prominent alternative to the image of hard sex and power that predominated in womenswear. His style revolved around exotic interpretations of the Orient, the Renaissance and the turn of the 20th century, and has proved to be a lasting influence.

 INFLUENCED BY

KEY
- fashion designer
- fashion house/brand
- artistic influence
- cultural influence

• Cristóbal Balenciaga
Preferring to stay out of the limelight, Balenciaga was an artisan who developed a design philosophy centred on the traditions of craft, much in the same way that Gigli preferred to make unique clothing through experimentation.

• Issey Miyake
Miyake is an artisan who believes that the slow and constant development of a core philosophy is better than following trends. This, and the fact that his clothing functions so well, has similarities to Gigli's work.

• Yohji Yamamoto
Yamamoto has a similar attitude about feminine strength, and shares Gigli's philosophy that women's clothes should not necessarily define their sexuality.

■ Antiquity and art
Gigli was inspired by a variety of historical periods and the artwork during those times. He was sensitive to the sensuality of German expressionism, as well as the fabrics and shapes from the Renaissance. The richness and allure of Byzantine and ancient Greek art were also significant in his aesthetic choices.

ROMEO GIGLI
Italian
(1949 Faenza)

	Born December 12th into an aristocratic family in northern Italy.	Travels to New York and designs a menswear collection for Piero Dimitri. Returns to Italy and freelances for several companies.	Starts his eponymous company in Milan.	Enters into a distribution agreement with Japanese department store chain Takashimaya. Opens a boutique in Milan.	Starts showing in Paris, opens a showroom there and launches the fragrance Romeo di Romeo Gigli.
CHRONOLOGY	**1949**	**1978–79**	**1983**	**1987–88**	**1989**

 INSPIRED

• Marc Jacobs for Louis Vuitton
The spirit of Gigli's aesthetic was present in Jacobs's Louis Vuitton Autumn 2005 collection (right), with rich, deep colours and an emphasis on large, draped, soft collars.

• Haider Ackermann
Ackermann consistently creates collections that focus on an alternative to sexy and flashy clothing for women. He and Gigli share a philosophy of quiet intelligence and sensuality.

• Marios Schwab
In Schwab's Autumn 2007 collection (right), Gigli's influence can be seen in the soft shoulders and relaxed silhouettes – elegant, wearable and sophisticated.

Romeo Gigli had a unique vision of women's expressions of strength and intelligence in an era when women were delving into a man's world in earnest for the first time. The overall expression of strength and power that most designers offered to women in the 1980s was what fashion writer Anne Hollander referred to as the 'new androgyny'. As a physical manifestation of equality, women were meant to resemble men in their toned bodies, wide shoulders, and linear hard-edged clothing.

Romeo Gigli designed for women who were not defined by their feminine body, yet took advantage of all that is inherent in being a woman. Gigli's woman in the 1980s and 1990s was intelligent, gentle, artistic and wise, with a self-confident sensuality and strength.

CELEBRATING FEMININITY

Taking his aesthetic cues from the antiquarian books that were a part of his childhood as the son of a bookseller, as well as from his Italian heritage, Gigli used richly coloured and textural fabrics to provoke an ephemeral and romantic feeling. Inspired by a variety of cultural or ethnic dress, he created a signature look in silhouette and detail that celebrated the feminine, but did not objectify or sexualize the wearer.

Gigli's frequent use of specialized textile and craft techniques – such as his use of Venetian glass for accessories, or his fondness for gold-infused textiles – helps to imbue his work with an artistic quality. His steady development of a design philosophy also gave his pieces a distinctive aesthetic that was easily recognizable from that of other designers.

← Sensuality expressed

While being neither overtly sexual nor boring, Romeo Gigli exhibits a soft femininity in his Spring 1990 collection. The clothing wraps the figure, mirroring the soft curve of the hips with the gentle slope of the shoulder. The textile, colour and shape reinforce one another for a unified interpretation of Gigli's woman.

'I was thinking I would like my dress to be free of time.'

Romeo Gigli

● Mariano Fortuny

Fortuny is by far the most obvious influence on Gigli's work. Both Italian designers were inspired by antiquity, and Byzantine and ancient Greek dress. Fortuny the artisan created textiles that were rich and delicately ornate, with a soft, feminine colour palette.

● Madeleine Vionnet

Vionnet understood the haptic qualities in rich colours, textures and fabrications. She was also influenced by antiquity and the beauty of the Grecian form.

● Paul Poiret

Poiret took advantage of ethnic dress as well as richly coloured and decorated fabric to create an allure that suggested strength and self-possession, also major hallmarks of Gigli.

1990	1991	1996	1999	2004	2009
Launches a diffusion line called G Gigli and opens a New York store.	Separating from his business partners, Gigli restructures his company to create Romeo World.	Launches a jeans collection.	IT Holdings, an Italian manufacturer, buys a majority share of Gigli's company.	Gigli loses the rights to his own name, and leaves the company he founded.	Starts a new company called Io Ipse Idem, which loosely translates as 'Myself, More Than Myself'. It is received well by the fashion press.

● Alexander McQueen

McQueen flew to Italy in the hope of working for Gigli, the hottest designer in the late 1980s and early 1990s. McQueen learned from Gigli that quiet fashion can make a powerful statement.

● Alberta Ferretti

Ferretti is known for her fondness of Greek dress inspirations and her rich colour palettes, both influenced by fellow Italian Gigli.

● Dries Van Noten

Van Noten has carried on Gigli's tradition of utilizing craft practice and ethnically diverse inspirations to inform the design process for women in the 21st century. Van Noten also shares Gigli's definition of women's beauty and strength.

● Christopher Kane

In his Autumn 2007 show, Kane showed several dresses that had similarities to the rich colours and textures that were so prevalent in Gigli's collections.

INHERENT STRENGTH

Romeo Gigli was unable to balance the demands of international distribution and lost the rights to his own name in 2004. He launched a new collection called Io Ipse Idem for the Autumn 2009 season, first showing menswear and then womenswear. It met with a warm reception by the fashion press and loyal customers. In 2010, Gigli focused on menswear and did not present a womenswear collection.

Ultimately, Gigli's understanding of women and their inherent strength, which is different from that of men but equally powerful, was to win out and become more of a norm than a deviation. Designers were strongly influenced by Gigli's sense of aesthetic, centred in craft, and this influence continues to be seen in collections on the catwalk today.

→ Softness and strength

The ability to suggest soft femininity as well as strength has been an influence that Gigli has imparted to designers such as Christopher Kane. In this piece from Kane's Autumn 2007 collection, he wraps the figure in a soft knit that is richly coloured and textured.

Christian Lacroix approaches fashion with a love of the artistry, research and process involved in creating the luxurious finished product. For him, couture is emblematic of all that he appreciates about clothing, style and femininity. It is through Lacroix's influence that many contemporary designers have come to appreciate the art form of couture, as well as Lacroix's ability to create a confection of fabric.

INFLUENCED BY

KEY
- ● fashion designer
- ◆ fashion house/brand
- ■ artistic influence
- ❖ cultural influence

● Vivienne Westwood
Westwood uses historical dress to make a point about contemporary times. She reinvents historical costume by combining it with an array of other influences, which is something that Lacroix also does.

● Paul Poiret
Poiret believed in the fantasy of couture, and resisted the notion that beautiful dresses could be created for a mass market. Although Lacroix has a more realistic and contemporary outlook on the importance of couture, the two designers share a love of the fantasy, embellishment and exoticism that are possible in couture.

● Cristóbal Balenciaga
Balenciaga would not work in a fashion industry that did not have couture, because perfection of cut and construction as well as experimentation were not possible in a ready-to-wear market. The two designers also share a love of Spanish dress and culture.

● Yves Saint Laurent
Later in Saint Laurent's life, he decided that couture was the only real way fully to express individuality and scope in dress. Lacroix certainly learned his love of theatricality from Saint Laurent.

CHRISTIAN LACROIX
French
(1951 Arles)

	Born May 16th in Arles, southern France.	Works at Hermès and then as an assistant to Guy Paulin.	Alongside publicity agent Jean-Jacques Picart, begins working on haute couture at Jean Patou.	Launches his own house with financial backing from luxury goods company LMVH.	Launches a ready-to-wear collection, an accessories line and C'est la Vie! fragrance. Designs costumes for several theatre productions.
CHRONOLOGY	**1951**	**1978–80**	**1981**	**1987**	**1988–90**

INSPIRED

◆ Rodarte
In the same way that Lacroix hopes to keep the couture tradition intact, the Mulleavy sisters of the label Rodarte combine a contemporary aesthetic with tradition in their handcrafted pieces (right).

● John Galliano
Galliano is undoubtedly influenced by Lacroix's sense of the dramatic. Galliano also has a fondness for the 1980s pouf skirt that Lacroix perfected in his time at the house of Patou.

● Alice Temperley
The British designer pulls together historical references, trends and cultural influences to provide her customer with a light, imaginative taste of fantasy in the same way that Lacroix has consistently done.

◆ Clements Ribeiro
The British and Brazilian design duo is known for using a diverse assortment of colour, pattern, print and cultural references, also hallmarks of many Lacroix collections.

For Christian Lacroix, the love of couture is not elitism or snobbery. The fact that only the extremely wealthy can afford such things is beside the point. For Lacroix, it is really about the artistry involved in creating a couture masterpiece and the ability to express individuality: 'My work is based on individuality and self-expression. It is not exactly antifashion but it is contrary to the way fashion is. My fashion is much more a way of living life with your roots and finding your own true self, than having to put a logo on your back.'

THE ROLE OF COUTURE
Lacroix is attracted to the inherent qualities of this one-of-a-kind craft and the endless variations that are possible. Within his career, Lacroix has cowritten several books about his process and inspirations. Mood boards, quick sketches and fabrics help to explain this designer and couturier, who is enraptured by every stage and process involved in the creation of a garment.

Couture has regularly been predicted or declared dead since the 1960s, yet loyal adherents such as Lacroix continue to stay true to the practice, believing that the potential of such an art form has not yet been fully explored or defined: 'At the end of the 20th century, couture will survive if it manages to situate itself coherently between luxury ready-to-wear, which it must not be, and radical creativity, which is not its role... A handmade straight skirt doesn't mean very much. The future lies between the two because the individual desire for a unique and handcrafted garment will always exist... I want to continue to believe that being different remains the key to everything.'

← Lavender lux
Referencing both the Belle Époque and 1950s screen sirens, combined with the sweetness of spring lilacs, Lacroix gathers fabric into this restrained but extremely glamorous concoction for his 1995 Spring collection.

'In these violent and desperate times, the only salvation lies in sincerity and total loyalty towards one's passions. Couture is my passion.'

Christian Lacroix

● Charles James
James was famous for his structured gowns that created a shape for the women wearing them. Although Lacroix does not impose body shapes, he often creates pieces that are rigid in order to achieve an interesting shape.

◆ Biba
Lacroix has cited Biba as an early influence that accounts for his love of mixing historical time periods with a downtown gypsy aesthetic that often appeared in his ready-to-wear and diffusion collections.

● Elsa Schiaparelli
Lacroix said, 'I want to get back to the position where couture becomes a laboratory of ideas, the way it was with Schiaparelli forty years ago.'

Publishes several books. Launches Bazar diffusion line, a jeans collection and a textiles line.	*Becomes creative director for the house of Pucci, as well as designing his own collections.*	*LMVH sells his company to duty-free retailer Falic Fashion Group.*	*The house of Lacroix is forced to go into protection after reporting a huge loss.*
1992–96	**2002–05**	**2005**	**2009**

● Jean Paul Gaultier
Gaultier began his career in ready-to-wear, sharing the belief of many that couture was a dying art, but recently he has begun to share Lacroix's enthusiasm for couture and has created his own couture collection. Conversely, Gaultier's influence can be seen in Lacroix's ready-to-wear collections.

● Alexandre Herchcovitch
The Brazilian designer's Spring 2007 collection featured brightly coloured patterns and prints inspired by diverse places such as Africa, South America and Europe. Although the two designers have a very different aesthetic, they share a common pursuit of cultural references in colour, shape or silhouette.

● Alber Elbaz for Lanvin
In his Spring 2010 collection, Elbaz created swirling masterpieces of brightly coloured short dresses that are reminiscent of the type of aesthetic that Lacroix is so famous for.

PURITY AND ECSTASY

Despite Lacroix's devotion to the past, his work has become postmodern in its complexity and multicultural influences. Steeped in what it means to be French, Lacroix loves to explore the rich array of European culture, historical time periods and art movements.

His clothing explores volume, shape and texture, in a wide array of strong vibrant colours. He says, 'Personally I've always hovered between the purity of structures and the ecstasy of ornament.'

→ Modern couture
Alber Elbaz received a great deal of praise for his Spring 2010 collection for Lanvin. The clothing seems to take the experimentation and craft of couture, and translate it for a ready-to-wear market, which has always been what Lacroix cares about most. The result is a seemingly spontaneous creation with superb craftsmanship.

Dries Van Noten has combined craft practice with business to create one of the more influential fashion companies of the 21st century, whose influence can be seen on countless catwalks. He has been able to achieve a dynamic balance between making wearable and innovative clothing, and has explored the global society for inspiration without becoming derivative or costume.

 INFLUENCED BY

KEY
● fashion designer
◆ fashion house/brand
■ artistic influence
❖ cultural influence

● Calvin Klein
Klein is known for his sexually based advertising and jeans, but in the 1990s his collections often exhibited a sensitive colour palette, beautiful textiles and interesting print techniques – also seen in Van Noten's collections (right).

● Yves Saint Laurent
Saint Laurent was one of the first established designers to use ethnic dress as a source of inspiration, something that has become a hallmark of Van Noten's work.

● Emanuel Ungaro
The French couturier was famous for mixing subtly coloured floral prints. Van Noten also uses this idea, but mixes ethnic prints and colours to reflect a global perspective.

◆ Byblos
Alan Cleaver and Keith Varty were known for being inspired by a diverse array of cultures and using bright colours in their work for Byblos, which seems to have made an impression on Van Noten.

DRIES VAN NOTEN
Belgian
(1958 Antwerp)

	Born in Antwerp. His father owns a menswear shop; his grandfather is a tailor.	Graduates from Antwerp's Royal Academy of Fine Arts.	Shows a menswear collection in London with five other Royal Academy graduates; they become known as the Antwerp Six. Van Noten starts selling his collection to stores internationally: Barneys in New York, Pauw in Amsterdam and Whistles in London. He opens a tiny boutique in Antwerp's gallery district, and creates men's and women's collections with the same fabrications.
CHRONOLOGY	**1958**	**1980**	**1986**

 INSPIRED

● Nicolas Ghesquière for Balenciaga
In some of Ghesquière's collections, such as Autumn 2007, the designer has uncharacteristically abandoned his futuristic aesthetic to use an ethnic inspiration – perhaps an influence from Van Noten.

● Phillip Lim
Lim's Spring 2010 collection features suits, colours and silhouettes that are reminiscent of Van Noten's Spring and Autumn 2009 collections, as well as Van Noten's popular bracelet necklace from Autumn 2008.

● Bryan Bradley for Tuleh
Bradley has cited gardens and nature as inspiration, as seen in his Spring 2009 collection (left). Van Noten shares the same inspirations, with the result that there is a strong similarity between the two designers' work.

Dries Van Noten makes clothes that are practical yet beautiful, innovative yet classic. His collections are intended to be wearable and useful clothing for the contemporary environment, but are also based on a craft heritage: 'I really try and live in the now. It's not that I like to live in a fake world or that I don't respect the past or tradition, but I make clothes for now.' The craft elements of his designs, in the form of prints, embroidery and silhouette, are never overwhelming or used purely on principle; rather, they are used as decorative details.

CRAFTSMANSHIP AND EXPERIMENTATION
For Van Noten, both the product itself and the process of creating that product are equally riveting and require the same attention. For him, research development and creation allow for experimentation and a focus on the haptic and sensual world that fabrics, colours and textures provide: 'Craftsmanship is one of the collection's points of departure. Especially with fabrics, just think of embroidered scarves, colour effects, prints. However, sometimes we really have to search for a solution to a certain problem, and sometimes new ideas emerge from the possible solutions, or a new inspiration. So it works two ways.'

CULTURAL INFLUENCES
Van Noten uses craftsmanship from diverse cultures, but prefers not to travel to places to experience these cultures directly. He believes that travelling to a destination might destroy the romantic, imaginary world he has created. By doing this, the culture that is of interest can be influential on his designs, but does not overwhelm them. The final creation can be an amalgamation of many cultures,

Heirloom chic
Dries Van Noten's
trendsetting Autumn 2008
collection suggests an eclectic
combination of sentimental
heirloom pieces being put
to new uses, such as
favourite bangles being worn
as a necklace. Van Noten's
collection is a celebration
of craft, individual expression
and emotional connections
in an ever-changing world.

→ Multiple influences

In this look from Van Noten's Autumn 2002 collection, the influence of Romeo Gigli can be seen in the rich use of textiles and texture, as well as the soft drape around the shoulders. Kenzo Takada's love of ethnicity and colour are also effortlessly combined by Van Noten to create an original look.

INFLUENCED BY

KEY
- ● fashion designer
- ◆ fashion house/brand
- ■ artistic influence
- ❖ cultural influence

● Romeo Gigli
Gigli popularized the combination of rich fabrications, colours, textures and prints. The silhouettes were often romantic and classically styled, or with an air of ethnic exoticism that has also become significant in the work of Van Noten.

● Kenzo Takada
Takada created fun and fanciful prints and colours throughout the 1970s and 1980s. Van Noten has adopted the same aesthetic mix.

DRIES VAN NOTEN CONTINUED

CHRONOLOGY	1989	1990	2000
	Moves to a five-storey former department store in dilapidated condition in a rundown neighbourhood of Antwerp. Restores the building, complete with antique fixtures, and keeps the old name Het Modepaleis (which coincidentally had been his grandfather's greatest competition).	Opens a showroom and press office in Paris, and then a showroom in Milan.	Moves to a large warehouse that now houses a showroom, design offices and an archive library, as well as marketing, production, accounting and distribution departments.

INSPIRED

● Vera Wang
Wang's use of prints and accessories (right) shows the influence of Van Noten. Wang, known for her rich colour sense, depends on a colour palette similar to that of Van Noten.

● Paul Smith
Van Noten is known for combining a variety of materials, colours and prints in one look, inspiring Smith to send men down the catwalk in floral shirts, checked jackets and python-print trousers in Autumn 2005.

● Thakoon Panichgul
For his Spring 2010 collection, Panichgul drew upon Van Noten's expert use of prints to create interesting textures.

● Peter Som
Som's collections have an overall romantic look, but for the Spring 2010 season he used diverse prints, borrowing from the trend set by Van Noten.

techniques and craft practices, combined with an approachable European aesthetic: 'I aim to create fashion that is neutral in such a way that each person can add his or her own personality to it. It's about fashion that doesn't overwhelm your own personality.'

BRAND EXCLUSIVITY

In a fashion world that is dominated by corporate takeovers and financial backing, Van Noten is unique as one of the few designers who has not succumbed to big business. His privately owned company is still in Antwerp, though he shows in Paris. He has not focused on licensing agreements, and believes that accessories should account for only a small amount of his company's creative energy.

In a seemingly antithetical approach to economic good sense, Van Noten does not use advertising, realizing that this enhances the exclusivity of his brand. He also refuses to use himself as a marketing tool: 'I think I tell enough about myself when I make my clothes and when I show them. I don't need people to buy clothes for who I am; I prefer them to buy things that I create.'

GLOBAL APPRECIATION

Van Noten provides an extremely successful model for many young designers, who recognize his balance between innovation and financial success. Both designers and customers alike respond to the international content and global appreciation that manifest in Van Noten's beautiful, approachable and wearable clothing.

→ Retracing steps

In his Spring 2010 collection, Van Noten decided to return to ethnic diversity as a primary focus, after showing several collections in which there were only geometric prints and no overt ethnic references. The prints Van Noten used in Spring 2010 inspired a flurry of designers to use multiple layers of prints and bright colours.

● Issey Miyake

The two designers focus on craft and usability as the primary concerns of their design philosophies. Both also feel that innovation stems from craft practice and an exploration of materials, but without losing sight of comfort and ease, as seen in this Spring 1996 look from Van Noten (right).

● Halston

Halston made his name for designing saleable and wearable chic clothing that was not contingent on any other marketing tool. This is a business and directional path that Van Noten has decided to adopt.

Opens a boutique in a 17th-century building in Paris.	Opens a boutique in Tokyo.
2007	**2009**

◆ United Bamboo

Design duo Miho Aoki and Thuy Pham have been influenced by Van Noten's rich colour sense and use of a relaxed, draped silhouette. They have also clearly been influenced by the accessories that often appear in Van Noten collections, such as round glasses and silk head wraps.

← Ease and wearability

United Bamboo's Spring 2010 collection featured the typical Van Noten accessories of round glasses and head wraps. Beyond this, the primary influence that Van Noten has had on this young company is the ease and wearability that has become such a signature for the Belgian designer.

'I am a little naive but I don't like the idea of showing things that you don't sell in a store.'

Dries Van Noten

Francisco Costa has been able to take an established company such as Calvin Klein, which helped to define fashion in the latter half of the 20th century, and successfully bring it into the 21st century. Costa's combination of practicality with dressmaker details, sensuality and experimentation has made him an influential voice in the dialogue of fashion.

INFLUENCED BY

KEY
- ● fashion designer
- ◆ fashion house/brand
- ■ artistic influence
- ❖ cultural influence

● Oscar de la Renta
De la Renta hired Costa as a design assistant. Costa has said that de la Renta taught him about fabrication and shared his design aesthetic, for which Costa will always be grateful.

● Tom Ford for Gucci
Ford recruited Costa to design for Gucci, which gave Costa more exposure to savvy business practices as well as to the fashion press.

● Cristóbal Balenciaga
Balenciaga is undoubtedly a major influence for Costa, who approaches fashion with a similar eye for experimentation, as well as the planar treatment of fabric on the figure.

● Giorgio Armani
Armani's aesthetic can be seen in the herringbone patterns and reliance on a minimalist navy colour palette in Costa's Autumn 2006 collection (left).

FRANCISCO COSTA
Brazilian
(1961 Guarani)

	Born May 10th in Guarani, Brazil. His mother owns a childrenswear factory.	*Moves to New York after the death of his mother. Attends Hunter College by day to study English, and takes night classes at the Fashion Institute of Technology.*	*Enrolls in the degree programme at the Fashion Institute of Technology.*	*After graduating, designs knitwear and dresses for a licensee of Bill Blass.*
CHRONOLOGY	**1961**	**1986**	**1990**	**1992**

INSPIRED

● Alexandre Herchcovitch
Echoing Costa's American football-inspired Spring 2007 collection, fellow Brazilian Herchcovitch also used the sport as inspiration in Spring 2010 (right), utilizing strong and often voluminous shapes.

● Brian Reyes
Reyes has an aesthetic similar to that of Costa, in which classics have a subtle twist or display a level of experimentation. Both designers enjoy experimenting with colour and patterns.

● Alber Elbaz for Lanvin
Elbaz has garnered an outstanding reputation for many explorations into drape and detail similar to those of Costa.

● Marios Schwab
Schwab examined dressmaker details and volume in his Spring 2010 collection, both of which are staples of Costa's aesthetic.

Francisco Costa is an influential figure in contemporary fashion for melding an emphasis on craft with simplicity of silhouette, providing a sensual and artistic interpretation of modern dress. His diverse work background has provided him with a unique perspective on how to combine big business with a more artisanal approach. Costa worked for Oscar de la Renta at the house of Balmain in Paris, learning couture techniques and acquiring a deep appreciation for fabrication and colour. Conversely, the proudly commercial Tom Ford employed Costa to design eveningwear for Gucci. Costa's experiences have resulted in a designer who understands the importance of both business and craft.

ARTISTRY AND CRAFT
The fashion industry in the latter half of the 20th century largely abandoned the practices of couture because of the impracticality of multiple fittings and the expense involved. There evolved a greater focus on clothing that was efficient in use, easily produced, sleek and minimalistic in order to achieve the greatest margin of profit. Design companies sought to expand with licensing agreements and diffusion lines, and to create a brand that was both aspirational and affordable. Although this is no less the case today, Francisco Costa has shifted away from minimalism and an almost generic aesthetic to create clothing that suggests a more artistic and personal journey.

Costa takes cues from designers such as Hussein Chalayan and Alexander McQueen, who are interested in abstract thought, as well as couturiers such as Cristóbal Balenciaga and Madeleine Vionnet, who were immersed in craft. The result is clothing that is thoughtfully produced, but without ever forgetting the provenance of the Klein brand.

← Soft geometry

In many of his recent collections, Francisco Costa has been exploring geometric form and manipulations of surface texture as they relate to the natural figure. This Autumn 2010 piece is soft and wearable, but gives a new shape to the feminine figure.

'I only do what I do. For me, it is a craft. It's got to be my own thing – otherwise, I would never be successful.'

Francisco Costa

● **Issey Miyake**

Miyake is known for his attachment to craft practice and his experimentation in fabrications, characteristics that have differentiated Costa from many of his big-name contemporaries.

● **Helmut Lang**

Lang seemed to be an influence in Costa's all-white Spring 2007 collection, in which the clothing layered sheer fabrics and textures.

● **Miuccia Prada**

Prada effortlessly balances the practical aspects of fashion with the artistic and experimental, and in this sense has paved the way for designers such as Costa.

Works for Oscar de la Renta, overseeing the Signature and Pink labels, as well as Pierre Balmain haute couture and ready-to-wear.

Recruited by Tom Ford to serve as senior designer for eveningwear at Gucci.

Becomes creative director for Calvin Klein womenswear.

1993 **1998** **2002**

● **Tomas Maier for Bottega Veneta**

Maier has established a name for himself for his attention to dressmaker details. In Spring 2010, Maier created several pieces that resembled Costa's all-white collections.

● **Nicolas Ghesquière for Balenciaga**

Ghesquière sent out a collection for Spring 2010 that used layers of shape and colour that closely resembled Costa's Spring 2007 collection.

● **Raf Simons**

Simons has been able to take a well-established house such as Jil Sander, with an extremely clean-cut brand image, and introduce a more personal vision with great success. The ability to do so was navigated earlier, by designers such as Costa for Calvin Klein.

FORM AND CONSTRUCTION

Francisco Costa's work continually explores form and construction, producing clothing that is both wearable and progressive in its scope. His work bears a marked sensuality, begging to be worn and touched. As Costa himself says, 'I drape a lot. I cut. I have to touch. For me it's almost impossible to start without that.'

The fact that Costa designs for such an established and important company as Calvin Klein means that he is able to pave the way for other designers who are hoping to explore new forms of construction and fabrication. This is particularly important in American fashion, where there is a long tradition of business taking precedence over craft-based innovation. Costa bridges the gap between an artisanal approach and business success.

← Alternative forms

This piece from Spring 2010 demonstrates how Tomas Maier uses a reductionist palette while also delving into alternative forms – both signatures of Costa's work. Both designers create clothing that does not sacrifice aesthetics for wearability.

CHAPTER 4

FUTURISTS

CARDIN ∘ RUDI GER
THIERRY MUGLER ∘ N

Technology often captures the imaginations of artists, designers, writers and illustrators, who illuminate contemporary ideas by exploring the possibilities of the future. Fashion has always had designers who are intrigued by reflecting our hopes and anxieties about the future, and use such ideas to propel the dialogue of fashion forward in a new way.

SPACE AGE

In the 1960s, designers such as Pierre Cardin and André Courrèges were attracted to the possibilities associated with space. The space race between the Soviet Union and the United States entered into pop culture as a symbol of societal fears about the mastery of science and technology, and resulted in an enraptured public that was enlivened by the possibilities of the future. For these designers, the quest for space travel allowed them to explore the society in which they lived, and gave them a venue for suggesting alternatives.

Pierre Cardin created clothing that explored cut, form and silhouette in a manner that was new to the world of couture. The results were often devoid of natural form, and created a dialogue of expression centred on product and use. For André Courrèges, space and technology suggested a more rational approach to all parts of life. Courrèges believed that it was not rational for women to exist only in dresses and uncomfortable high-heeled shoes, so he advocated trousers or tights and flat shoes. His aesthetic mirrored the linear forms so often associated with technology, helping to define our understanding of a futuristic look.

CHALLENGING THE NORMS

A little later in the 1960s and early 1970s, Rudi Gernreich used the vocabulary of futurism and technology to critique the society of his era. In response to a period of intense upheaval in views on women, sexuality and personal freedoms, Gernreich suggested styles of dress for a more enlightened society.

Thierry Mugler was interested in many of the same ideas, even if he was not as altruistic in his goals as Gernreich. In the 1980s, Mugler saw a chance in futuristic dress to create clothing that challenged the norms of sexuality and highlighted his connections to gay culture.

POP CULTURE FUTURISM

In contemporary terms, designers such as Nicolas Ghesquière, designing for the house of Balenciaga, uses the house tradition of experimental fabrics, precision cut and a disregard of trends as a platform for his own investigations of futurism and technology. He is often influenced by pop culture's media interpretations of the future, and uses the symbols of these interpretations as a metaphor for his own ideas of protection and empowerment for women.

INNOVATIVE WAYS OF DRESS

It is essential to understand that fashion will not always exist in its current form. All of the designers in this chapter suggest a realm of possibilities that offer new and innovative ways of dress made possible by technological advances. By engaging in the dialogue of futurism and technology, designers help to suggest the next step in fashion.

Pierre Cardin has expanded the role of the traditional couturier by delving into licences, businesses and products well beyond fashion, yet with a constant aesthetic sense and philosophy of approach. While becoming one of the richest fashion designers of all time, Cardin has explored what it means to marry business with creativity, and explored what fashion will become in the future.

INFLUENCED BY

KEY
● fashion designer
◆ fashion house/brand
■ artistic influence
❖ cultural influence

● **Elsa Schiaparelli**
Schiaparelli employed Cardin as a cutter and tailor, but her influence can be seen in Cardin's desire to explore the controversial or unaccepted.

● **Christian Dior**
As an assistant to the couturier, Cardin was influenced by Dior's use of structured form to create an architectural base that allowed for fabric manipulations otherwise not possible.

● **Cristóbal Balenciaga**
Balenciaga seems to have been Cardin's greatest influence throughout his career – for example, the sculptural, clean-edged silhouettes of Cardin's early career.

● **Yves Saint Laurent**
Saint Laurent was a contemporary of Cardin, but as a leader of French fashion design, Saint Laurent's aesthetic held sway on other designers' catwalks, as seen in Cardin's Spring 1996 collection (right).

PIERRE CARDIN
Italian
(1922 Venice)

CHRONOLOGY	1922	1945–46	1950	1954	1959
	Born July 7th in Venice.	Moves to Paris and works briefly for Jeanne Paquin and Marcelle Chaumont in minor positions. Becomes an apprentice cutter and tailor for Elsa Schiaparelli, and then head of tailoring for Christian Dior.	Opens his own couture house in Paris.	Introduces the popular bubble dress and opens a boutique in Paris.	Expelled from the Chambre Syndicale de la Haute Couture, the governing body of the French fashion industry, for showing a collection outside of his salon. He is later reinstated.

INSPIRED

● **Hannah MacGibbon for Chloé**
MacGibbon's Spring 2009 collection (left) featured scalloped edges like those that had appeared prominently in Cardin's Spring 1970 couture collection.

● **Giorgio Armani**
Armani has expanded his fashion empire into hotels, resorts and restaurants, which is a trail first blazed by Cardin, who purchased the famous Belle Époque restaurant Maxim's in Paris in 1981.

● **Halston**
Halston was one of the first designers in the United States to experiment with licences, from which Cardin had been making money in France since the 1960s.

● **Thierry Mugler**
Like Cardin, Mugler has often preferred making a dramatic statement over producing wearable clothing. Mugler also became famous for his performance shows, as first done by Cardin.

Pierre Cardin's career extends from the mid-20th century to the dawning of the 21st century, and the designer continues to be recognized for his influence on the fashion industry. Due to the longevity of Cardin's career, his aesthetic and style have changed monumentally over the course of the decades, from elegant to utilitarian, theoretical and artful.

HUMAN SCULPTURE
Throughout these permutations, Cardin has continually sought to explore the figure's relationship to its surroundings. From large collars and sheath dresses in the 1950s and 1960s to the sci-fi overextended shoulder of the 1980s, Cardin has made the figure into a human sculpture.

Cardin has used his aesthetic to interpret each decade's zeitgeist – design for all in the 1960s, a clean-edged aggres-

siveness for the sexual revolution of the 1970s, and large shoulders and suggestions of power in the 1980s. Since the 1990s, Cardin has positioned himself as a purely theoretical designer. Trading on his amazing name recognition, he continues to make money on his many licences and business ventures, and so has the luxury of creating clothing that explores his futuristic interests.

SPACE AND FORM
Cardin's interest in space and form has led him to experiment and produce a wide array of architecturally unique buildings, furniture, interiors and accessories that reinforce the look of his clothing. Cardin has expanded into the hospitality industry, buying the famous French restaurant Maxim's, and created hotels and resorts for a total experience. To Cardin, all design is the same: 'I like designing out of context,

← Sleekly timeless
This piece from Pierre Cardin's Autumn 1969 collection is a sleek interpretation of the maxicoat and minidress. Although completely functional, the quilted leather trim lends an air of futurism that extends the outfit from a 1960s trend to a look of timelessness.

'The clothes I like the best are the ones I invent for a life that doesn't yet exist: tomorrow's world.'

Pierre Cardin

● André Courrèges
Courrèges interpreted the youth movement for couture, blending elements of science fiction and futurism, which clearly had an influence on Cardin's work.

● Mary Quant
Quant had an impact on Cardin as one of the first designers to focus on the youth market in the 1960s. She also emphasized the use of nontraditional materials, such as plastic, which Cardin embraced.

● Issey Miyake
Miyake had a large impact on Western designers, with his use of abstract shapes in the 1970s. Cardin was one of the first French designers to explore the Japanese aesthetic.

Against the rules of the Chambre Syndicale, he launches ready-to-wear for men and then women.	*Opens Espace Cardin as a space for artistic ventures. Begins showing all his collections there.*	*Introduces haute couture furniture, or 'Utilitarian Sculptures'.*	*Presents a collection in Red Square, Moscow, to an audience of 200,000.*	*Awarded the French Légion d'honneur.*
1961–63	**1970**	**1977**	**1991**	**1997**

● Claude Montana
Montana embraced the large shoulders and sense of the dramatic that were so important in Cardin's work in the 1970s and 1980s.

● Nicolas Ghesquière for Balenciaga
Ghesquière is influenced by Cardin's use of geometry and alternative fabrications, and the sense of futurism that came to pervade so much of Cardin's work.

→ Polished futurism
Nicolas Ghesquière's Spring 2007 collection for the house of Balenciaga references the work of Cardin in the late 1960s. Ghesquière suggests the Cardin brand of futurism in the emphasis on black and white, as well as the use of horizontal and vertical lines in the silhouette.

without the limitations of angles, corridors, rooms or walls. It's all the same to me whether I'm doing sleeves for dresses or table legs.'

AESTHETIC SCOPE

Cardin's desire to expand his aesthetic scope beyond clothing has meant that, in many cases, his influence in the fashion industry has been decreased. Due to the vast numbers of licences, Cardin cannot consistently control the quality of the products that bear his name, often resulting in a cheaply made item or a watered-down version of a distinctive idea. However, despite the shortcomings of Cardin's business practices, his overall influence is a lasting and important contribution to contemporary design, and what design will become in the future.

Rudi Gernreich was interested in the future, and perfectly represented the shifting paradigm of 1960s youth culture. Influenced by the emotive and expressive movements in art and dance during the 1950s and 1960s, Gernreich was a proponent of letting dated ideas of beauty and propriety fade into history.

 INFLUENCED BY

KEY
- ● fashion designer
- ◆ fashion house/brand
- ■ artistic influence
- ❖ cultural influence

● Emilio Pucci
A fellow athlete, Pucci was the only other designer as interested as Gernreich in doing away with constricting constructions in garments.

■ Dance
Gernreich's early training as a modern dancer gave him a lifelong interest in movement unhindered by constricting undergarments or clothing construction.

❖ Asian, Indian and Russian dress
As a participant in the experimental 1960s and 1970s, Gernreich was interested in ethnic, cultural and spiritual diversity and acceptance. For example, Gernreich's influences included Indian dress (right), which could be seen in his use of silhouettes that mimicked the sari, mehndi make-up, and Indian prints and colours.

RUDI GERNREICH
American
(1922 Vienna, Austria)

CHRONOLOGY	1922	1938	1949	1951
	Born August 8th in Vienna. His aunt runs a high-fashion dress shop.	Escapes from the Nazis, moving to California with his mother. Becomes a naturalized citizen a few years later.	Abandoning a career in dance, he works for coat-and-suit firm George Carmel in New York. Finding it difficult to conform to the custom of copying French designers, he is eventually fired.	Forms a partnership with manufacturer Walter Bass to design for JAX boutique in Los Angeles. His line of loose-cut, tight-belted gingham and cotton tweeds quickly sells out.

 INSPIRED

 **Ethnic silhouette**
One of the most well-known and referenced early collections from Dries Van Noten is Autumn 1996, which included several interpretations of Indian dress. Asian dress was a continual interest and reference for Gernreich, too. Neither designer ever travelled to India, but they used the best of the relaxed but sensuous silhouette for Western dress.

● Dries Van Noten
Van Noten often uses ethnic inspiration and mixes graphic prints much in the same way Gernreich did, as well as placing an emphasis on wearable, comfortable clothing for the modern woman. Gernreich often used Japanese, Thai and Indian dress as a source of inspiration. Van Noten's clothing is never clingy or overtly sexy, and although Gernreich occasionally pushed the boundaries of taste, the two designers share an understanding of how clothing interacts with the body and the ultimate comfort of being in one's own skin.

Rudi Gernreich's influence can be felt not only in the diverse style directions of his work but also in the emphasis he placed on the body underneath the clothing. His ideas have helped to solidify our present fashion environment, one in which freedom of the figure and an acceptance of nudity is commonplace. Rudi Gernreich was interested in producing affordable clothing for those who were most open to his ideas: the young.

LIBERATION OF THE BODY
The events that were part of Gernreich's childhood had a great effect on the way in which he approached fashion later in life. Having escaped Nazi-invaded Austria, he moved to Los Angeles, California, with his mother. Gernreich was influenced by Hollywood style and glamour, as well as the expressive and often politically minded beatniks, intellectuals

■ Modern art

Gernreich was drawn to the emotional and expressive focus of modern artists from movements such as abstract expressionism, op art (right) and pop art. He used bold, graphic shapes, fabrics and themes in his clothing that echoed the work of many of these artists.

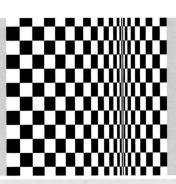

Takes his new line to New York. Sally Kirkland, fashion editor for Life magazine, encourages him to take his collection to Marjorie Griswold, who helped Claire McCardell. He designs the first bra-free swimsuit.

Starts designing swimwear for Westwood Knitting Mills.

1952

1955

◆ Dolce & Gabbana

Dolce & Gabbana mix prints and experiment with many of the same themes that Gernreich was attracted to, such as the negotiation of moral attitudes toward sex and nudity as well as futurism.

● Cynthia Rowley

Rowley is known for her sense of humour and use of bright, bold colours. In her Spring 2009 collection, she used the knits and cutouts that Gernreich was famous for.

← Japanese schoolgirl

Gernreich was influenced by both ethnic dress and popular culture. In his Autumn 1967 collection, Gernreich combines both influences in his use of the pop culture icon of the Japanese schoolgirl. The backpack, shorts and knee-high socks call attention to the schoolgirl inspiration, while the dress offers a youthful look in the desired aesthetic that is suitable for any age.

← Topless bathing suit
The 1964 topless bathing suit embodied Gernreich's primary philosophy of freedom for the body. For him, nudity was not about sexuality, and the bathing suit was not about objectifying women. On the contrary, Gernreich was hoping that his clothing would lead to self-actualization and acceptance.

INFLUENCED BY

KEY
● fashion designer
◆ fashion house/brand
■ artistic influence
❖ cultural influence

● Claire McCardell
McCardell created clothing for 'real women' that was affordable and easy to wear. She helped to develop the concept of mix-and-match separates that was fundamental to Gernreich's work. She was the first designer to focus on the need for relaxed and casual clothing, which she referred to as 'play clothes', and she was also the first to take all foundation construction out of garments, which revolutionized swimwear. Gernreich concentrated a great deal on knits and swimwear, pushing the boundaries of comfort and morality. For him, as for many other designers, McCardell's work opened the possibilities for perfecting casual wear.

RUDI GERNREICH CONTINUED

	Starts designing collections for the Ted Saval division of the General Shoe Company.	Expands his accessories collections, believing that accessories are just as important as the clothing.	Forms his own clothing company, G.R. Designs, Inc.	Introduces the infamous topless swimsuit. Launches the 'no-bra' bra that has no boning or padding, and allows women to achieve the support they need without exaggerating their breasts.	Featured on the cover of Time magazine.
CHRONOLOGY	1957	1958	1960	1964	1967

INSPIRED

● Halston
Gernreich used knits as a primary fabrication, which opened the door for designers such as Halston to use them liberally throughout his career. Both designers recognized not only the comfort and ease of movement that knitwear affords but also how well the drape of a knit looks on a young, thin form.

● Alexandre Herchcovitch
In his Spring 2007 collection (right), Herchcovitch showed several different patterns inspired by Africa and his native Brazil, coupled with graphic black-and-white accessories and some 1960s and military details, themes that were also present in many Gernreich collections.

and artists who were expressing their outrage at post–World War II society. The introduction of the birth-control pill, women's rights and the gay liberation movement inspired Gernreich to create clothing for 'modern, sexually liberated women'.

As Gernreich said, 'The era of fashion dictatorship is gone and with it the authoritarian approach to clothes. Everywhere structures are breaking down. We have discovered that nakedness isn't necessarily immoral, that it can have a logical and decent meaning. The body is a legitimate dimension of human reality and can be used for a lot of things besides sex. Slowly, the liberation of the body will cure our society of its sex hangup. Today our notions of masculine–feminine appeal are in people, not in clothes.'

DESIGNER AS TECHNICIAN

Later in his career, Gernreich was convinced that 'the creative part of fashion is gone'. He believed that the new breakthrough in clothing would be technological: 'Once the sewing machine has been replaced, once a designer can spray on clothing or transmigrate fabrics to the body, new things will happen. The designer will become less of an artist, more of a technician. He'll be more like an architect or engineer, with a sound background in chemistry. There will be no need for sewing machine operators or cutters; other machines will do this work. Knowledge of machinery such as computers will therefore be essential.'

← Plastic cutouts

Gernreich and two (different) models reenact the shot used for the cover of the December 1967 issue of *Time* magazine. The knit minidresses with peekaboo plastic cutouts are both futuristic and body-revealing. Being featured on the *Time* cover was a rare honour for a fashion designer. One of the models on the actual cover was Peggy Moffitt (right), who was Gernreich's lifelong friend, model and muse.

● Mary Quant

Quant focused on creating affordable clothing. She, along with André Courrèges, introduced the miniskirt that was also essential to the Gernreich customer.

● André Courrèges

Like Gernreich, Courrèges worked with graphic, geometric shapes to create clothing that reflected the changes in youth culture, and the definition of femininity in the new modern age.

After *Life* magazine asks him to design what people will be wearing in 1980, he instead presents designs for the year 2000. The magazine publishes his predictions that clothing will be functional and people will stop being so concerned with their appearance.

Dies of lung cancer on April 21st.

1970

1985

● Norma Kamali

Kamali has done a great deal of work with mass-market venues, such as Walmart. The designer follows in the footsteps of Gernreich to create good design for everyone.

● Peter Jensen

Like Gernreich, Jensen displays a sense of play and humour in his work, and experiments with the boundaries of good taste, attracting a younger customer.

'Fashion has got to be relevant to women today. To desire the past is to negate the present and future as well.'

Rudi Gernreich

→ Beauty abstracted

Gernreich's conception of the future included large tentlike robes that would abstract the figure when it became no longer aesthetically pleasing. These large graphic shapes often found a place in Gernreich's ready-to-wear – he wanted women to feel comfortable even if they no longer had the ideal body type.

André Courrèges brought couture into the space age, creating clothing that attempted to address the changing roles of women, society and culture, and treating fashion as a functioning product rather than frippery. An enormous influence in the 1960s, Courrèges continues to inspire designers today.

INFLUENCED BY

KEY
● fashion designer
◆ fashion house/brand
■ artistic influence
❖ cultural influence

● Edward Molyneux
Molyneux was a couturier in the 1930s who used clean, unadorned lines, and was known for his simplicity and taste, all of which influenced Courrèges.

■ Modern architecture and civil engineering
Courrèges admired architecture that fulfilled the dual criteria of functionality and simplicity, which he strove to emulate in his own collections. The rationality and strict planning of civil engineering can be seen in the sharp geometric lines of his clothing. Like a street planner, he approached fashion design as a balance between function and aesthetics.

● Cristóbal Balenciaga
Balenciaga trained Courrèges in all aspects of design, teaching him to draw, cut, sew and fit. Courrèges said, 'Balenciaga was very exacting, very very hard to please,' yet he stayed at the house for 10 years, learning from and being influenced by the master.

● Emilio Pucci
In the 1950s, the Italian aristocrat introduced trousers within his ski-inspired collections, as well as pedal pushers for a lazy walk on the beach. This helped to pave the way for Courrèges in the 1960s.

ANDRÉ COURRÈGES
French
(1923 Pau)

CHRONOLOGY	1923	1945	1950	1961	1963
	Born March 9th in Pau.	*After studying civil engineering, he decides to go into fashion. Moves to Paris to work for Jeanne Lafaurie.*	*Begins working for the house of Balenciaga.*	*Opens his own couture house, based in his tiny apartment.*	*Introduces the concept of trousers for every occasion, suggesting the radical idea that they are suitable for both casual and formal events.*

INSPIRED

● Emanuel Ungaro
Ungaro trained at the house of Balenciaga, replacing Courrèges there. He was later employed by Courrèges as an assistant. Ungaro's work in the 1960s was reflective of Courrèges's style and focus.

● Claude Montana
Courrèges was a source of inspiration for Montana's work in the 1980s, which comprised clean, unadorned lines and shapes, and rejected the ever popular colour black.

● Miuccia Prada
Prada often relies on Courrèges innovations, such as his clean geometry and silhouette shapes, as seen in this piece from the Autumn 2002 Miu Miu collection (left).

● Rudi Gernreich
Like Courrèges, Gernreich used a lot of knits, and focused on miniskirts as a way to allow young women freedom of movement. The two designers also developed body stockings and preferred flat-footed boots.

André Courrèges wanted to create clothing that was suitable for the changing times, abolishing the past and embracing the possibilities of the future and technology. Courrèges was called the 'Le Corbusier of Paris couture', referring to the influential architect so closely associated with the tenets of modernism. Courrèges was a true modernist designer, desiring a break from past ideas of fashion, wanting clothing to be truly efficient and rejecting any extraneous decoration. Courrèges approached fashion as a product designer, understanding that a truly futuristic notion of clothing centred on function and usability.

TROUSERS FOR ALL OCCASIONS
Both Courrèges and Mary Quant have a claim on the introduction of the miniskirt in 1965, which allowed young women a sense of movement and comfort not afforded by many designers. However, Courrèges was also a proponent of trousers for all occasions, realizing that women's roles were changing to become more active and independent: 'Something has to happen to women's clothes. Clothes are no longer designed for the life women lead. All women want to look young and short skirts help you to do so, but skirts cannot get any shorter and still be decent. As for trousers, they are comfortable and practical for living today and, if they are beautifully cut, can flatter a woman's figure and be every bit as feminine as anything else she wears.' Today, the idea of women wearing trousers for any occasion is commonplace, but in the 1960s, Courrèges was introducing a radical idea.

← Wearable today

The clean black-and-white graphics in this 1960s outfit are typical of most of Courrèges's work. In the 1960s, Courrèges managed to be successful in suggesting what women would wear in the future. His emphasis on long skinny trousers and an easy-to-wear boxy silhouette makes this ensemble wearable today.

> 'Luxury in clothes to me has no meaning. It belongs to the past.'
>
> André Courrèges

● Coco Chanel
Chanel's primary goal was to simplify clothing to answer the needs of women. She also preferred simplicity and specific means of decoration. Courrèges would have learned from the work of Chanel, with whom he shared so much in common.

● Pierre Balmain
Balmain's experiments with clean, linear shapes in the late 1950s would have influenced Courrèges. In turn, Balmain was inspired by the graphic lines of Courrèges in the late 1960s.

● Christian Dior
Dior created architectural pieces of clothing that also reflected his love of poetry and nature, a dichotomy also seen in Courrèges's work.

1964	1965	1967	1972–73	2002–08
His Spring collection becomes known as the Space Age collection. Emanuel Ungaro, who had replaced Courrèges at Balenciaga, comes to work for him.	Introduces the miniskirt (a claim shared by Mary Quant).	Launches Couture Future, a ready-to-wear line, in frustration at the number of copies of his work that are appearing in department stores.	Designs clothing for the employees at the Munich Olympics. Launches his perfume Empreinte and Courrèges menswear.	Branches into other areas, such as developing alternative-fuel cars and holding a sculpture exhibition.

● Nicolas Ghesquière for Balenciaga
Ghesquière relies on precision cut and unornamented details (right) to suggest futuristic, forward-thinking clothing, which shows the influence of Courrèges.

● Yves Saint Laurent
Saint Laurent was inspired by Courrèges's uncompromising rejection of the past while still existing within the parameters of the Chambre Syndicale, the governing body of the French fashion industry.

● Marc Jacobs
Jacobs is continually inspired by the 1960s and the sense of futurism that defined the work of Courrèges.

← Shape and detail

Although this look from Marc Jacobs's Pre-Autumn 2010 collection for Louis Vuitton has traces of Chanel, another clear influence is Courrèges, as seen in the heavy graphic lines and the short miniskirt. The repetition of shape and detail is an obvious Courrèges trademark.

LINEAR GEOMETRY AND USABILITY

Courrèges had a relatively short career in the sense of a traditional couturier, but his work continues to provide visual language and metaphors for our contemporary idea of futurism. His reliance on white geometric forms and spare decoration has influenced everything from science-fiction films to popular culture, yet his influence did not stop at his linear geometric aesthetic.

Courrèges was one of the first French designers to shift the focus on clothing away from pure art to a functional, usable garment: 'The woman who interests me doesn't belong to any physical type. She lives a certain life, however. She is active, moves fast, works, is usually young and modern enough to wear intelligent clothes. When people buy my clothes, they buy a way of life, a philosophy.'

Thierry Mugler has an alternative vision of what it means to be a designer, encompassing theatricality, science fiction and subversive sexuality, yet his influence is often seen in the work of contemporary designers. This influence encompasses the connections between art and fashion, and the fashion show as a performance piece.

 INFLUENCED BY

KEY
● fashion designer
◆ fashion house/brand
■ artistic influence
❖ cultural influence

● **Adrian**
There is no doubt that Mugler was influenced by the over-the-top glamour of the costumes Adrian created for the world's most renowned film studio, MGM, at the height of its influence.

● **Travilla**
Travilla constructed gowns for actresses in the 1950s, including Marilyn Monroe and Jane Russell, that displayed all the curves but also formed an impenetrable armour. The same can be said for much of Mugler's work.

● **Madame Grès**
Grès's exceptionally sculpted gowns appeared effortless and easy to wear. Mugler has said that he admired Grès and her stunning gowns.

● **Yves Saint Laurent**
Saint Laurent often played with the connection between masculine and feminine as represented by the choice of fabric. Mugler continued that exploration in his own work.

● **Christian Dior**
Dior constructed glamorous gowns displaying swags of fabric, but also utilized sharp tailoring and sculptural forms. Both have helped to inform Mugler's work.

THIERRY MUGLER
French
(1948 Strasbourg)

	Born December 21st in Strasbourg.	Studies dance at Strasbourg's School of Fine Arts.	Moves to Paris and works as a window dresser while also making clothing for himself and friends.	Launches his first line, called Café de Paris.	Founds his eponymous company, launching a women's collection the following year.	Launches menswear collection.
CHRONOLOGY	**1948**	**1966–67**	**1970**	**1973**	**1974–75**	**1978**

→ **INSPIRED**

● **Riccardo Tisci for Givenchy**
Tisci has shown bondage-inspired collections, such as Spring 2009 (right), as well as garments with long sheaths of hair in Autumn 2009 that are a mixture of inspirations from Mugler and Martin Margiela.

● **Alexander McQueen**
The two designers share a primary philosophy and therefore have many similarities in aesthetic. Their clothing provides protection, creating warrior women who are fierce, strong and impenetrable, and who own their sexuality. McQueen followed Mugler's example by providing controversial and uncomfortable images of women to drive a point home.

● **Rosemary Rodriguez**
In 2008, Rodriguez was appointed to reopen the Mugler atelier. She has continued to explore the fierce angular suits that constituted Mugler's more approachable and saleable looks.

Thierry Mugler was consistent in his sources of inspiration, from insects, Hollywood glamour and S&M to Russian constructivism, robotics and cyborgs, which is why it is so easy to spot his influence on contemporary designers. Although a major portion of his notoriety was based on the fantasy costumes that he created to express these inspirations, his day clothing also exemplified the woman of the 1980s.

EMPOWERING WOMEN
Mugler was among the first of many designers to reflect a new breed of women, who were no longer ladylike or fragile flowers needing to be wrapped in delicate and precious fabrics. Women in the 1970s and 1980s were redefining their place in the world, and seeking to be equal to men in every way. Mugler suits featured large shoulders, hard

angular lines and bright colours that were clearly inspired by the glamazons seen in Hollywood films, and the sharp tailoring that trailed Christian Dior's New Look of 1947. The models were as aloof as the angular clothes they wore, and were posed throughout the 1980s in Mugler's cold and remote photographs. For any woman wishing to feel empowered by her clothing, Mugler's vision was irresistible.

REDEFINING FASHION
Mugler played with the desire for validation and expression to create a new vocabulary in fashion: 'I did make clothes because I was looking for something that did not exist. I had to try and create my own world.'

Having immersed himself in visions of style and glamour of the past, Mugler wanted to create clothing that defined the wearer in a new way, questioning what constituted

← Too funky
Mugler's iconic motorcycle corset, seen here during an anniversary show in 2007, first appeared on the catwalk in Spring 1992 as well as featuring in George Michael's 'Too Funky' video.

Having photographed his own advertising campaigns, Mugler publishes Thierry Mugler: Photographer, a book of photographs in a Stalinist propaganda style that at the time is seen as controversial.

Directs video for George Michael's song 'Too Funky', featuring several iconic Mugler creations, most notably his motorcycle corset.

1988

1992

● Christophe Decarnin for Balmain
Decarnin created clothing in his Spring 2010 collection (right) that borrowed from the 1980s contributions to fashion of Mugler, Katharine Hamnett and Gianni Versace.

● Gareth Pugh
Autumn 2008 saw samurai warrior women march down the British designer's catwalk. Mugler often used the exoskeleton of insects as an analogy of protection and aggression.

good and bad taste and levels of acceptability. One such example would be his attachment to PVC, which has always been associated with S&M and the dominatrix. Instead, Mugler sought to redefine the use of PVC, calling it an elegant and staple fabric: 'It reminds me of skin in its shine and sharpness.'

HUMANS AND MACHINES

Mugler introduced pieces in his fashion shows that questioned the connections between humans and machines, as exemplified by the motorcycle corset featured in George Michael's 'Too Funky' video. Mugler also famously sexualized the robot by placing a woman in a metal and clear plastic costume. By exposing the flesh, Mugler was asking what was real or created about human interaction.

→ Suppressed Victoriana
This look from Mugler's Spring 1999 collection references the Belle Époque and the sexual repression characteristic of the 19th century. With her veiled face, the model is both exposed and constrained, yet is so forceful in her stance and sexuality that she is undoubtedly in control.

'I like to make people dream
and to tell a story.'

Thierry Mugler

← **Lady cyborg**
Mugler's Autumn 1995 lady cyborg takes its explorational lead from designers such as Pierre Cardin, who was not necessarily interested in wearability so much as in advancing an idea within our social context.

INFLUENCED BY

KEY
- ● fashion designer
- ◆ fashion house/brand
- ■ artistic influence
- ❖ cultural influence

● **Vivienne Westwood**
Westwood combines elements of raunchy sex and gentrification in a way that Mugler has also consistently explored.

● **Pierre Cardin**
Cardin's work is associated with abstracted shapes on the figure, and incorporates a heavy science-fiction element. These influences can be seen in Mugler's work.

● **Paul Poiret**
Poiret was not as concerned with the wearability of his clothing as with the effect that it had. Mugler's work is often so sculpturally rigid that it acts as armour visually and metaphorically, while not always being comfortable.

THIERRY MUGLER CONTINUED

CHRONOLOGY	1997	1998	2003	2008	2009
	Enters into a lucrative contract with French fragrance company Clarins to produce the perfume Angel.	Releases a second book of photography called Fashion, Fetish, Fantasy.	Closes his couture house because of a decline in sales, and focuses on other artistic projects as well as expanding his fragrances.	Rosemary Rodriguez, formerly of Paco Rabanne, becomes designer of the house of Thierry Mugler.	Mugler designs sets and costumes for Beyoncé Knowles's 'I Am…' world tour and videos.

INSPIRED

◆ **Dolce & Gabbana**
For Autumn 2007, the design duo showed a homage collection to the work of Mugler, with structured nipped metal belts, references to S&M and high-shine fabrications.

● **Nicolas Ghesquière for Balenciaga**
Ghesquière showed cyborg legwear in his Spring 2007 collection that called to mind Mugler's work with robotic metal and plastic.

→ **Voluptuous machine**
Dolce & Gabbana's Spring 2007 show exhibited several armour-like dresses in an overall metallic-heavy collection. Not only is this dress reminiscent of Mugler's Autumn 1995 lady cyborg, but it also suggests a far more voluptuous body than this model naturally has.

PERFORMANCE ART

Before Mugler, fashion shows had traditionally been more of a way for buyers and celebrities to have a first look at a designer's collection. Mugler used the fashion show to expand the natural connections of couture by exploring its inherent theatricality as performance art – something that designers such as John Galliano, Viktor & Rolf and Alexander McQueen have heartily embraced.

With the mind of an artist, Thierry Mugler was never content to limit himself just to the creation of clothing. His career has encompassed photography, costume design and film and stage directing, suggesting that clothing was simply one of the means Mugler used to create his unique vision.

Nicolas Ghesquière blends popular culture with innovations in fabric and craft to give us a glimpse of what is to come in the future of fashion. Since he designs with a futuristic aesthetic and creates such experimental shapes and fabrics, Ghesquière looks like he is 10 steps ahead of everyone else – and he usually is.

INFLUENCED BY

KEY
- ● fashion designer
- ◆ fashion house/brand
- ■ artistic influence
- ❖ cultural influence

● Jean Paul Gaultier
Ghesquière said of his time working for Gaultier: 'It [assistantship] was about coffee and not much drawing. But I was looking at everything… I learned that fashion is putting together many, many things, crossing the universe of arts, movies and music.'

● Azzedine Alaïa
Alaïa uses sex to redefine strength and power for women. Much of the same style ideas and philosophies show up in the work of Ghesquière.

● André Courrèges
Courrèges took the aesthetic from his training at Balenciaga and focused it on space and futurism, making him a large influence on Ghesquière. Ghesquière's Spring 2009 Balenciaga collection (left) references the short dress and geometric motifs that often appeared in Courrèges's work.

NICOLAS GHESQUIÈRE
French
(1971 Comines)

CHRONOLOGY	1971	1986	1991–93	1995		1997–98
	Born May 9th in Comines in northern France.	Starts various internships, such as for Agnès B and Corrine Cobson.	Works as design assistant to Jean Paul Gaultier.	While freelancing at various fashion houses, he enters the Balenciaga house via the licensing department, where among other things he designs mourning clothes for the Japanese market.		Promoted to creative director of Balenciaga, with his first collection being Spring 1998. Also becomes head designer for Trussardi.

INSPIRED

● Francesco Scognamiglio
Scognamiglio's collections have been consistently influenced by the futuristic hard tailoring that is prevalent on Ghesquière's runway.

● Giles Deacon
Each season, a reference to Ghesquière's work seems to surface in Deacon's shows, primarily in the structured tailoring and use of volume.

● Julien Macdonald
Macdonald has been influenced by Ghesquière's precision cut and fondness for structured, hard-looking fabric.

→ Proportions and color

For his Autumn 2008 collection, Francesco Scognamiglio sent out several wool coat dresses with long leather gloves that are reminiscent of Ghesquière's interpretations of Balenciaga's work, such as the proportions and colour choice.

In a 2006 *New York Times* article, Cathy Horyn said, 'If Nicolas Ghesquière isn't the most important designer of his generation, it is hard to think who would be!' This statement is largely the result of Ghesquière's overwhelming influence and his ability to start trends. His work is a fine balance of technical innovation, familiarity with the old ways, and concepts that are both forward looking and approachable.

FAMILIAR METAPHORS

For many in the press and fashion audience at large, the new ideas explored by some designers seem so abstracted that they will never be adopted, much less understood. Ghesquière, however, makes such ideas seem within reach, because he uses metaphors for futurism that borrow from the science-fiction pop culture of the past. An apt analogy might be the early home computer's similarity to the look of

← Futurist couture

Nicolas Ghesquière's Autumn 2010 collection for
Balenciaga received high praise for its deft balance of
futurism and relevance for the contemporary context.
Throughout the collection, Ghesquière treated fabrics
so that they would appear rigid, although in reality
they are soft and luxurious to wear.

● Cristóbal Balenciaga

As the couturier whose name is on the door where he works,
Balenciaga's work exerts a massive influence on Ghesquière.
Balenciaga's spirit lives on most importantly in Ghesquière's innovations
and experimentation in form, fabric and construction. Ghesquière
bounces effortlessly between the archives of the house and his
own, more contemporary influences, so that the outcome is
never derivative.

In addition to other positions, becomes head designer for Callaghan. Launches the Balenciaga Classic bag line.	*Collaborates with French artist Dominique Gonzalez-Foerster on the design of new flagship Balenciaga stores in Paris and New York.*
1999–2000	**2003**

◆ Proenza Schouler

The two young American designers
Jack McCollough and Lazaro Hernandez
have been influenced by Ghesquière's
use of drape, geometric tailoring,
fabrications and 1960s references
in many of their collections, such
as Autumn 2009 (right).

a television set. Early computer users felt more comfortable
because the new, intimidating technology looked like an
object that was already familiar to them and user-friendly. As
Ghesquière comments, 'I always want a surprising way to go,
but beneath that I want to try and say the same things;
I think in a way you always have to use the same thing in
fashion but you must find a new way to tell it.'

LEGACY OF INNOVATION

Ghesquière has also been able to balance his work for an
important and iconic house such as Balenciaga with his own
ideas of what fashion should become: 'The history of the
house is incredible, which means I can work with a lot of
freedom. Cristóbal Balenciaga discovered so many things,
was so inventive, it's astonishing. I can work on something
and then look back through the archives and find it already.

→ Solar power
Ghesquière's Spring 2009 collection for Balenciaga
was inspired by the 1970s sci-fi television show *Battlestar
Galactica* and the 1982 film *Tron*. The French designer was
attempting to make the jacket look as if it were made of
solar panels. This collection, among others, began major
trends that reverberated throughout the fashion industry.

 INFLUENCED BY

KEY
● fashion designer
◆ fashion house/brand
■ artistic influence
❖ cultural influence

● Yves Saint Laurent
Ghesquière's Autumn
2009 collection, with
its mix of hard tailoring,
draping and prints, paid
homage to Saint Laurent,
who was the first to
combine art, popular
culture and couture to
reflect a new generation.

● Hussein Chalayan
Like Ghesquière,
Chalayan pushes forward
the dialogue of futurism
and technology in fashion.
The two designers
influence and respect
each other's work.

NICOLAS GHESQUIÈRE CONTINUED

*Launches several new Balenciaga collections: menswear, accessories,
shoes and Balenciaga Edition, which features items inspired by the
house's haute couture archives. Introduces the capsule collections
Balenciaga Knits and then Balenciaga Pants [Trousers].*

CHRONOLOGY   **2004–05**

 INSPIRED

**● Bryan Bradley
for Tuleh**
Bradley's Spring 2010
collection shows the
influence of Ghesquière
in the brightly coloured
crisp silk jackets and skirt
suits that hung off the body
in a style often seen on
the Balenciaga catwalk.

◆ Acne
Ghesquière's penchant
for padded-shin
trousers and futuristic
metal boots can clearly
be seen in the young
label Acne.

'I don't think couture fits our world. I don't think
it fits our time. Anyway I have the luxury of using
the couture techniques in my ready-to-wear.
One thing about couture is the craft… For me
the craft is really what's making the difference.'

Nicolas Ghesquière

→ **Natural road warrior**
Ghesquière was interested in creating young, urban looks for his Spring 2010 collection for Balenciaga. He used several innovative and eco-friendly fabrics, such as vegetable-dyed leather and hemp. The collection also exhibits Ghesquière's other consistent inspiration of athletic sports.

● **Thierry Mugler**
Mugler, known for his futurist approach to fashion that often borders on costume, would have influenced Ghesquière in the 1980s. Ghesquière's Spring 2007 collection (left) featured plastic and knit fabrications that are suggestive of the robotics or machine parts that could be seen in Mugler's work.

● **Martin Margiela**
Ghesquière is said to admire Margiela's work greatly, and personally wears his menswear. The influence on Ghesquière's work can be seen in the experimental approach to craft.

Further capsule collections include Balenciaga Silk, Balenciaga Leather and Balenciaga T's (a T-shirt collection).

Launches Balenciaga Denim and Balenciaga Black Dress capsule collections. Receives the Insignes de Chevalier de l'Ordre des Arts et des Lettres, in recognition of his contributions to the French cultural inheritance.

2006–07	2008

● **Vera Wang**
Wang is often influenced by Ghesquière's use of positive and negative space, as well as his draping techniques.

● **Thakoon Panichgul**
In his Spring 2010 collection, Panichgul was influenced by Ghesquière's references to activewear and symbols of sci-fi futurism. In this example (left), it can be seen in the type of fabrication and graphic constructional qualities of the shoulder and chest, which have an armour-like quality.

I am very respectful of Balenciaga, but that is another time and it is my vision of what Balenciaga is now. For me it's about evolution, not revolution.'

Ghesquière has fully embraced the interest in fabric innovation that Balenciaga began. For one collection, he might mix wool crepe, gabardine and felt with foam or jersey to make a fabric that has the body or form of neoprene but is comfortable to wear in an everyday setting. He also uses fabrics such as radzimir, a stiffer weave of silk, as well as a crinkled fabric similar to matelassé that is made using a heat-shrinking process. Ghesquière affixed metallic pieces to a knit to create his famous robot leggings for the Spring 2007 collection; for Spring 2010, he used leather to suggest a type of armour and stiff hoods that helped to maintain anonymity against the prying eyes of 'big brother'. He says, 'I have always liked the idea of protection.'

NEW IDEAS AND CONCEPTS

Nicolas Ghesquière understands that the lineage of the house of Balenciaga is about experimentation and development. The original designer's idiosyncrasies, such as a refusal to accept new practices in business or expansion, are just that: peculiarities to the man, not the company.

Having come into a house that had struggled since the retirement of 'the master', Ghesquière has done a great deal to make Balenciaga profitable, adopting the standard business practices of the 21st century. He has opened several diffusion mini-collections, and launched a fragrance as well as a successful menswear collection. Couture, which Cristóbal Balenciaga defended so stubbornly, is a practice that Ghesquière feels has no relevance in contemporary society. What the house does offer is a legacy of creative play, and the advancement of new ideas and concepts.

CHAPTER 5

MODERNISTS vs. POSTMODERNISTS

Modernist and postmodernist philosophies are the principal frameworks and influences on 20th-century design. Modernism traces its roots to the latter part of the 19th century and defines a remarkable set of changes within society. Modernism embraced technology and reflected a desire to eliminate extraneous decoration or ornament, and reorder the world under a universal system of rational thought.

Postmodernism, with its revival of ornament and traditional techniques, developed towards the latter half of the 20th century, when modernist principles began to falter in the face of a diversified culture that was based on multiple perspectives and philosophies.

REVISING FASHION

The modernist versus postmodernist debate played out in fashion across the entire span of the 20th century and beyond into the 21st century. The designers in this chapter approach their work via a reinterpretation of the historical context of fashion through either a modernist or postmodernist philosophy. They either see

clothing history as no longer relevant, or they see it as a rich resource that should be included and explored, but repurposed for a new era. In both cases, the designers use these fundamental perspectives to revise clothing around contemporary issues.

THE MODERNISTS

Designers such as Jil Sander and Helmut Lang came into prominence in the 1990s, when there was a backlash against the excesses of the 1980s. In essence, history was repeating a minicycle of the 19th-century Victorian era moving into the modernist 20th century – the 1980s had been marked by a rise of conservatism, attention to class differences and materialism, and in reaction the 1990s brought with it a sense of inclusion, desire for diversity and atonement.

These minimalist designers created many new fashion trends that relied on the use of little or no ornament, monochromatic colour palettes and clean silhouettes. They defined the new woman of the era by creating clothing that did not rely on historical references. Narciso Rodriguez, for example, designs within that minimalistic framework, but plays with thresholds of detail, positive and negative space, and graphic detail to bring a modernist perspective into the 21st century.

THE POSTMODERNISTS

The postmodernist designers, such as Vivienne Westwood, Gianni Versace, Katharine Hamnett and John Galliano, have always sought inspiration in different historical time periods. A simplified explanation of postmodernism is the appropriation or juxtaposition of many styles in order to create a new style. Within those appropriations, the original meaning is found to be no longer relevant, so new meanings are assigned.

The postmodernist designers are known for carrying out careful research in clothing and textile museums, and combining this research into multiple levels of reference. Consequently, they are not interested in re-creating history, but instead in combining several different references to create a wholly new idea of fashion that fits effortlessly into a contemporary context.

Vivienne Westwood is a study in contrasts, from her love of tradition to never being reverentially historical, from her involvement in punk to being famous for creating stunning ball gowns, and finally as a designer who uses traditional icons of suppression as contemporary symbols of feminine strength and sexuality.

INFLUENCED BY

KEY
- ● fashion designer
- ◆ fashion house/brand
- ■ artistic influence
- ❖ cultural influence

● Christian Dior
Dior was at his zenith when Westwood came of age. She remembers experimenting with her own versions of Dior's 1947 New Look as a teenager, and discovering her own sense of sexuality. Despite her involvement with alternative forms of beauty in the form of punk and her later interpretations of style, Dior and his focus on womanly hips, bust and waist have come to define Westwood's ideal beauty for women. Westwood has often copied versions of the bar suit that appeared in Dior's New Look collection, reinterpreting it for contemporary usage.

■ Malcolm McLaren
The two met in 1965 and collaborated on many artistic and business endeavours that introduced Westwood to the idea of fashion design as a serious career choice. (Right: McLaren and Westwood, 1981.)

VIVIENNE WESTWOOD
British
(1941 Glossop)

CHRONOLOGY	1941	1965	1970	1972	1974
	Born April 8th in Glossop, England.	Meets Malcolm McLaren, who later becomes manager of punk group the Sex Pistols.	Opens a shop, Let It Rock, in London with McLaren, selling teddy boy clothing. Westwood also pulls apart vintage pieces, makes patterns and creates copies.	Renames shop Too Fast To Live, Too Fast To Die. Creates first slogan T-shirts targeted at disaffected youth.	Renames shop Sex, selling clothing and S&M paraphernalia. Westwood customizes clothes, but does not design any.

INSPIRED

● John Galliano
Galliano is a fellow postmodernist, who also sees the connection between historical ideas and contemporary times. Like Westwood, Galliano is fascinated by changing ideas of sexuality, and uses historical fashion to express those ideas.

● Gareth Pugh
The young iconoclastic British designer owes much to the likes of Westwood for her work in the punk scene and the sense of theatricality she promotes in her fashion shows.

➔ Historical seduction

For the Dior Autumn 2004 couture collection, John Galliano creates an alluring play on ultra-feminine sexuality. Similar to Westwood, Galliano is exaggerating the body shape that makes women uniquely feminine. The model is both armoured and exposed, with the sensuous furs reinforcing the delicacy of her chest and hands.

Vivienne Westwood has become inspirational to countless other designers by creating fashion on her own terms. Punk's focus on the questioning of all things is a grounding philosophy of Westwood's, as she sets about examining all facets of fashion, society and sexuality, never taking an idea for granted or assuming knowledge.

Vivienne Westwood has recognized that certain questions routinely get asked, but the answers change constantly: What is femininity? What is sexy? What does it mean to be strong? How are clothes used as symbols of all these ideas? By attempting to understand sexuality as it existed in the past, Westwood interprets how it is best expressed now.

UNCONVENTIONAL CONSTRUCTIONS
One approach that has proved successful for Westwood has been to study techniques of construction. However, she is not

- **Elsa Schiaparelli**
Like Westwood, Schiaparelli experimented with the dichotomy of fashion and the absurd. Schiaparelli always pushed the boundaries of taste to attempt a new understanding of beauty.

- **Rei Kawakubo**
Kawakubo's introduction to fashion in the 1980s seems to have had a large influence on the work of Westwood. Although Kawakubo approaches fashion very differently, the two designers are both interested in alternative notions of beauty and aesthetics.

Renames shop Seditionaries – Clothes For Heroes, which launches the punk look.

Renames shop World's End. Holds her first catwalk show, the Pirate collection.

1976   **1981**

- **Jean Paul Gaultier**
Gaultier has Westwood to thank for playing with innerwear as outerwear to express alternative ideas of sexuality and female power. Gaultier has since pursued the idea and is himself famous for the concept.

- **Heatherette**
Richie Rich and Traver Reins create collections that are based on the club scene of New York and feature fearless and humorous clothing, such as a skirt with oversized googly eyes or the statement T-shirt that Westwood popularized in the 1970s.

← **Hail to the British**

For her Autumn 1995 collection, Vivienne Westwood played with various plaids and applied them to 19th-century silhouettes. The plaid, silhouette and accessories declare a particular British sensibility, giving the model a firm air of aloof power, but with a sense of humour.

→ Rejection of androgyny
From the Autumn 1994 collection, this outfit highlights masculine characteristics of dress: broad shoulders, suit waistcoat and solid plaid fabric. However, these masculine features only call attention to the model's feminine shape. The bull ring in the nose is a symbol of submission to a large and potentially dangerous beast. Perhaps Westwood is opening a challenge?

 INFLUENCED BY

KEY
● fashion designer
◆ fashion house/brand
■ artistic influence
❖ cultural influence

● **Coco Chanel**
Westwood said, 'Chanel probably designed for the same reason that I do: a certain perversity and irritation with orthodox ways of thinking.'

❖ **Menswear**
Westwood utilizes women's historical costume to express ideas of femininity, but also uses menswear as a rich resource for exploring sexuality and power, since the contrasts call attention to feminine attributes.

VIVIENNE WESTWOOD CONTINUED

	Shows Nostalgia of Mud (Buffalo) collection in Paris; she is the first British designer since Mary Quant to show there.	Moves to Italy and negotiates a deal with Giorgio Armani to finance her collections.	Opens Vivienne Westwood boutique, selling the couture Gold Label collection, which is chosen to show at the prestigious Tokyo Fashion Summit.	Awarded an OBE (Officer of the Order of the British Empire).	Launches Man, a menswear label, in Milan.
CHRONOLOGY	**1982**	**1984**	**1990–91**	**1992**	**1996**

→ INSPIRED

◆ **Viktor & Rolf**
The design duo seems to have a love/hate relationship with fashion, as demonstrated in their Autumn 2008 antifashion collection (right), that compels them to participate in the arena, but also causes them to become harsh critics of the capricious nature of the business. The pair often presents statement fashion shows that delve into matters of image, celebrity and tradition. Westwood paved the way for Viktor & Rolf by initiating concept fashion shows that call into question ideas of image and sexuality. All three designers use fashion as a means of expressing larger social questions.

● **Jean-Charles de Castelbajac**
Castelbajac was influenced by the work that Westwood and McLaren were doing in their shop in the 1970s. Castelbajac became known for his art-to-wear clothing, on which he affixed objects of meaning, something he admired in Westwood's early customized T-shirts.

interested in tailoring as a technique, but rather in the 'push and pull of the garment against the body', recognizing that our haptic or sensual relationship with fabric directly affects how we perceive ourselves and others.

It is evident in many of her collections that she is using unconventional construction techniques to achieve a whole new understanding of drape, often resulting in an over-the-top approach to glamour. This postmodernist combination of historical influences with modern applications enables her to create clothing that is relevant in a contemporary context.

CRINOLINES AND CORSETS
For someone who has been forcefully independent in her private life as well as in her career path, Vivienne Westwood rejects the 1980s version of ideal androgynous notions of female power. 'I've never thought it powerful to be like a

second rate man. Femininity is stronger, and I don't understand why people keep plugging this boring asexual body.' Westwood came of age when Marilyn Monroe was a favoured female icon and Christian Dior redefined femininity.

Many of Westwood's collections use symbols that contradict the conventional ideas of female emancipation, such as her revival of the crinoline and the corset, or her interpretations of Dior's 1947 New Look. In fact, Westwood is a prime example of a postmodern feminist philosophy – own your sexuality, and revel in the notion of difference and individualism. Within this philosophy, there is an acknowledgement that sex appeal and absurdity are almost synonymous; an example would be the extreme contortions that the body can be forced into in the name of beauty.

Westwood is also known for her use of iconic British symbols, from her company logo of a royal orb and sceptre

'I am a great believer in copying – there has never been an age in which people have so little respect for the past. By trying to copy technique, you build up your own technique – I was able to finally produce a silhouette that has never been done before, nor could it have been, because it was a synthesis put together in the present.'

Vivienne Westwood

● **Madeleine Vionnet**
Vionnet approached the concept of draping with the eye of an experimenter, often rejecting established rules to achieve her goal, which Westwood surely adopted as a philosophy.

■ **16th- to 19th-century dress**
History in all its forms is a primary source of inspiration for Westwood, particularly image and sexuality as expressed through clothing. She is known to spend countless hours in clothing museums, poring over historical garments.

Launches first fragrance, Boudoir, followed later by Libertine. Launches the ready-to-wear Red Label to coincide with the opening of her first shop in New York.

A retrospective of her work opens at the Victoria & Albert Museum in London.

1998–2000

2004

◆ **Dsquared²**
Brothers Dean and Dan Caten often play with gender roles and sexuality, much like Westwood. In their Autumn 2007 show, they played with homoerotic icons in the form of female clothing, creating a larger question about enticement and attraction.

● **Alexander McQueen**
Apart from the similarities in working-class background, the two designers both embrace a questioning and critical stance towards the fashion world, but are routinely inspired by the transcendent beauty of couture and drama inherent in fashion.

⬆ Experimental drape
Having never pursued a course in fashion construction, Westwood relies instead on experimental drape to achieve innovations in design. In this Autumn 2005 ball gown, Westwood combines her own investigations into the manipulation of fabric with 19th-century dress inspirations.

to the creation of her own tartan plaid named MacAndreas in honour of her husband. The designer sees the humour but also respects the traditions of British culture, much in the same way as she approaches historical dress.

QUESTIONING AUTHORITY

The collections that Westwood has introduced in the last several years have become increasingly political, taking on issues of governmental policies, global warming and environmental activism. She continues to use her signature looks, from her experimental cuts and draping techniques to her graphic T-shirts that started in the early 1970s. What is important about Vivienne Westwood's work is that she makes us think and question authority, yet respect the past to understand our future.

Jil Sander was an incredibly important modernist designer in the 1990s, with a clean no-nonsense aesthetic in beautiful neutral colours and luxurious fabrications. In Jil Sander's collections, women could find essential items of clothing that looked professional but were also comfortable, helping them to have the utmost confidence and self-possession.

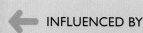 INFLUENCED BY

KEY
● fashion designer
◆ fashion house/brand
■ artistic influence
❖ cultural influence

● Madeleine Vionnet
Sander has said that she has always admired the work of Vionnet, and has undoubtedly been influenced by Vionnet's emphasis on usability.

● Christian Dior
Dior was a master craftsman who took historical references and reduced the decorative elements in order to create designs that would function in a modern context. Sander has clearly been influenced by this transition, as well as Dior's treatment of fabric and silhouette.

● André Courrèges
Courrèges was known for clean space age design, with only the essentials of decoration – a philosophy similar to Sander's, as can be seen in the clean, graphic lines of this Autumn 2004 piece (left).

JIL SANDER
German
(1943 Wesselburen)

	Born Heidemarie Jiline Sander on November 27th near Hamburg.	Graduates in textile design from Krefeld School of Textiles, near Düsseldorf.	Opens a boutique in a Hamburg suburb, selling Thierry Mugler and Sonia Rykiel.	Launches her eponymous line and sells it in her boutique.	Launches Jil Sander cosmetics, and Pure Woman and Pure Man fragrances.	Offers her company on the Frankfurt Stock Exchange, allowing for rapid expansion of product and stores.
CHRONOLOGY	**1943**	**1963**	**1967**	**1973**	**1979**	**1989**

→ INSPIRED

● Donna Karan
Karan was very influenced by the clean silhouettes and colour palette of Sander's collections in the 1990s. Sander's influence can also be seen in the rich fabrications and minimalist aesthetic on Karan's catwalk (right).

● Helmut Lang
As a contemporary of Sander, and as a designer with a very similar philosophy, Lang would undoubtedly have been influenced by Sander's slightly earlier work.

● Miuccia Prada
In Prada's early collections, the influence of Sander's minimalist aesthetic was very prevalent, as well as Sander's approach to experimentations with fabric and shape.

Jil Sander approaches fashion in the true sense of what it means to be a designer – her work could never be confused with being art or a political endeavour. Instead, Sander formulated her collections from a perspective of deep admiration for women.

REINVENTING MINIMALISM
Sander used her method of design to create a product that proved to be essential in its look and function, and was characteristically modern in concept. She embraced any difficulties that arose during the design process as a chance to develop solutions to clothing problems and evolve new ideas. Sander was consistently able to reinvent the subtleties of minimalism, and offer a fresh perspective on unadorned, well-designed clothing: 'The difficulties that you have as a designer are important for design. Resolved difficulties open up new ideas;

create tensions from which something unexpected can evolve. So there is no real reason to give up if you are able to work creatively with difficulty.'

Using herself and other professional women of her acquaintance as a point of departure, Sander created an aesthetic that translated not only into what women needed in the present context, but also into long-lasting, well-used designs that looked towards the future. She says, 'Firstly I am inspired by something, and I don't know where it comes from. Secondly, by something that lies behind me. And thirdly, by everything that could shape the future. We need to learn to decipher and translate the symbols, signals and hieroglyphs that tell us about the future.'

● Coco Chanel
Chanel created practical, wearable clothing that functioned perfectly in an active woman's life. Chanel relied on a basic formula for all her clothing, allowing for a unified and consistent look—something that could also be said about Sander.

● Hubert de Givenchy
Givenchy believed in simplicity and refinement, which can easily be seen in Sander's collections.

Opens flagship store in Paris, followed by stores in Milan and then Chicago.

Launches menswear in Milan.

1993–95

1997

● Ann Demeulemeester
Demeulemeester has explored the intersection of menswear and womenswear, choosing the best of both to create a new type of clothing. Demeulemeester's work owes a lot to the minimalist creations of Sander in the 1990s.

● Narciso Rodriguez
Rodriguez has always tried to reduce the amount of detail and decoration in his clothing to only the most essential, much in the same way as Sander.

← Texture play
By reducing ornament to its most essential, colour and texture become primary in the aesthetic appeal of the clothing. For the Autumn 1997 collection, Sander unconventionally pairs two different fabrics in a monotone colour palette. The texture and warmth of the wool sweater is reinforced next to the sensuous velvet skirt.

'I think there is always a need for pure design. With pure design, you don't need so much decoration.'

Jil Sander

→ Skin and fabric connections

Jil Sander's ultimate challenge was always to make clothing comfortable and easy to wear. This piece from Spring 2000 suggests nudity in the colour, slickness and light ethereal weight of the fabric. Sander calls attention to the close connections of skin and fabric with the deliberate detail on the shoulders.

 INFLUENCED BY

KEY
- ● fashion designer
- ◆ fashion house/brand
- ■ artistic influence
- ❖ cultural influence

● Yohji Yamamoto
Yamamoto consistently reinvents his core philosophy, which is that the fabric must not define the figure, but rather that the figure should dictate the fabric's drape or shape. Sander has admired Yamamoto's philosophy, preferring to place comfort and movement as a high priority in her creative process.

JIL SANDER CONTINUED

CHRONOLOGY	1999–2000	2003–05
	Prada Group buys a majority holding of Jil Sander. Reports of disagreements surface immediately, and Sander leaves the company.	*Returns for three seasons to rave reviews, but leaves after disagreements continue. Belgian designer Raf Simons is named creative director of Jil Sander.*

 INSPIRED

● Raf Simons
Simons has become extremely successful and influential as the heir to the Sander name. Having originally trained as an industrial designer, Simons approaches fashion from the same point of view as Sander, exploring shapes, fabrications and simplistic ornament, all with a keen eye towards what women and men need from their clothing.

● Calvin Klein
Klein began to use a great many heather-coloured fabrics in the 1990s, which was a trademark of many of Sander's collections. Klein appreciated Sander's minimalist approach to fashion and her use of a reductionist colour palette.

→ Roots in textiles

Raf Simons's Spring 2010 collection for Jil Sander not only addresses the beauty of simplicity, but also highlights Sander's early education and work in textiles, from which she continued to derive the most inspiration.

SOFT COLOUR PALETTE AND FABRICS

Jil Sander defined the 1990s colour palette, with soft heathered greys, taupes and navy blues, all in monochromatic variations and shades. The details were subtle and understated, with soft silhouettes that wrapped around the body rather than defining it. By appealing to the senses through colours and soft fabrics, Sander was able to create beautiful clothing that was both feminine and refined, as well as suggesting power and authority.

Approaching design as a true measure of modernist function, beauty was defined by the wearer and all design elements were intended to compliment the figure: 'You cannot produce beauty just for itself. Beauty is created when the parts are in a relationship to each other and "sit". Beauty in design is also connected with the dignity of the wearer.'

→ **Functional femininity**

Jil Sander's Spring 2004 collection had a functional ease that is often taken for granted in menswear. Like the work of Giorgio Armani, Sander's piece borrows the ease of a man's casual jacket to create a women's garment that could quickly become indispensable.

● **Cristóbal Balenciaga**

Balenciaga was known for his experimentations with fabric technology and innovative cutting techniques, which Sander has clearly studied.

● **Giorgio Armani**

Armani revolutionized suits for women, and paved the way for designers such as Sander to create clothing that was neither androgynous nor masculine, yet borrowed from men's clothing for purposes of functionalism.

British private equity fund Change Capital Partners buys Jil Sander from the Prada Group, making it a private company once again.

Sander announces that, with the financial backing of Uniqlo from Japan, she is opening a fashion consultancy firm.

2006   **2009**

● **Phoebe Philo for Céline**

After having taken a hiatus from designing to be with her family, Spring 2010 brought Philo back into the fashion limelight with a highly celebrated collection for Céline. The silhouettes were clean and precise, with no excess ornament and in a subdued colour palette (left) — all trademarks of Sander's work.

AUTONOMOUS BUSINESSWOMAN

In an attempt to expand to international status, Sander offered her company on the Frankfurt Stock Exchange in 1989. The stocks were bought by the Prada Group, and Jil Sander lost the rights to her own name — a fate that has affected several well-known designers. In a series of attempts to reconcile with the new owners after disagreements over management, Sander made a brief comeback in 2003, but then decided that her successor Raf Simons would be capable of directing the company in the 21st century without her assistance. In the interest of being an autonomous businesswoman who is celebrated in her design philosophy, Jil Sander has reemerged as an independent design consultant.

Gianni Versace helped to cement Italian fashion on the world stage, setting trends in the 1980s and helping to define an aesthetic that has become synonymous with his name. Versace referenced history, translating ideas and messages from the past to become relevant and meaningful in contemporary society.

INFLUENCED BY

KEY
- ● fashion designer
- ◆ fashion house/brand
- ■ artistic influence
- ❖ cultural influence

● **Coco Chanel**
Chanel was referenced by Versace in collections where he played with the iconic imagery of the Chanel suit – for example, he made it in a baby blue synthetic plush for his Autumn 1994 collection.

● **Christian Dior**
In his Spring 1994 collection, Versace played with iconic Dior suitings and the idea of polite society.

● **Madame Grès**
Grès was one of Versace's all-time favourite designers. Many of his eveningwear pieces were inspired by her virtuosity with fabric.

● **Emilio Pucci**
Pucci became famous for his colourful optical print silks and his love of short, flirty dresses and slim silhouettes. Versace's own aesthetic was largely based on seemingly random combinations of colourful prints (left). Both Italian designers were also interested in intersecting art with fashion.

GIANNI VERSACE
Italian
(1946 Reggio di Calabria)

CHRONOLOGY	1946	1964	1972–78	1978
	Born December 2nd in southern Italy.	*Begins working in his mother's tailoring studio while studying architecture.*	*Begins a career in fashion in Milan, freelancing for companies such as Callaghan, Genny and Complice.*	*Creates his own company, with his brother Santo as the business manager and his sister Donatella as muse. Shows a womenswear collection at the Palazzo della Permanente art museum in Milan, quickly followed by a men's collection.*

INSPIRED

● **Alexander Wang**
In his Autumn 2009 collection, Wang's downtown girl grew up with the help of figure-wrapping dresses reminiscent of Versace's bondage dresses.

● **Charlotte Ronson**
It is inevitable that as young designers such as Ronson reference the 1980s (left), a major source of inspiration will be Versace.

● **Giles Deacon**
In his Spring 2010 collection, Deacon had several pieces that referenced a Versace approach to the covering of the figure, as well as Versace's penchant for bright colours and metallics.

● **Bryan Bradley for Tuleh**
For his Spring 2009 collection, Bradley used several bold animal prints that were reminiscent of Versace.

Gianni Versace was a quintessential postmodernist. An extremely simplified definition of postmodernism as the combination of several different looks, ideas, philosophies or aesthetic qualities to form a whole new product reached its height in the 1970s and 1980s when Versace was defining his own style. Versace did this by combining historical periods, materials, fabrications, shapes and silhouettes, together with moral and social ideas, plus his love of pop culture, art and rock 'n' roll.

EXPERIMENTING WITH SYMBOLS AND FABRICS
For Versace, the best way of understanding contemporary society was through the lens of history. Historical references never led to costume or slavish reinterpretations in his work, but instead formed a basis for experimentation. Versace understood that by playing with a historical reference, he might be able to communicate a message all the more strongly about the present. For example, by using crosses and references of chain mail, Byzantium and the Crusades, Versace called attention to the duality of the iconic vision of women as the contrasting virgin/whore, and the ability of contemporary women to take control of their own sexuality and not be embarrassed or castigated.

Additionally, Versace had a real love of all things Italian, and was inspired by his nation's rich heritage of art and culture. Italy is known for its exquisite printed silks and expensive textiles, and these surfaced in his work in the form of richly coloured animal prints, florals and geometric shapes, as well as lace, beading and embroidery. However, Versace's respect for the materials did not stop him from experimenting with fabrics such as vinyl, denim for eveningwear and metal mesh.

← Notoriously sexy
The notorious Autumn 1992 bondage look helped to cement Versace's reputation as being highly sexualized, allowing women to flaunt their bodies as a way of owning the constant male gaze and inevitable objectification that comes with it.

'A knowledge of history makes you see things as they are.'

Gianni Versace

● Jean Paul Gaultier
Gaultier was an important designer in the 1980s, and was at the forefront of calling attention to the sexualized figure. He often mixed and matched prints, colours and fabrics, which undoubtedly influenced Versace.

● Elsa Schiaparelli
Schiaparelli's influence on Versace can be seen in surrealistic touches, such as the mixing of patterns, colours and subject matter of prints.

● Cristóbal Balenciaga
In Versace's Spring 1991 collection, he did several short baby-doll dresses that Balenciaga premiered, but made them his own through references to pop culture and symbols of lingerie. In the Spring 1987 collection, he referenced Balenciaga's flamenco-style dresses.

1982	1985	1989–91	1992	1994	1997
Starts designing costumes for theatre productions, such as Maurice Béjart ballets.	*Launches Istante diffusion line aimed at young professionals. London's Victoria & Albert Museum holds a Versace exhibition.*	*Introduces Versus diffusion line, designed by Donatella for a younger market, and his Signature fragrance.*	*Shows the infamous Bondage collection that catapults him to superstar status.*	*Launches Home Signature collection.*	*Shot dead outside his home in Miami Beach on July 15th. Santo Versace remains business manager; Donatella takes over as creative director.*

◆ Dolce & Gabbana
The design duo has long played with brazen sexuality, metallics, animal prints and bold colours, all signatures of the Versace aesthetic.

◆ Dsquared²
Canadian twins Dean and Dan Caten have become famous for their sexy hard-glam look that references pop culture and, invariably, Versace.

● Tom Ford
Ford has referenced Versace as a source for potent sexuality and glamour.

● Donatella Versace
Since her older brother's death, Donatella has carried on the Versace label. She continues to create clothing that closely resembles her brother's sexy and glamorous aesthetic.

INDIVIDUAL STYLE

Versace wanted women to feel strong, sexy, and independent in his clothing. He expressed this not only with the silhouette and fabrication, but also by his own attitude of distinctiveness: 'Fashion has to be free to express personality and individuality. I always look for people who are out of the crowd, who are individuals, who are free, who have a real sense of style, which means their own sense of style.'

→ Power glam continued
Donatella Versace carries on in her brother's footsteps, providing high-glam sex appeal. From the Autumn 2007 collection, this dress makes reference to both flowing nightgowns and ancient Greek dress. In either case, the wearer is completely in control.

Katharine Hamnett designs clothing that can become part of a sustainable solution to environmental concerns, taking early leadership in areas that so many in the fashion industry are reluctant to embrace. Hamnett's influence can be seen on many designers' catwalks, from her emphasis on environmental responsibility to her contributions to the quintessential 1980s look.

INFLUENCED BY

KEY
- ● fashion designer
- ◆ fashion house/brand
- ■ artistic influence
- ❖ cultural influence

■ Postmodernism
The architectural movement that quickly spread to art and design in the 1970s and 1980s defined Hamnett's aesthetic, as seen in the way that she combines evening and day looks, repurposes cultural icons and combines historical styles. (Right: The postmodernist combination of futuristic glass pyramid and Renaissance style is shown at the Louvre Museum in Paris.)

● Jean Paul Gaultier
Gaultier creates a dialogue about gay culture and gender politics by bringing together a wide variety of styles to create collections that defy expectations. Hamnett uses her political and feminist interests to accomplish the same thing.

● Claire McCardell
McCardell used a lot of metal hardware in her designs, as well as trying to make clothing that was economical and easy to wear – also characteristics of Hamnett's work.

KATHARINE HAMNETT
British
(1947 Gravesend)

CHRONOLOGY	1947	1964–69	1969–75	1979–83	1989
	Born Katharine Appelton on August 16th.	Studies fashion in Stockholm, Sweden, and then London's Central Saint Martins.	Sets up fashion business, Tuttabankem, with friend Anne Buck.	Launches eponymous label. Invents stonewashing, distressed denim and stretch denim. Introduces her first protest T-shirt.	Stops manufacturing her collections and moves business to licensing in Milan. Researches social and environmental impact of manufacturing.

INSPIRED

● Stella McCartney
McCartney is the most well-known designer to embrace Hamnett's environmental and sustainable message. McCartney is often inspired by the 1980s and Hamnett's work from that time. In her Autumn 2002 collection, McCartney sent a bride down the catwalk with 'Trouble and Strife' boldly printed on her gown, and she used a large 'Yes' as a backdrop to her Spring 2010 fashion show, mirroring Hamnett's Autumn 1993 Yes collection.

◆ Antoni & Alison
The British design duo show the influence of Hamnett in their frequent use of bold, graphic shapes and patterns, and their line of T-shirts bearing amusing slogans.

● Wichy Hassan for Miss Sixty
Hassan relies heavily on the look and feel of Hamnett's work from the 1980s, in her focus on denim, sporty street style and overall aesthetic.

● Henry Holland
Holland's debut Autumn 2007 show revealed the influence of Hamnett, when he caused a stir by sending slogan T-shirts down the catwalk, poking fun at fellow designers and models.

Katharine Hamnett's contribution to trends in fashion was greatest in the 1980s, when style innovation was her primary objective. Inspired by a postmodernist combination of street style, politics, pop culture and art, along with a mishmash of historical styles, she created a look that helped to define the whole era.

DENIM AND SLOGAN T-SHIRTS
The 1980s will always be associated with the popularity of denim and its many treatments and variations, such as bleaching, distressing and stretch denim, all of which Hamnett introduced. Hamnett is also associated with the popularization of the military look, the use of parachute silk and utility fashion. By far her most notable contribution was the slogan T-shirt, which continues in popularity and importance today. Sartorially proclaiming a political belief, personal opinion or even a musical preference defined the politically correct 1990s, and is connected to personal blogs, MySpace and other online sharing sites in contemporary culture.

SUSTAINABLE MANUFACTURE
In more recent years, Hamnett's contribution to fashion stems from her commitment to sustainable options for the manufacture of fabric and clothing. When searching for more economical ways of manufacturing her clothing, Hamnett realized some unsettling truths that compelled her to alter the focus of her career: 'Buddhist philosophy talks about the need for "right" livelihood (making a living without hurting anyone or anything). I thought I wasn't hurting anyone by making clothes but when I did the research I realized I was wrong. I was horrified and felt a moral imperative to do something.'

→ Sustainability now

This Autumn 2003 dress is typical of the evolution of Katharine Hamnett's style, which is always simple and wearable, but also flirtatious and appealing to her constant audience, the youth market. In many instances, the youth market is more open to Hamnett's ideas of sustainability.

• Vivienne Westwood

Westwood was an early proponent of using shock value to communicate an idea, something that Hamnett has also done. In turn, Westwood has taken Hamnett's lead and become more environmentally sensitive.

• Gianni Versace

Versace used metal, leather and shine to create clothing in the designer market that suggested sex, freedom and fun. Hamnett's collections, such as Spring 1996, often had similarities.

• Mary Quant

Quant sought to create her company on her own terms, and provided a much-needed focus on fun, youthful, affordable clothing – something that Hamnett has also embraced.

• Rudi Gernreich

Gernreich's experimental approach to fashion emphasized youth's ability to change and meld to the times. Hamnett was influenced not only by his aesthetic but also by his reliance on the young to change the tide of fashion.

Moves her fashion shows to Paris and then Milan, before returning to London. Travels to New York to give lectures on the dangers of cotton production.

Cancels most of her licences in order to manufacture her own collection, Katharine E Hamnett, which is launched online. The E stands for environmental and ethical.

Signs a contract with Tesco supermarket for an ethical organic cotton collection. Becomes involved in projects studying corporate social responsibility in the fashion industry.

1990–95   **2004**   **2006–07**

◆ Libertine

For their Spring 2006 collection, the young designers sent out Hamnett-style slogan T-shirts praising British poets and Queen Victoria, and celebrating the British love of the pub.

◆ Emma Cook

Sharing Hamnett's environmental concerns, Cook has made a name for herself by using recycled and found fabrics for a young, trendy customer.

◆ Blaak

The design duo sent clothing down the Spring 2003 catwalk that was inspired by Hamnett's work in parachute silk and oversized shirts.

Hamnett spends a great deal of time lecturing and teaching, as well as sourcing and developing new business practices for a sustainable future. As a major name in the fashion industry who focused on environmental causes early on, Hamnett has paved the way for younger designers who hope to create changes in the industry. Hamnett's 1980s chic appears on many catwalks as a new generation of designers is inspired by all her innovations, from style to environmental causes.

← Iconic contribution

Libertine's Spring 2006 collection references not only Hamnett's contribution of the slogan T-shirt, but also her mixing of several style references, such as daywear with eveningwear, and the flash and glitter so popular among 1980s designers.

'Industry runs the planet and the fashion industry is the fourth largest. How we design and consume fashion to an extent decides our future.'

Katharine Hamnett

Helmut Lang was known for two things in the 1990s – modernism, and playing with the sexuality and power of women's image. For these reasons, Lang became one of the most influential and copied designers of the last decade of the 20th century.

INFLUENCED BY

KEY
- ● fashion designer
- ◆ fashion house/brand
- ■ artistic influence
- ❖ cultural influence

● Azzedine Alaïa
Alaïa is known for his body-conscious designs, his refusal to be constrained by the schedule of Paris Fashion Week, and the sexuality infused into each of his pieces. Lang's Spring 2001 collection seemed to be a homage to Alaïa, featuring bandage-type wrapping, trousers with slits up the side and short A-line skirts – all Alaïa signatures. Lang also adopted a similar attitude towards the intricacies of the fashion business as Alaïa.

● Rei Kawakubo
Lang has said that he very much admires Kawakubo. The two designers' aesthetics often do not seem remotely similar, but what Lang learned from Kawakubo was her intellectual approach to the subject of fashion.

● André Courrèges
The space age designer of the 1960s preferred playing with positive and negative space, as well as a simplified colour palette and silhouette, all of which influenced Lang's aesthetic.

● Yohji Yamamoto
Yamamoto often treats fabric architecturally, and is frequently concerned with the interplay between fabric and body. Lang expresses it differently, but the philosophy is still an obvious influence.

HELMUT LANG
Austrian
(1956 Vienna)

	Born March 10th in Vienna.	*Having switched from banking to fashion design, he opens the boutique Bou Bou Lang in Vienna, where he sells his own designs. Creates T-shirts specifically shaped to achieve a particular fit.*	*Presents a collection at the Paris Vienna Exhibition at the Centre Pompidou in Paris. After much success, he launches his eponymous label.*	*Moves his company from Paris to New York, the first-ever intercontinental move of a fashion company.*
CHRONOLOGY	**1956**	**1979**	**1986**	**1997**

INSPIRED

● Max Azria
In Azria's Spring 2010 collection (right), several dresses were in the signature white that Lang preferred, and played with layers and opacity in a way similar to Lang.

● Narciso Rodriguez
Rodriguez has come to be known for his minimalist look, with an attention to positive and negative space, as exemplified in Lang's work.

● Nicolas Ghesquière for Balenciaga
The French designer has a clean, precise aesthetic, and a penchant for playing with technologically advanced fabrics. He also seems to prefer the long, lean silhouettes that Lang was so famous for.

● Francisco Costa
Costa has played with the layering of fabrications and the geometric application of fabric to the sinuous figure, similar to Lang's own investigations.

Helmut Lang's work was supremely simple in silhouette, yet he is often talked about alongside more conceptual designers, such as Rei Kawakubo or Martin Margiela, whose work is not nearly as clean and precise. The primary reason for this is that Lang's aesthetic was not based in the ideas of mass production or saleability, but rather in a minimalist concept that is far more intellectual and artistic in its connections to a modernist philosophy.

SLEEK ELEGANCE

Lang's loyal following in the 1990s was primarily caused by how the clothing made women feel as professionals in the post-women's movement of the 1970s and 1980s. Reflecting the impending millennium, as well as a rejection of the opulence and gigantic shoulders of the 1980s, Lang's version of sleek, hard and refined elegance quickly found a willing audience. As the designer himself noted, 'I don't believe that fashion evolves on its own. There are more radical social changes behind it.'

Lang often used layers of sheer fabrics, or 'peek holes' in places such as elbows or the side of the leg, to examine the sexuality inherent in skin and exposure. In his Spring 2002 collection, Lang showed the knit rib finishes of a cardigan hung around the model's neck and attached to the waist. The reminder of the piece of clothing calls attention to the hidden mysteries of the figure – skin is sexualized because it is hidden under clothing.

REDUCED COLOUR PALETTE

Despite the undercurrent of sexuality in all his collections, Lang emphasized the androgynous nature of his women's collections. Using a reduced colour palette consisting

← **Clothing as protection**

The subtle connection between fabric and body in Helmut Lang's Spring 1999 collection can almost be missed. The noticeably gauzy qualities of the jacket and shirt do not cover or protect the rather androgynous model. Lang is questioning the ability of clothing to hide who we really are, but with secrets eventually being revealed.

● **Jil Sander**
Sander was one of the first designers to espouse a reductionist view of fashion, becoming known for her subdued colour palette and superior fabrications. Lang was influenced by the clean, simple lines of Sander's silhouettes.

● **Cristóbal Balenciaga**
Both designers rejected the spotlight and were interested in nontraditional fabrications, as well as extremely simplified advertising campaigns that usually consisted of only their names being displayed.

● **Ann Demeulemeester**
Introduced to the world around the same time, the two designers have several traits in common. They are both known for their reductive colour palette, sticking mainly to black and white, as well as their androgynous men's and women's collections.

1998	1999	2000	2002–05	2006
Presents his collection on an internet broadcast before New York, Paris and Milan fashion weeks. Other designers follow his lead; the New York shows now take place six weeks before those in Europe.	*Prada Group buys a 51% stake in Lang's company.*	*In another unprecedented move, Lang advertises in National Geographic instead of a fashion magazine.*	*Prada switches Lang's showings back to Paris. Lang eventually resigns, saying that the company is getting too big.*	*Prada sells the Lang brand to Japanese fashion group Link Theory Holdings.*

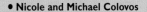

● **Tom Ford**
Responding to Lang's clean, modern aesthetic, Ford has praised Lang for his intellectual approach to fashion, while at the same time creating wearable and approachable clothing.

● **Miuccia Prada**
In the mid-1990s, Lang's minimalist aesthetic was so popular that he was setting all the trends of the moment. The Prada Spring 1998 collection showed clean and unadorned pieces in white or monochromatic subtle colour.

● **Nicole and Michael Colovos**
The American/New Zealand couple, formerly the designers for their own collection Habitual, took over as creative directors of the house of Lang in 2006. They have attempted to capture the essence of the Lang aesthetic, while moving the company forward with their own interpretations.

primarily of black, white or cream, Lang created womenswear that was not effusively feminine. The combination of the austere look combined with the undercurrent of sexiness helped to define women as powerful and equal, while not resorting to trying to look like a man.

← **Skin and cloth**
Michael and Nicole Colovos are tapping into Lang's examinations of the connections between skin and cloth. In this Spring 2010 piece, the clingy, drapey fabric conforms to the figure, but does not define it.

'Androgyny is an idea from the past. Women are feminine in many different ways. Maybe the biggest achievement of the last years is that there are many more attitudes of being a woman.'

Helmut Lang

John Galliano has enjoyed critical acclaim from the fashion press, and celebrity status among the fashionistas of the world, largely because of his ability to interpret the past in a larger-than-life way and create the excitement of couturiers of yesteryear. His collections offer romance and theatrical imagination that affect all facets of the fashion industry.

 INFLUENCED BY

KEY
- ● fashion designer
- ◆ fashion house/brand
- ■ artistic influence
- ❖ cultural influence

❖ Historical events
Galliano finds relevant connections between historical and contemporary time periods, such as the French Revolution and the 1980s London club scene, and uses them to create postmodern masterpieces.

❖ Eclectic cultures and art
Cultures such as the African Maasai (right) and those of Mongolia, China and Japan have all inspired Galliano. His collections also reveal the influence of artists of the Belle Époque, such as Giovanni Boldini, James Whistler and John Singer Sargent, as well as Amedeo Modigliani, Anthony Van Dyke, Johannes Vermeer and Gustav Klimt.

■ Theatre
Having worked in the theatre during college, Galliano takes the view that fashion is a story – an image or identity that we affect to manipulate the viewer.

JOHN GALLIANO
British
(1960 Gibraltar)

Born November 28th in Gibraltar to a Spanish mother and Gibraltarian father.	*Moves to London with his family. As a foreigner who is uninspired by school, he reverts into fantasy and make-believe, which has a clear influence on his later career.*	*Attends City and East London College to study design and printed textiles. Finds inspiration from London's burgeoning club scene.*	*Graduates from Central Saint Martins. While studying, he works as a dresser in the National Theatre.*
CHRONOLOGY **1960**	**1966**	**1976**	**1984**

 INSPIRED

● Zac Posen
The young designer has a romantic but never sentimental view of women and their clothing. Both he and Galliano have a particular sense of the spectacular that is executed with confidence in their eveningwear. Posen has also adopted Galliano's approach to alternative constructions and draping techniques that allow them both to create arresting interpretations of history. The two designers share an eye for richly coloured and textured fabrications.

● Anna Sui
In her Autumn 2009 collection, Sui combined historical and cultural eclecticism in much the same way as Galliano, producing a rich and ornate collection.

 Delicately voluminous
For his Spring 2008 collection, Zac Posen chose a lightweight and delicate fabric to create high drama in construction and colour, both of which are often seen in Galliano's Dior collections. Posen's manipulation and contortion of the ombré print suggests the beauty and romance of a mermaid in the deeps of the ocean.

The fantastic qualities of fashion design that make imaginations flow and hearts stop are often found in connection with John Galliano. Galliano approaches the process of design in such a focused, almost obsessional way that the results of his creativity cannot help but excite and enthuse.

EVOLUTION OF IDEAS
Galliano began to experiment with the cutting of fabrics and alternative ways of putting pieces together during his college days at Central Saint Martins and his part-time jobs in the National Theatre in London: 'My fashion has been a constant evolution of ideas which I began to explore before I had left college. All that experimental cutting led me to understand precisely how a jacket had been put together in the past; how to put it together correctly in the present and then, from that, I was led to dismantle it and reassemble it in a way

← Historical virtuosity

There is no other designer who can so successfully evoke the stunning beauty of couture from the 1950s. For the Dior Spring 2010 couture collection, Galliano melds the influence of Christian Dior with that of couturier Charles James, together with early 20th-century American fashion and beauty icons Millicent Rogers and the Gibson Girl.

• Christian Dior
As designer at the house of Dior since 1996, Galliano has mined the archives of Dior's creations, making them relevant for today's market and times.

• Madeleine Vionnet
Galliano received early recognition for his interpretations of bias-cut dresses that were clearly inspired by Vionnet.

With backing from Johann Brun, Galliano creates a static show called Afghanistan Repudiates Western Ideals, followed by catwalk shows The Ludic Game, Fallen Angels and Forgotten Innocents.

1984–86

• Alexander McQueen
Perhaps Galliano's greatest rival in fantastic shows, love of the dramatic and fascination with tragically strong women, McQueen's own career path often touched Galliano's.

• Oscar de la Renta
Although de la Renta is of the old guard of fashion, Galliano's extreme construction and heady optimism, as seen in his collections for Dior, seem to have had an effect on the Dominican designer.

'Early on, I realized how important it is to just be curious. You mustn't be frightened or hide behind preconceived ideas. You have to experiment. You just do it and it's beautiful because you discover an energy that feeds you. There are no rules.'

John Galliano

→ Denise's ghost
The Autumn 2008 John Galliano collection is the result of a rich array of influences, from Kubla Khan's pleasure dome to 1930s bias-cut dresses – and, of course, Paul Poiret. This piece looks as if it were designed for Poiret's muse and wife, Denise.

INFLUENCED BY

KEY
- ● fashion designer
- ◆ fashion house/brand
- ■ artistic influence
- ❖ cultural influence

● Paul Poiret
Poiret has been cited by Galliano as a major source of inspiration, rivalled only by Christian Dior. The exoticism, richly ornate quality and tragic romanticism of Poiret's clothes find fertile ground in Galliano's historically driven collections. Galliano often uses colour, silhouette and fabrication from Poiret as a basis for his collections, adding other time periods, female icons or other designers' work to convey the message or idea he wants to communicate. Galliano's showman tendencies, relying on extravagant shows with a costumed appearance of the designer at the end, echo Poiret's fantastic parties.

JOHN GALLIANO CONTINUED

CHRONOLOGY	1986	1991	1993	1995–96
	Receives funding from Danish entrepreneur Peder Bertelsen, whose company Aguecheek also backs Katharine Hamnett.	Relocates to Paris.	Anna Wintour, editor of American Vogue, introduces him to Portuguese fashion patron Sao Schlumberger. Galliano is then introduced to John Bult and Mark Rice of venture firm Arbela Inc., who agree to back his own label.	Appointed to the house of Givenchy, owned by luxury goods company LMVH. He is the first British fashion designer to head a French house. After a year, LMVH moves him to the house of Dior.

INSPIRED

● Olivier Theyskens
Theyskens is known for his red carpet dresses that are favoured by socialites and actresses alike. The dresses often recall a Galliano influence, utilizing historical references as well as an ornate treatment of fabric and surface embellishment (left).

● Junya Watanabe
In Watanabe's Autumn 2002 collection, he showed 1930s-inspired bias-cut dresses that Galliano had already made popular. The two designers have also worked with denim patchwork to create interesting new silhouettes not often associated with denim.

● Erdem Moralioglu
The young designer's Spring 2009 collection was about clothes that were 'soft and hyper romantic but a little bit surreal', which would clearly point to Galliano collections of the past.

that would point to the future. I never saw any point in stopping at the way in which conventional wisdom decreed a jacket should be cut.'

RESEARCH AND RECURRING THEMES
Galliano famously engulfs himself in research and points of inspiration. Every detail of his collections has Galliano's attention, from the invitations and the story lines his models are instructed to follow to his own appearance in costume at the end of his fashion shows.

Galliano's postmodernist array of style influences and sources of inspiration are wide and varied, but there are several recurring themes that he examines and reinterprets. Certainly, historical fashion is important, from his graduation collection called Les Incroyables, referring to the fashion dandies of the 18th century, to homage

collections inspired by Christian Dior. Strong and stylish women of the past play prominently in his design work, as he co-opts traits and thoughts, and translates them effortlessly into pieces for contemporary women.

Galliano also seems to be attracted to the dramatic displays of non-Western countries, as can be seen in his collections inspired by Russia, the Maasai people of Africa, Japan, China, Mongolia and Egypt, to name but a few. Galliano is looked to not merely for his love of things stylish, but also for his choice of iconography that has relevance to a contemporary audience. Not slavishly focused on one concept, Galliano melds the fruits of his research to create completely new ideas, a design process that is ultimately postmodern in philosophy.

→ **The new Belle Époque**

For the Dior Autumn 2010 ready-to-wear collection, Galliano played with the hunting theme that had inspired his Dior Spring 2010 couture collection, but this time combined it with the mystery and audaciousness of the Belle Époque, the soft romance of the 18th century and a sense of sex in the boudoir.

● **Japanese designers**

Rei Kawakubo and Yohji Yamamoto have inspired Galliano to explore alternative shapes in silhouettes, and approach the draped body in a way that is very different from that of most Western designers.

❖ **Female sexuality**

Designers such as Jean Paul Gaultier, Vivienne Westwood and Azzedine Alaïa all deal with the dichotomies inherent in female sexuality, and have influenced Galliano in his own explorations.

Creates his first collection for Dior, marking the 50th anniversary of the introduction of Dior's New Look and the opening of the house. Galliano wins British Fashion Designer of the Year Award for an unprecedented fourth time.

Awarded the French Légion d'honneur.

| **1997** | **2009** |

● **Luella Bartley**

Like fellow British designer Galliano, Bartley combines cultural and historical iconography, and twists them into something new and contemporary. This Spring 2009 piece (left) hints at Galliano's influence by referencing the 1950s, using historically inaccurate colours and deconstructionist techniques for a postmodernist look.

FAIRY-TALE FASHION

The ability to play with and combine so many rich style influences from the past allows Galliano to create a romance and excitement that is not often felt in the contemporary fashion market. Couture of the first half of the 20th century was rarefied and stunning in its preciousness, but many current designers correctly focus on the saleability and usefulness of clothing.

The functionalism of fashion is so fully ingrained in the fashion business at present that the impracticality of John Galliano's confections can sometimes be a shock. The sheer theatricality of his fashion shows, which cost millions to produce, have come under criticism for their wastefulness. However, the house of Dior continues to be successful, selling merchandise and licences to those who want to feel the brilliance of fairy-tale fashion.

Narciso Rodriguez creates collections that help women look their best and function in their everyday lives. This seems like a simple idea, but it is an ever-present challenge, because simplicity is often the hardest to achieve. The result is a loyal following of women, helping to establish Rodriguez as an important and influential name in fashion.

INFLUENCED BY

KEY
● fashion designer
◆ fashion house/brand
■ artistic influence
❖ cultural influence

● **Cristóbal Balenciaga**
Rodriguez has said that Balenciaga holds the greatest influence over him. This is clear, with the two designers sharing a similar quest to reduce the decoration within a garment to only the most essential.

● **Donna Karan**
Rodriguez has said that he originally went to Parsons School of Design because of his admiration for Karan's work. He later went on to work for Karan at Anne Klein.

● **Calvin Klein**
Rodriguez worked for Calvin Klein for four years, and learned valuable lessons about marketing and simplicity of design, as can be seen in the precise geometry of this piece from Spring 2010 (right).

● **Geoffrey Beene**
Rodriguez has clearly been inspired by Beene's use of geometry on the figure to create a signature feminine aesthetic that speaks of strength and precision.

NARCISO RODRIGUEZ
American
(1961 New Jersey)

	Born January 27th in Newark, New Jersey, to Cuban American parents.	*Graduates from New York's Parsons School of Design, then freelances at various companies before joining Donna Karan at Anne Klein.*	*Works as a womenswear designer at Calvin Klein.*	*Appointed design director of New York–based knitwear company TSE. Also becomes design director of Cerruti in Paris. Becomes noticed after designing the bias-cut dress that Carolyn Bessette wears to marry John F. Kennedy Jr.*
CHRONOLOGY	**1961**	**1982–85**	**1991**	**1995**

INSPIRED

● **Antonio Berardi**
The British-trained designer sent out several pieces that use bold graphic shapes in his Spring 2010 collection (right), reminiscent of Rodriguez's work.

● **Jonathan Saunders**
In his Autumn 2007 collection, the British designer used his signature bright colours to shape the figure in a way that Rodriguez is also known for.

● **Giles Deacon**
Spring 2009 saw several pieces that used bold, graphic black and white as well as seaming inspired by Rodriguez's work.

● **Phoebe Philo for Céline**
For her Spring 2010 collection for Céline, Philo shaped the figure with well-proportioned geometry, just as Rodriguez does.

Narciso Rodriguez is steeped in the history and essence of American design, but with an understanding of European traditions and materials. Having studied at New York's Parsons School of Design and worked for iconic American designers such as Donna Karan and Calvin Klein, he has also successfully served as designer for Cerruti in Paris and Loewe in Spain. The result is a wonderful combination of artistic and business practices.

SELF-POSSESSED FEMININITY
For Rodriguez, the modern requirement of fashion design is the creation of wearable, functional collections that communicate precision and strength, yet with a subtle femininity. Rodriguez's type of femininity does not hope to be androgynous or remotely masculine, but also does not suggest girlishness or a sense of frippery. Rodriguez's woman represents the most contemporary version of feminism. She is not a woman who needs big shoulders and dark colours to feel powerful; rather, she is comfortable and self-possessed in her femininity. Rodriguez's modernist aesthetic also functions for a woman who has a realistic figure rather than that of a model – something that undoubtedly inspires loyalty in women who wear Rodriguez's clothing.

ARCHITECTURAL GEOMETRY
Rodriguez achieves this new sense of femininity and wearability by creating architectural geometry for the figure: 'What I relate to is the creation of a form from structure and material. Although I don't use direct architectural references in my work, I approach designing a garment in much the same way an architect approaches designing a building, with seaming for structure to create interesting fit lines and shape.' Rodriguez

← Futuristic precision
With the application of architectural geometry to the figure in this Autumn 2006 piece, Rodriguez suggests futuristic precision like that of André Courrèges in the 1960s. This graphically arresting look allows the wearer to make a subtle but powerful entrance.

'I think something can be very classic and be completely modern.'

Narciso Rodriguez

● André Courrèges
Courrèges took the tailoring and design aesthetic from his training at Balenciaga and transformed it for the youth of the 1960s. This interpretation of Balenciaga's work can also be seen in contemporary designers, such as Rodriguez.

● Adrian
The Hollywood designer became famous for helping actresses to look their best by means of well-placed seam lines, colour or bold graphics, all of which Rodriguez has learned from.

● Claire McCardell
McCardell continually strove to reduce the amount of decoration on her clothing, partly because of wartime fabric restrictions, but more importantly as a way to make the clothing more wearable – a lesson Rodriguez seems to have absorbed.

1997	2003	2006	2007	2009
Launches his eponymous collection, financed by Italian manufacturer Aeffe. Also becomes design director for Spanish leather goods company Loewe.	Launches fragrance with Shiseido Beauté Prestige International, called For Her.	Ends partnership with Aeffe, in debt by $1 million to suppliers, citing mismanagement as the primary reason.	Liz Claiborne Company acquires 50% of the Rodriguez label, with Rodriguez in complete creative control. Launches For Him fragrance.	Michelle Obama wears Rodriguez on stage for her first appearance as first lady.

● Michael Kors
Fellow American Kors often uses seaming and bold colours to help shape the female figure, as well as sharing Rodriguez's wearable sensibility.

◆ Proenza Schouler
The design duo looks to Rodriguez as an interpreter of the French aesthetic of the mid-20th century for a contemporary consumer.

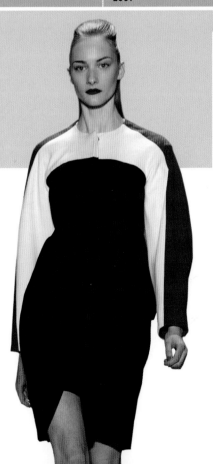

● Prabal Gurung
This young designer has been showing only since 2009 but has skyrocketed to fashion's hot list for his Autumn 2010 collection. The collection featured several graphically geometric shapes that closely resemble many of Rodriguez's collections.

← Wearable femininity
This jacket from Prabal Gurung's Autumn 2010 collection combines a favorite colour palette of Rodriguez with a sensible approach to fashion that is feminine, but also exudes power and strength.

uses colour, shape and form to allow for multiple body types: 'I design primarily in black and white as I find it is the boldest graphic way to present a clean silhouette.'

Rodriguez continually develops new interpretations of his modernist philosophy, allowing for a well-developed collection each season: 'It [design philosophy] is the inspiration that seems to carry through as the foundation from which I build each season's collections. In a very subtle way it is always there.'

CHAPTER 6
CONCEPTUALISTS

SCHIAPARELLI ○ REIKA
McQUEEN ○ VIKTOR

The designers in this chapter represent a group of conceptualists whose primary objective is to advance the dialogue of fashion on an intellectual or philosophical basis. They are often accused of creating art that does not meet the requirements of commercially viable design. Many of them do indeed display artistic impulses, but most would emphatically claim that they are creating a product that is to be worn.

THE INFLUENCE OF ART
Fashion design in the 20th century reflected many of the same artistic developments that art and literature focused on. Artistic movements, such as surrealism in the 1920s and 1930s, focused on the liberation of the unconscious and the embracing of the emotional. Elsa Schiaparelli incorporated elements of surrealism into her clothing, as well as participating in several collaborations with artists such as Salvador Dalí and Jean Cocteau. Schiaparelli's work was appreciated on multiple levels, from comic relief to a commentary on the often confusing and chaotic time period.

CONCEPTUAL INVESTIGATIONS
Rei Kawakubo and Martin Margiela, two highly conceptual contemporary designers, often use clothing and style as a way to express their ideas on beauty, image and women's personal relationship to the clothing they wear. In the contemporary context, clothing as a form of environmental protection or as a way to conform to society's moral attitudes is a given. The more tenuous association is how clothing affects identity and perceptions of self. Viktor & Rolf are designers who examine and critique the fashion industry itself, the impact of celebrity culture, fashion's connection to the art world, and the importance of couture, among many other investigations.

Conceptualist Alexander McQueen saw clothing as a metaphor for survival, and examined the complex relationship between victim and aggressor. McQueen explored several common themes in his work, including the relationships between men and women, the tensions between humans and nature, and the dynamics between aggression, anger and submission.

EXPLORING TECHNOLOGY

Hussein Chalayan has explored a wide diversity of themes, such as feelings of loss and the displaced sense of self within the constructs of a larger culture. Chalayan references many subject areas, including philosophy, science, religion, politics, aeronautics and digital media, for a diverse view of our present existence. His work, like that of many in this chapter, takes advantage of a wide variety of technological innovations, and as a result has been featured in an extraordinary number of exhibitions because of its breadth and virtuosity.

THE INFLUENCE OF ART

Although the designers in this chapter advance the conceptual theories of dress, they are still beholden to the need for profit. As a result, these conceptual designers spend a great deal of time creating monetary ventures to support their more creative endeavours. They often adopt the status of a celebrity designer for branding, marketing and licensing purposes, offering consumers an identity of stylish and artistic intellectualism.

Elsa Schiaparelli is best known as a designer who defied traditional notions of austere, serious clothing in exchange for a lighthearted, humorous, yet uniquely elegant style that has made her eternally influential. One of the first designers to collaborate with contemporary artists, Schiaparelli will always be associated with the surrealist movement that typifies the tumultuous 1930s.

INFLUENCED BY

KEY
- ● fashion designer
- ◆ fashion house/brand
- ■ artistic influence
- ❖ cultural influence

● **Madeleine Vionnet**
Vionnet's emphasis on the long lean figure can be seen in the silhouettes that Schiaparelli created. Vionnet's sense of independence and business acumen were also extremely important to Schiaparelli.

● **Jeanne Lanvin**
Lanvin was a couturier when there were very few women as heads of companies. Schiaparelli said in her autobiography, 'If Mme Lanvin was able to succeed, perhaps I might also succeed!'

❖ **Hollywood**
The bottle of Schiaparelli's perfume Shocking is modelled on Mae West's voluptuous figure (left: 1943 advertisement for Shocking). Schiaparelli was drawn to the theatricality and sense of the unreal that was so prevalent in 1930s Hollywood.

ELSA SCHIAPARELLI
Italian
(1890 Rome)

CHRONOLOGY	1890	1912	1919–21	1925
	Born September 10th in Palazzo Corsini in Rome.	Studies philosophy at the University of Rome until she publishes a book of sensual poems that scandalizes her family. Goes to London to become a nanny.	Marries and moves to New York. Becomes pregnant and is abandoned by her husband.	Schiaparelli and her daughter return to Paris. Schiaparelli approaches the house of Maggy Rouff for a design position, but is told that she 'would do better to plant potatoes than to try and make dresses', as she lacks the obvious talents of a couturier.

INSPIRED

● **Walter Van Beirendonck**
In Van Beirendonck's Autumn 2006 collection, he created hoodies and trousers that featured a cartoonish skeleton (right), much like the black jacket Schiaparelli created with Salvador Dalí, with a trapunto spine and ribs down the back.

● **Thierry Mugler**
Mugler was inspired by insects, robots and space, creating a surreal collection of clothing that pays homage to Schiaparelli, who first realized the beauty of such things.

◆ **Viktor & Rolf**
Viktor & Rolf have created fashion shows that are more like art performances, and are consistently inspired by the unusual and odd. Shows like their Autumn 2005 collection, in which models appeared as if already in bed, or their antifashion stance for the Autumn 2008 collection, in which the clothing exhibited giant stuffed 'NO's and used staples as a main component of construction, follow in the surrealistic legacy of Schiaparelli.

Elsa Schiaparelli's best-selling perfume is called Shocking, a name that reflects how the designer preferred to be seen. Schiaparelli strove to shock and to question what it meant to be a couturier in Paris, the ultimate city of fashion. Having no formal training, Schiaparelli approached fashion with a sense of experimentation, whimsy and the ridiculous. For her, there were no rules to be broken, just her own perceptions and sense of style.

FASHION AS AN ART FORM
A true product of the modern age at the beginning of 20th century, Schiaparelli wholeheartedly believed that new interpretations of art, dress, design and indeed society at large were needed for the changing future. Nowhere was this enthusiasm for the novel as evident as in her collaborations with artists such as Salvador Dalí, Francis Picabia, Christian Bérard, Man Ray and Jean Cocteau. Their artwork as well as their attitudes and philosophies affected Schiaparelli, and inspired her to approach fashion as an art form.

Starting with her trompe l'oeil sweaters that featured a bow tie or scarf, to the iconic 1937 lobster dress created with Dalí, Schiaparelli always found beauty and truth in the bizarre. Although her clothes were always supremely elegant and wearable, Schiaparelli preferred to question the accepted ideals of beauty. For example, her 1938 insect necklace looked like a beautiful semiprecious configuration around the neck when viewed from far away, but closer inspection revealed that the jewels were life-size copies of insects.

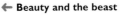

← **Beauty and the beast**

The iconic lobster dress, created in collaboration with Salvador. Dalí, exemplifies Elsa Schiaparelli's understanding of grace and elegance, while refusing to become mired in sanctimonious seriousness. It is as if Schiaparelli is suggesting that there is nothing more beautiful on a woman than a sense of humour.

■ **Contemporary artists**

Artists, such as Salvador Dalí (right), Jean Cocteau, Christian Bérard, Francis Picabia, Man Ray and others, were not only Schiaparelli's friends but also her collaborators, inspiring iconic pieces that define her style, such as the lobster dress that she created with Dalí.

Wears a tromp l'oeil bow-tie sweater that she has designed. She immediately has requests for copies.	Opens her own house, Pour le Sport, focusing on knit daywear and simple blouses.	Adds eveningwear to her collection, and officially becomes a couturier.
1926	**1927**	**1931**

● **Yves Saint Laurent**

Saint Laurent was inspired by Schiaparelli's consistent modern art inspirations to imbue his own collections with a rich variety of contemporary art influences throughout his career.

● **Cristóbal Balenciaga**

Balenciaga remembered going to see Schiaparelli's collections when he was a young couturier in Spain. Later, in his Paris collections, Balenciaga was known for using experimental fabrications, just as he had seen in Schiaparelli's collections.

'Dress designing, incidentally, is to me not a profession but an art. I find that it is a most difficult and unsatisfying art, because as soon as a dress is born it has already become a thing of the past.'

Elsa Schiaparelli

➜ Protected beauty

This 1937 Schiaparelli evening coat, designed in collaboration with the acclaimed surrealist artist and writer Jean Cocteau, plays with shapes to create two faces and a vase for cut flowers. Cocteau is suggesting a telling metaphor, comparing the protected beauty of the flowers to that of a woman. The silhouette and use of strong shoulders were to become Schiaparelli signatures.

 INFLUENCED BY

KEY
- fashion designer
- ◆ fashion house/brand
- ■ artistic influence
- ❖ cultural influence

● Paul Poiret

An early supporter of Schiaparelli, Poiret is said to have given her a dress free of charge because he liked her sense of the dramatic. From the couturier, Schiaparelli would inevitably have been attracted to the flights of fantasy and artistic collaborations for which Poiret was so well known. Schiaparelli must also have observed Poiret's flair for publicity and sense of the dramatic, which enabled both designers to garner attention and clients. For all of the adornments that Poiret and Schiaparelli displayed in their collections, at the heart they both believed in simplicity of line, construction and silhouette.

ELSA SCHIAPARELLI CONTINUED

Collaborates with surrealist writer and artist Jean Cocteau to design a jacket and evening coat. Introduces her first perfume, Shocking. The bottle is modelled after the torso of Mae West.	*Collaborates with surrealist artist Salvador Dalí to produce the famous lobster dress, then other pieces in her Circus collection.*

CHRONOLOGY	1937	1937–38

 INSPIRED

◆ Aquilano Rimondi

The young Italian duo featured an obvious homage to Schiaparelli in their Autumn 2009 collection, in the form of sharp and exaggerated shoulders and fitted waists (left).

THEMED ACCESSORIES

Schiaparelli liked working within themes, such as for her Circus, Pagan and Astrological collections. For these and others, she would often devise special buttons and accessories that would reinforce the theme. The buttons took the form of clowns, balloons, animals, insects, zodiac signs and lollipops. She famously created a series of hats that looked like a high-heeled shoe turned upside down, a telephone or a chess piece.

SILHOUETTE AND SHAPE

Despite the surrealistic touches in her work, Schiaparelli was extremely successful during the 1930s, until World War II forced her to close her atelier. Her steady stream of clients included society women and Hollywood stars, such as Marlene Dietrich, Claudette Colbert and Norma Shearer.

Beyond the humour and sense that everything must be turned on its head, women came to Schiaparelli for her approach to silhouette and shape. She was a proponent of the full shoulder that allowed women the appearance of narrow hips. She lengthened the figure by relying on a long thin skirt that has become synonymous with this time period. She was so associated with the silhouette that, after the war, she eventually closed her house for good, refusing to accept the changes that Dior's full-skirted New Look of 1947 had brought.

Elsa Schiaparelli's influence continues to inspire in the contemporary context as an increasing array of designers experiment with the melding of art and fashion and question ideas of beauty and propriety.

→ Playful voyeurism

This 1949 satin hat by Schiaparelli suggests a reciprocal notion of voyeurism – the objectification of the wearer, but also of the audience as viewed through the peephole. A sense of playfulness is suggested rather than anything sinister, because of the shape of the hat being reminiscent of a young boy's ball cap.

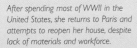

● Jean Patou

Patou was known for his sporty clothing that emphasized physical fitness in an era largely devoid of those considerations. His influence was clearly felt by Schiaparelli when she opened her Pour le Sport atelier in 1927.

● Coco Chanel

Chanel inspired the burgeoning designer to consider the knit dressing that Chanel had made so popular. For her part, Chanel dismissed Schiaparelli as 'the Italian artist who makes clothes'.

■ Architecture

Schiaparelli said, 'Clothes have to be architectural!... The body must never be forgotten and it must be used as a frame for the building.'

After spending most of WWII in the United States, she returns to Paris and attempts to reopen her house, despite lack of materials and workforce.

Writes her memoirs, Shocking Life. Closes her house, unable to compete with the new direction of fashion.

Dies in Paris on November 13th.

1944

1954

1973

◆ Dolce & Gabbana

The Italian duo's collection for Autumn 2009 was a clear homage to Schiaparelli. The collection featured exaggerated shoulders and the colours black and her signature hot pink. The collection also included hats and scarves that looked like opera gloves, and buttons that were nontraditional and emblematic of Schiaparelli's love for the surreal. Although this collection was overt, Dolce & Gabbana have often toyed with instilling their collections with humour and camp, from their love of 1950s sex bombs to the space oddities of their Autumn 2007 collection.

● Alexander McQueen

The British designer exhibited several collections that examine Western ideas of beauty, and venture into the surreal and unbelievable.

← Pink homage

In Dolce & Gabbana's Autumn 2009 collection, pink gorilla-style hair becomes a chic and stylish shrug, gloves become a necktie and novelty buttons are used in a homage to their fellow Italian designer Elsa Schiaparelli.

Rei Kawakubo has dramatically influenced the Western perspective on body adornment and the meaning of clothes, as well as the Japanese conception of what it means to be a woman in a male-dominated society. Kawakubo has helped to foster intellectualism in fashion, and her influence can be seen in a wide variety of designers' collections.

INFLUENCED BY

KEY
- fashion designer
- fashion house/brand
- artistic influence
- cultural influence

❖ **Japanese philosophy and culture**
Fundamental to Kawakubo's work is the Japanese concept of wabi-sabi (acceptance of transience and imperfection, and finding beauty in them); the traditional Japanese way of dress and the wearability of the kimono (right); and the emphasis on quiet contemplation of abstract ideas.

REI KAWAKUBO
Japanese
(1942 Tokyo)

	Born October 11th in Tokyo.	Graduates from Keio University after studying philosophy, literature and fine art. Works for a brief time as a stylist.	Starts creating women's cl[othing] under the name Comme [des] Garçons, which means 'Like [Boys'].			
CHRONOLOGY	**1942**	**1964**	**1969**	**1975**	**1978**	

INSPIRED

● **Hussein Chalayan**
Kawakubo serves as a model for conceptual thought, a philosophical approach to design and a revisiting of ideas rather than an attachment to trends, all of which Chalayan is known for in his own right.

● **Marc Jacobs**
Kawakubo has been a major influence on the New York designer, as can be seen in Jacobs's collections for Autumn 2006 and Spring 2008 (left). This dress reflects Kawakubo's influence, such as in the incongruous placement of fabric on the figure. The dress is feminine and doll-like, overwhelming the model and not fitting in the traditionally accepted manner for Western dress. The sash references both Western decorative details and the Japanese obi.

● **Martin Margiela**
Margiela was extremely influenced by Japanese designers in his formative years, identifying with the deconstructionist philosophy that Kawakubo helped to introduce.

Rei Kawakubo's Comme des Garçons fashion shows are often the subject of a great deal of head scratching by many buyers and journalists, who may not understand the clothing or the message that is being communicated. Kawakubo shuns the spotlight, rarely coming out to take a bow at the end of her shows. Journalists who hope to learn the secrets of her thought process or meaning are often answered cryptically, resulting in more confusion. However, every season they return, because they all seem to recognize that, although they may not understand Kawakubo's collection at first glance, they are witnessing something that will influence other designers and have a considerable impact on future fashion.

FASHION IS NOT ART
It may seem that Kawakubo approaches fashion as if it were art – full of experimentation, open-ended questions and a desire to explore larger issues. However, despite her perceived connection to artistic, conceptual fashion, Kawakubo does not want her work to be considered art for art's sake, or as forsaking function. She says, 'Fashion is not art. You sell art to one person. Fashion comes in a series and is more of a social phenomenon. It is also something more personal and individual, because you express your personality. It is an active participation; art is passive.'

Kawakubo's work has been featured in countless museum collections, exhibitions and publications, because of the incredible artistic perspective she brings to each of her collections. Her statement that fashion is not art might actually be more of a defensive reaction than a belief, since conceptual designers are continually being forced to prove that their clothing is wearable and approachable, even though it stems from an intellectual approach.

← Surrealism and pop culture

This piece from the Comme des Garçons Autumn 2007 collection includes obvious references to the work of Elsa Schiaparelli in the form of hands clasping the model's chest. In 1937, Schiaparelli collaborated with surrealist artist Jean Cocteau to create a jacket with a porcelain hand acting as a closure. Kawakubo has also used pop culture in the form of cartoonish ears, just as Schiaparelli referenced 1930s culture.

• Elsa Schiaparelli

Although Kawakubo might not align herself with the fitted silhouette and Western aesthetic of Schiaparelli's work, she often plays with surrealistic elements and disjointed ideas, much in the way that Schiaparelli did in the 1930s. Kawakubo has experimented with scale, colour, symbolism and popular culture to make her audience reevaluate established ideas. Schiaparelli aimed to shock or surprise as a function of self-expression, which is Kawakubo's primary aim. Schiaparelli also represents an ideal model of female self-determination to the autonomous Kawakubo.

Opens her first store in Paris and begins to manufacture her clothing in Paris.	*Junya Watanabe, Kawakubo's most well-known protégé, begins designing the Comme des Garçons Tricot knitwear line.*
1982	**1987**

• Ann Demeulemeester

Kawakubo has been associated with the colour black and the adoption of many gender-neutral looks. Demeulemeester has clearly been influenced by the Japanese designer's aesthetic, creating her own look based on many of the same principles.

• Alexander McQueen

The British designer said many times that he greatly admired the work of Kawakubo. Both designers have created an aura of strength and reserve for their female customers, while approaching fashion with a larger political statement in mind.

'I don't have a definition of beauty. I don't have an established view of what beauty is, as my idea of beauty keeps changing.'

Rei Kawakubo

→ **Japanese aesthetic**
Kawakubo is inspired by Japanese culture and symbolism. In this piece from her Spring 2007 collection, she uses geisha-inspired make-up on the model's face, and the large red sun from the Japanese flag on the clothing.

← **INFLUENCED BY**

KEY
● fashion designer
◆ fashion house/brand
■ artistic influence
❖ cultural influence

● **Yohji Yamamoto**
Yamamoto was one of Kawakubo's greatest champions early in her career. He encouraged her to debut with him in Paris, and to forge her own path.

● **Issey Miyake**
Miyake was the first Japanese designer to be introduced to the West who also held on to the aesthetics of the East. Miyake has set an example of a designer/artist collaborative, with a steadfast belief in his own personal philosophy, which has undoubtedly influenced Kawakubo.

● **Vivienne Westwood**
Westwood's early work with the punk movement provided fertile ground for the introduction of Kawakubo's work to the West.

REI KAWAKUBO CONTINUED

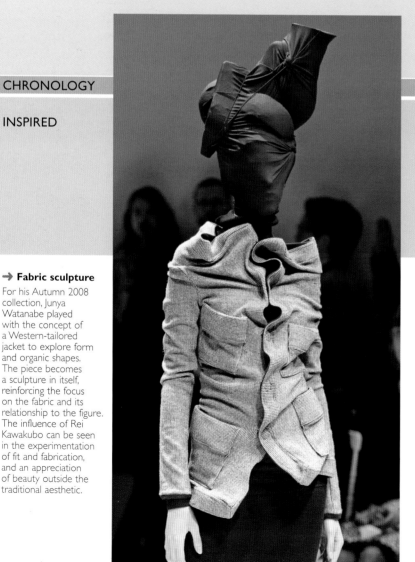

CHRONOLOGY

→ **INSPIRED**

→ **Fabric sculpture**
For his Autumn 2008 collection, Junya Watanabe played with the concept of a Western-tailored jacket to explore form and organic shapes. The piece becomes a sculpture in itself, reinforcing the focus on the fabric and its relationship to the figure. The influence of Rei Kawakubo can be seen in the experimentation of fit and fabrication, and an appreciation of beauty outside the traditional aesthetic.

Launches Comme des Garçons SHIRT diffusion line.	Starts publishing a bi-annual magazine, Six (standing for "Sixth Sense"), that features inspiring images but has very little text.	Becomes a guest editor of the visual arts magazine Visionaire.
1988	**1990**	**1996**

● **Junya Watanabe**
Watanabe said of Kawakubo, 'Rei has taught me everything about how to create.' Kawakubo gave Watanabe funds to start his own collection, but their business relationship does not include advice or input by the more renowned designer. In fact, Kawakubo does not know what Watanabe is doing from season to season. From her, Watanabe has learned to question all established ideas and, most important, to experiment, letting the results vary and breathe a life of their own. Like his teacher, Watanabe revisits concepts and has formulated a philosophy all his own.

SEARCH FOR BEAUTY
From the start, Kawakubo has questioned several facets of contemporary society in both Japan and the West, namely feminism and the inherent concerns of image and position. Although she is often associated with fellow Japanese designers Yohji Yamamoto and Issey Miyake for bringing a significant Japanese influence to Paris, Kawakubo has become unique in her feminine perspectives. She continually confronts idealized or prescribed beauty: 'I want to see things differently to search for beauty. I want to find something nobody has ever found… It is meaningless to create something predictable.'

The inequalities that all women face are often a source of inspiration for her: 'I never lose my ability to rebel, I get angry and the anger becomes my energy for certain. I would not be able to create anything if I stopped rebelling.'

→ **Inside decoration**

For her Autumn 2010 collection, Rei Kawakubo said that it was about 'inside decoration'. Although this baffled many in the press, it seems that it is in fact a continued study of identity and protection through clothing. This can be seen in the armour-like quality of the quilting in this ensemble, and the manipulations of fabric into folds or wrinkles, perhaps suggesting the juxtaposition of youth, beauty, and idealized body shapes.

■ **Architecture**

Kawakubo is married to an architect, and works very closely with architect Takao Kawasaki in the development of all her stores (left: Comme des Garçons store in Aoyama, Tokyo). The designer's clothing has an architectural feel, as she explores the relationship of the body with the shell that covers it.

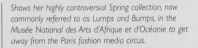

Shows her highly controversial Spring collection, now commonly referred to as Lumps and Bumps, in the Musée National des Arts d'Afrique et d'Océanie to get away from the Paris fashion media circus.

Tao Kurihara takes over from Junya Watanabe as designer of the Comme des Garçons Tricot knitwear line.

Becomes a guest designer for fashion retailer H&M, designing clothing for men, women and children as well as a unisex perfume.

1997   **2005**   **2008**

◆ **Armand Basi One**

Marcus Lupfer's Autumn 2009 collection for the small label Armand Basi One experimented with large shapes, dark colours and some deconstructionist elements (right), paying homage to the 1980s work of Kawakubo.

◆ **Rodarte**

Sisters Kate and Laura Mulleavy have learned from Kawakubo to experiment with fabrics, shapes and notions of idealized beauty. They have become known for their rich combinations of fabrics, textures and colours wrapped around the body in unconventional ways.

JAPANESE TRADITION AND AESTHETIC

Like her fellow Japanese designers, many of Kawakubo's aesthetic choices come from traditional Japanese dress, such as the kimono. The kimono is a unisex garment that largely eradicates the erogenous zones highlighted in European dress. The emphasis is on socially defining the person rather than evaluating their body proportions.

Kawakubo often draws upon Japan's rich craft tradition to experiment with the form of fabric, drape, construction and deconstruction. Her work also reflects the Japanese aesthetic philosophy wabi-sabi, which refers to accepting and finding beauty in the imperfect, impermanent or incomplete, and relies on asymmetry and discordance. Utilizing feminist philosophies, she questions ideal beauty, such as in her Spring 1997 collection, commonly known as Lumps and Bumps, that showed models with exaggerated shapes and contortions all over their bodies. At the same time, Kawakubo often translates aesthetic symbols and ideas from the West, combining or referencing them to form a post-modernist statement.

SHIFTING VALUES

Comme des Garçons has become a leading fashion house that has shifted the dialogue of female dress, prescribed aesthetic values and notions of beauty to become a major influence in the fashion industry. All of this influence would be hollow if it were not for the fact that the house is one of the most thriving, independently owned fashion companies, selling successfully not only in Japan but all over the world.

Martin Margiela is as famous for his complete rejection of the spotlight as for his involvement with the influential deconstructionist movement of the 1990s. He has influenced scores of designers with his philosophies, as well as inadvertently started trends, from ripped-up jeans to a reemphasis on shoulder pads.

 INFLUENCED BY

KEY
- ● fashion designer
- ◆ fashion house/brand
- ■ artistic influence
- ❖ cultural influence

● Cristóbal Balenciaga
Balenciaga was an extremely private man, and refused to participate in the media circus that is often focused on the designer. Margiela treated his atelier as Balenciaga did – as a place for experimentation and creative work – with the only public interaction focused on the finished product.

● Madeleine Vionnet
Vionnet spent her entire career creating technical innovations and examining the haptic relationship of clothing to the body, things that Margiela would have respected and learned from.

● Jean Paul Gaultier
Margiela was Gaultier's assistant for two years, and during that time undoubtedly began formulating his philosophies of identity through clothing.

● Ann Demeulemeester
As contemporaries, the two designers have influenced each other, not only in their aesthetic but also in the way that they query prescribed notions of style.

MARTIN MARGIELA
Belgian
(1957/59 Genk)

Believed to have been born on April 9th in 1957 or 1959 in Genk, Belgium. Margiela refuses to confirm these facts.	*Graduates from the Royal Academy of Fine Arts in Antwerp.*	*Freelances in Milan and Antwerp.*	*Works as an assistant for Jean Paul Gaultier.*	*Starts his own label, Maison Martin Margiela, in Paris with retailer Jenny Meirens. Shows his first collection, garnering a lot of attention.*

CHRONOLOGY	1957/59	1980	1980–84	1984–87	1988

 INSPIRED

● Alexander McQueen
McQueen was influenced by Margiela in his discomfort with celebrity, his relationship with craft, and the philosophical examinations that he created in his collections.

◆ Viktor & Rolf
The design duo has played with repetition, proportion and volume in ways that resemble the philosophies and work of Margiela.

● Helmut Lang
The retired reclusive Austrian designer was influenced primarily by Margiela's work focusing on the layers of cloth surrounding the body, as seen in Lang's Spring 2002 collection that featured layers of sheer fabrics (left). Lang's designs are a lot cleaner and more geometric than Margiela's almost earthy aesthetic, but both designers are intrigued by the connection between image, surface coverage and personal identity that make up a garment.

Martin Margiela has created a new understanding of fashion through his constant reinvention of his own singular ideas. Margiela participates in the fashion business, but only on his own terms – and with no deviation from them. Margiela has refused to answer personal questions or comment on anything other than what is related to his work, and does not allow himself to be photographed. Any questions that reporters may have must be submitted via fax and are answered in the plural, signed by Maison Martin Margiela.

Although at first glance it would seem that this tactic might be considered a ploy to garner more attention, it did in fact only hurt his early career. Since then, however, Maison Martin Margiela has garnered so much critical praise that his stubborn adherence to an idea has become an ingrained philosophy. This philosophy also extends to his fashion shows, with the faces of the models often covered so that the celebrity of the model does not overshadow the clothing that is on display.

CREATION AND CRAFT
Overarching themes behind Margiela's work are the act of creation and the relationship that we have with our clothing. In the most simple terms, deconstructionism refers to the inside appearing on the outside, so Margiela exposes darts, leaves hems unfinished or leaves shoulder pads exposed.

In a more pointed commentary, the designer calls attention to the development of traditional craft processes involved in fashion design by introducing clothing that appears unfinished or literally in the process of being assembled. For his Spring 1998 collection, Margiela displayed all the garments as if they were pattern pieces hanging on a dressmaker's hook. When placed on the figure, however, the

← **Act of creation**
The Spring 2006 Margiela collection saw models on platforms, with half of the garment finished and the other half still attached to the roll of fabric whence it came. This calls attention to the process of creation in relation to the idea of spontaneity, or lack thereof.

■ **Deconstructionist architecture**
The fashion design philosophies that Margiela has become famous for were first explored through deconstructionist architecture, which is noted for looking as if it is crumbling or falling down. It can also be recognized when elements from the inside, such as pipes or building materials, are displayed on the outside – or in the case of Margiela's designs, exposed darts and shoulder pads.

Becomes design director of Hermès. In his first solo exhibition, at the Museum Boijmans Van Beuningen in Rotterdam, he smears the clothing with bacteria that quickly destroys the cloth.

1997

● **Hussein Chalayan**
For his graduation from London's Central Saint Martins, Chalayan exhibited clothes that had been buried in his friend's back garden and dug up again. There is a clear resemblance to Margiela's 1997 exhibition of bacteria formations on fabric.

'Fashion is a craft, a technical know-how and not, in our opinion, an art form. Each world shares an expression through creativity though through very divergent media processes.'

Maison Martin Margiela

→ Clothing and identity
The clothes are hung off the front of the model in the Spring 2004 Margiela collection, examining clothing's ability to represent the individuality of the wearer. If we are forever using clothing to manipulate others' view of our identity, then what is the truth of who we really are?

 INFLUENCED BY

KEY
- ● fashion designer
- ◆ fashion house/brand
- ■ artistic influence
- ❖ cultural influence

● Rei Kawakubo
Kawakubo was a major influence on Margiela's early career in terms of deconstruction and the treatment of cloth that surrounds the figure. She has also had a lasting effect on his philosophy. Kawakubo's stubborn insistence that no question has a definitive answer, as well as her analysis of beauty, have perhaps been the most influential ideas to surface in Margiela's work.

MARTIN MARGIELA CONTINUED

CHRONOLOGY	2002		2003	2007	2008
	Renzo Rosso, owner of Italian clothing company Diesel, buys a majority stake in Maison Martin Margiela, allowing Margiela to expand internationally. Over the coming years, Margiela stores open across Europe and in the United States, Japan, Taiwan and Hong Kong.		Stops working at Hermès.	Launches a sunglasses line.	Forms a partnership with French cosmetics giant L'Oréal to create a line of perfumes. Launches a line of fine jewellery. The house celebrates its 20th anniversary.

→ INSPIRED

● Nicolas Ghesquière for Balenciaga
Ghesquière has embraced one of the key trends that has emanated from Maison Martin Margiela – the exaggerated shoulder (right).

● Olivier Theyskens
As part of the next generation of young Belgian designers, Theyskens has not yet clearly defined his path as a designer, but his early work shows a definitive influence from Margiela.

● Marc Jacobs
Jacobs was influenced by the work of Margiela in the 1990s, while Jacobs was working at Perry Ellis. Deconstructionism helped to inform Jacobs's famous Spring 1993 grunge collection for Ellis.

pattern pieces became a waistcoat or pair of trousers that were sewn together as if flat. In his Spring 2006 collection, models appeared with fabric that represented a garment but was still only a piece of fabric attached to the roll of cloth.

Additionally, Margiela has often used the mannequin or dressmaker's dummy as a source of inspiration, or simply as a garment in itself. To continue his theme in daily life, all of the people who work at Maison Martin Margiela, as well as the sales staff of his many international stores, wear an atelier lab coat as their uniform.

CYCLE OF FASHION

Many of Margiela's collections are created by reconfiguring old garments into new ones. This is not based on a sense of environmentalism; instead, Margiela is exploring the relationship that we have with the cycle of fashion, the need for

change and the eventuality of repetition. In the late 1990s, Margiela began experimenting with nonhazardous micro-organisms, culminating in the 1997 exhibition in which he smeared bacteria onto clothing, which quickly degraded the fabric to the degree that it became unrecognizable.

NOTIONS OF FEMININITY

Margiela also questions the idealized notions of femininity, weight, size and style attributes within the fashion industry. As Margiela himself notes, 'Femininity is a whole, a sum of many parts, a grouping of a multitude of mentalities, sensibilities, and sensualities.'

With his use of the dressmaker's mannequin in so many collections, Margiela is commenting on how the attributes of an inanimate object are being imposed on a living, breathing person. In his Spring 2000 collection, Margiela

→ Suppressed individuality

The Spring 2009 Maison Martin Margiela collection marked the 20th anniversary of the house that Margiela founded. This piece is inspired by Margiela's Spring 1999 collection, in which assistants held up large-format photographs of the clothing. The concept was revisited throughout Margiela's career, exposing fashion's relationship with the suppressed sense of individuality that dictates current style.

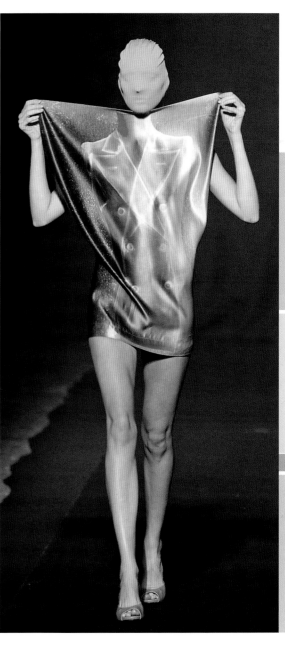

● Yohji Yamamoto

Margiela has adopted Yamamoto's philosophy that the cloth that surrounds the body does not need to define the figure. The two designers also share a sense of the romantic gothic.

■ Couture tradition

Margiela is inspired by the couture traditions of all designers, but is not derivative in any way to the designers he admires. The craft practice and tradition of couture are clearly integral to his work – indeed, the dressmaker's mannequin has been a frequent source of inspiration (left).

The book Maison Martin Margiela is published, archiving Margiela's entire body of work. Rumours surface of Raf Simons and Haider Ackermann being offered the job of heading the company; both decline to comment. Following speculation, it is announced that Margiela has not been contributing to recent collections; these have been handled by a team of designers who have worked with him in the past. It is later announced that Margiela has left the company.

2009

● Junya Watanabe

Watanabe refuses to speak to the fashion press and can perhaps be considered more hermetic than Margiela, who at least communicates by fax. Apart from the surface similarity, Watanabe has been influenced by Margiela's interpretations of their common mentor, Rei Kawakubo.

← Deconstruction revisited

This piece from Junya Watanabe's Autumn 2006 collection is a perfect example of how an idea can be morphed to create new explorations and outcomes. Rei Kawakubo influenced Martin Margiela in the early 1990s, with her deconstructed sweaters that were misshaped and holey. Watanabe has in turn been influenced by Margiela's input, and interprets the idea in a wholly original way.

introduced 'size 74', which was an imaginary size imposed on the collection of garments. In 1994, he introduced a collection based on dolls' clothing in which every detail, from the knit gauge to the snaps and fasteners, was magnified 5.2 times to human size.

PUSHING THE BOUNDARIES

Margiela has been an overwhelming influence on fashion as an industry, causing us to question ideas that we often take for granted, as well as pushing the boundaries of established practices, such as craft, style and image.

Alexander McQueen's impact is a force beyond trend or style dictate. Effortlessly melding fashion, art and concept with amazing tailoring and technical genius, McQueen took fashion forward and propelled the dialogue of fashion beyond clothing into a much larger realm.

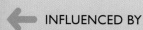

INFLUENCED BY

KEY
- ● fashion designer
- ◆ fashion house/brand
- ■ artistic influence
- ❖ cultural influence

● **Christian Dior**
McQueen displayed a similar talent for the extreme and sharp tailoring that Dior was known for, creating sculpted pieces that often shaped the body, rather than the body shaping the clothing, such as in McQueen's Spring 2009 collection (right).

● **Vivienne Westwood**
Westwood has been an extremely influential British designer, not only in terms of the way she achieved success, but also in her attitude. Westwood's connection to punk undoubtedly appealed to a young rebellious McQueen, who like Westwood was forced to negotiate the fashion industry as a bit of an outsider. Westwood has subsequently made a name for herself by referencing historical dress and manipulating it to mean something different in a contemporary context. McQueen also did this, preferring the grotesque Victorian era to Westwood's penchant for the 18th century.

ALEXANDER McQUEEN
British
(1969 London)

CHRONOLOGY	1969	1985–87	1988–89	1992
	Born Lee Alexander McQueen on March 17th in London.	Apprentices at Savile Row tailors Anderson & Sheppard and then Gieves & Hawkes. Moves on to theatrical costumiers Bermans & Nathans.	Becomes assistant designer to London-based Japanese designer Koji Tatsuno, then spends a year in Italy working for Romeo Gigli.	Graduates from London's Central Saint Martins. His degree collection is bought by Isabella Blow, fashion editor of British Vogue, who helps McQueen in his career.

INSPIRED

● **Jonathan Saunders**
Two days after graduating from London's Central Saint Martins, Saunders began working for Alexander McQueen. McQueen's influence on Saunders, now an independent designer, can be seen in the sophisticated combination of prints and cut.

● **Giles Deacon**
Deacon is building a substantial reputation as a designer who ventures into the perverse. In nearly every collection, Deacon has some element that needs a second look, such as Spring 2008's fabric printed with decapitated, still-bleeding Bambis. Shock tactics such as this have undoubtedly been influenced by McQueen.

◆ **Viktor & Rolf**
The design duo create artistic statements and presentations that revolve around a centralized concept. McQueen's influence is as a designer who put a great deal of thought into what he was trying to communicate through his clothing.

McQueen's work became more artistically and socially significant as he grew out of the need to shock, and opted instead for a thoughtful exploration and commentary on our world. Much has been made of his early life and background, which would not traditionally have led to a career as a couturier. In fact for many, McQueen's background has been the sole definition of his work up until recent years.

McQueen began his career with a great deal of vitriol towards the fashion industry by saying to the press, after the announcement of his new position at the house of Givenchy in 1996, that the founder of the house was 'irrelevant' and subsequently that his time there was a 'prison sentence'. Additionally, comments such as 'There is beauty in anger, and anger for me is a passion' hinted to his relatively young age for achieving such resounding success.

BALANCE OF POWER

McQueen's core inquiry throughout his career seemed to be centred on the balance of power, whether it be between men and women, beast/nature and humankind, technology and nature, or between humans as a species. Early in his career, he often relied on historical references, particularly corsets and Victorian dresses, that were slashed, torn or manipulated, so it was easy for critics to misunderstand his true intentions or concepts.

Claims of misogyny were levelled at McQueen, but it was later understood that he was in fact attempting to make women equal to men in their sexuality and power. Many of McQueen's collections featured women wearing armour or fierce jewellery, or displaying such a presence as to intimidate any oppressor. He said, 'I like men to keep their distance from women. I like men to be stunned by an entrance.'

Historical relevance
This stunning piece from McQueen's posthumous Autumn 2010 collection references the Middle Ages. Taking a step away from his recent focus on technology, McQueen designed the new collection using historical references, yet his virtuosity and incredible talents created a relevant piece for the 21st century.

'Fashion and art are coming closer together and there is an enormous amount of intermingling of the two that's unavoidable since both are visual stimulants.'

Alexander McQueen

 INFLUENCED BY

KEY
● fashion designer
◆ fashion house/brand
■ artistic influence
❖ cultural influence

● Rei Kawakubo
No designer who works within a conceptual framework has not been affected by Kawakubo. McQueen said publicly several times that he was extremely influenced by the work of the Japanese designer.

● Hussein Chalayan
As contemporaries, Chalayan and McQueen respected each other and were inspired by each other's work. Both also had similar experiences in attempting to balance the higher-concept pieces with the notion that they did not make wearable clothing.

ALEXANDER McQUEEN CONTINUED

	Becomes design director of the house of Givenchy, leaving in 2001.	Designs clothing for the cover of Icelandic musician Björk's Homogenic album.	Launches his own house under the patronage of the Gucci Group, which owns a 51% share in the company.	Awarded a CBE (Commander of the Order of the British Empire). Launches the fragrance Kingdom.	Launches his bespoke menswear line.
CHRONOLOGY	**1996**	**1997**	**2000**	**2003**	**2004**

INSPIRED

● Zac Posen
Like McQueen, Posen often references historical time periods, such as the 1940s and Victorian era in his Autumn 2009 collection (right), to suggest a new interpretation of beauty and sexuality.

● John Galliano
Galliano preceded McQueen at Givenchy. Both designers reference historical silhouettes, but McQueen deepened his conceptual base for Galliano to follow.

● Riccardo Tisci for Givenchy
Following in the footsteps of McQueen at Givenchy, Tisci has often referenced a type of warrior woman, as well as historical dress mixed with contemporary underworld symbolism.

● Rick Owens
Both designers initially rejected formal education in order to learn the trade from the ground up. They also shared an architectural approach to construction and a sense of the gothic romantic.

DICHOTOMY OF WOMEN

If women are not active in the hunt, then they are the ones being hunted; in his Autumn 1997 collection entitled It's a Jungle Out There, he referenced the Thompson's gazelle as a metaphor for the urban jungle. The Spring 1997 collection La Poupée featured the model Debra Shaw walking down the catwalk attached to a metal frame, resulting in a halting and contorted walk that called attention to her vulnerability.

Yet McQueen's woman was never defenseless; there is an ever-present threat of aggressive power or an active display of strength, as seen in the Spring 1999 collection when double amputee Aimee Mullins walked down the catwalk like any other model on legs created by the designer. Alexander McQueen inherently understood the fundamental dichotomy of women as that of a balance between sensitivity and strength, desire and dread, or reliance and independence.

CLOTHING AS A SYMPTOM

In his Spring 2009 Natural Dis-Tinction/Un-Natural Selection and Spring 2010 Plato's Atlantis collections, McQueen examined Charles Darwin's theory of natural selection and our relationship to nature.

Not necessarily wishing to declare a political statement, McQueen nonetheless created a dialogue centred on his chosen subject area. The designer voiced the dislocation and unease often caused by the rapid-fire technological, social and economic changes that affect our worldview. As McQueen said, 'Fashion is so indicative of the political and social climate in which we live, what we wear will always be a symptom of our environment.'

← Cyber chic

Many fashion designers are inspired by the idea of cyborgs, robots or mechanization of the human form, not least Alexander McQueen. Here, for Givenchy in Autumn 1999, McQueen creates an otherworldly being that borrows from the 1982 sci-fi film *Tron*.

→ Nature becomes woman

McQueen's Spring 2010 Plato's Atlantis collection was inspired by Charles Darwin's theory of natural selection. The incredible tailoring and manipulation of fabric suggest humans who become underwater beings, while stretching the connections between technology and nature – a theme that ran through McQueen's last shows.

● Romeo Gigli

As a young man of 20, McQueen learned from Gigli the power of the press, and that interest can often be more centred on the designer than the clothing itself.

● Martin Margiela

Early in McQueen's career, he was influenced by Margiela and refused to be photographed. He later abandoned the idea, but Margiela's examination of the relationship between creator and wearer had a lasting effect.

● Jean Paul Gaultier

Gaultier made his name by using sex and the female image in the context of clothing. McQueen undoubtedly learned from this, with his own work exploring that same subject area.

● Thierry Mugler

Mugler often referenced nature, particularly the exoskeleton of insects, to create armor for women, as well as giving theatrical presentations—both influential to McQueen.

2005	2006	2007	2009	2010
Launches the fragrance MyQueen. Creates a footwear collection with Puma.	Launches McQ diffusion line of denim-based ready-to-wear.	Enters into a partnership with Samsonite to create luxury travel gear.	Creates a collection for discount retailer Target that quickly sells out.	Found dead by suicide on February 11th.

● Gareth Pugh

As soon as the young British designer came onto the scene, the similarities to McQueen were obvious. Pugh uses diverse costume and historical references, such as samurai warriors, gothic romanticism and the Elizabethan era, and creates women who look as if they are plunging headlong into battle. Pugh also struggles with the press when they criticize his outlandish catwalk shows, as did McQueen.

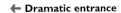

← Dramatic entrance

Gareth Pugh's Spring 2010 collection shows a flair for the feminine potential for drama in a sweeping dress that conforms to the figure. The headdress is both menacing and poetic as an allegorical bird of prey – something that also appeared in McQueen's Autumn 2006 and Spring 2008 collections.

BRIDGING OLD AND NEW

Like many of his notable contemporaries, McQueen was important as a herald of what is to become of fashion in the 21st century. He was a bridge between the old sense of fashion, as seen in his respect for Savile Row tailoring, and the new direction of the industry in the coming century, as he helped to propel fashion forward in terms of artistic statement and concept. The early death of McQueen, whose talents were unique in vision and genius, represents an astounding loss to the fashion world.

The two designers that make up Viktor & Rolf are representative of the shifts and study in contrasts of the present-day fashion industry. As relatively recent outsiders, their work often centres on an examination of what constitutes the fashion industry's as well as society's view of beauty, materialism and originality.

INFLUENCED BY

KEY
- ● fashion designer
- ◆ fashion house/brand
- ■ artistic influence
- ❖ cultural influence

● **Karl Lagerfeld**
For most of his career, Lagerfeld has been engaged in an aloof yet prophetic appraisal of style and luxury. Viktor & Rolf have cited Lagerfeld as a source of inspiration, not only for his virtuosity and prolific body of work, but also for his ability to manipulate fashion in such a new way. Lagerfeld has perfected the idea of branding and how to maintain an internationally recognized look for the corporate design houses he has worked for, most notably Chanel. Victor & Rolf play with these ideas as outsiders looking in, and as aspiring designers looking out.

● **Coco Chanel**
From Chanel, the design duo has learned the importance of the designer as the ultimate branding tool. Without releasing any personal material, they have been able to set up an aura of authority in much the same way that Chanel was able to do in her lifetime.

● **Cristóbal Balenciaga**
Viktor & Rolf's frequent use of sculptural shapes and experimental fabrics is reminiscent of Balenciaga's work. In their Autumn 2001 Black Hole collection, they used iconic silhouettes from Balenciaga, Chanel, and Saint Laurent to make a point about the timelessness of certain fashions.

VIKTOR & ROLF
Dutch
(1969 Geldrop & Donegan)

Viktor Horsting born May 27th in Geldrop and Rolf Snoeren born December 19th in Dongen, both in the Netherlands.	They graduate from the Arnhem Academy of Art and Design.	Win three prizes at the Salon Européen des Jeunes Stylistes during the Festival International de Mode et de Photographie at Hyères in France. Begin creating limited couture collections.	Begin producing fashion installations in European art galleries, starting in Paris.

CHRONOLOGY	1969	1992	1993	1994

INSPIRED

◆ **Albino**
The Autumn 2009 collection features luxurious fabrications in exaggerated shapes, similar to the work of Victor & Rolf.

● **Benjamin Cho**
Young New York designer Cho has utilized exaggerated romantic shapes contrasted with clean, simple silhouettes (right) that seem to be inspired in part by Viktor & Rolf.

● **Gareth Pugh**
Like Viktor & Rolf, this young British designer has a love/hate relationship with the fashion industry.

● **John Galliano**
Galliano is quoted as saying, 'I am here to make people dream, to seduce them into buying beautiful clothes' – a sentiment that is shared by Viktor & Rolf. The three designers delve into a self-conscious fantasy land that references history and glamour.

Viktor & Rolf started their career not in a boutique or by assisting other designers, but as couturiers who showed their small collections in galleries as artwork. Directly contradicting the established notion that clothing is created solely to be used, their early collections were never produced to be worn by private clients, nor created with comfort or usability in mind.

CLOTHING AS ART
The two designers were funnelling their ideas of clothing as art through the medium of fashion; they were expressing abstract ideas and concepts. Viktor & Rolf understood that branding was their key to success, and used the increasingly important art market to solidify their position. The practices they have adopted in the art world have become the crucial source of their inspiration, both in the subject areas of their collections and in their performance art. Their philosophies and style impulses, which suggest a fantasy world of fashion and femininity, portray enthrallment but also acknowledge shortcomings.

A RELEVANT MESSAGE
The centre of the Viktor & Rolf philosophy is the contemporary notion that we use clothing far beyond the need for protection or function, but rather as a means of self-creation: 'We don't think about what people "need". We think about what we would like to do or say, and try to understand whether there is some relevance to this message. A constant questioning of fashion itself as a system – and our place in it – is always at the root of our work, as is the tension between doubts about our chosen medium, on the one hand, and the hope and desire to create

Cutting edge

Viktor & Rolf's Spring 2010 Cutting Edge couture show features shaped and technically dazzling layers of cut tulle that suggest both weight and heft, but are also see-through and delicate. The emphasis on angular shapes in delicate fabric suggests the qualities of modern femininity – strength and fortitude, but beholden to biology.

→ **Fashion celebrity**

In the Autumn 2007 collection, entitled The Fashion Show, Viktor & Rolf called attention to the balance between the celebrity of the model and the exhibition of clothing. There also seems to be a commentary on the contemporary culture of celebrity and self-promotion.

INFLUENCED BY

KEY
- ● fashion designer
- ◆ fashion house/brand
- ■ artistic influence
- ❖ cultural influence

● Rei Kawakubo
Early in their career, Viktor & Rolf attempted to follow the philosophy espoused by Kawakubo, in which there is no reliance on historical conventions or references in fashion. They have also experimented with transformative shapes, questioning the idealized nature of feminine beauty.

● Martin Margiela
Margiela is keenly interested in the presence of the maker/designer in his work, and has often created collections that utilize and explore characteristics of the fashion industry. This philosophical approach that centres on the interaction of maker and final product has been very influential on Viktor & Rolf.

VIKTOR & ROLF CONTINUED

CHRONOLOGY	1997	2000	2003	2004	2005
	Show their Launch collection at the Torch Gallery in Amsterdam. The show consists of a miniature runway, boutique, photo studio, atelier and fictional perfume.	Create their first ready-to-wear collection, and last haute couture collection.	Launch menswear collection. Musée de la Mode et du Textile in Paris hold a 10-year retrospective of their work.	Launch Flowerbomb, their first feminine fragrance, in association with cosmetics company L'Oréal.	Open their first boutique, in Milan.

INSPIRED

● Francesco Scognamiglio
The Italian designer is fond of large ruffles and bows that outline or call attention to the feminine figure – also a recognizable feature of Viktor & Rolf's collections.

◆ Dolce & Gabbana
The Italian duo cited Elsa Schiaparelli as the primary influence for their Spring 2010 collection, which seems to have also been inspired by Viktor & Rolf's interpretations of the same concepts.

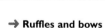

→ **Ruffles and bows**

In his Autumn 2009 collection, Francesco Scognamiglio explores new ways of building volume and presence in the often diminutive female figure. The model conveys the presence of a peacock in her ruffled fan of display, and mirrors the toying with excess that has also become a trademark of Viktor & Rolf.

something worthwhile, with beauty and meaning on the other.' Fashion is a self-conscious act of expression: 'Right from the beginning, fashion, for us, was more about the system of the fashion industry and its glamour. It was a naive way of escaping from daily reality.'

MEDIUM AND MESSAGE

Viktor & Rolf's influence is really just beginning, and the designers are increasingly having to balance art and fashion on the one hand with branding and business on the other: 'We want the fashion to be judged as fashion, and it has to function as such. But on top of that we personally like to express more through our work than the evolution of a style or a way of dressing. We are constantly facing the challenge of finding the balance where the medium – that is the clothes; fashion – does not get in the way of the message,

'We like to approach fashion as a broad medium that allows for many ways to express one's creativity. The brand that we have created is a result of that approach.'

Viktor & Rolf

● Thierry Mugler

The French designer is known for his science-fiction references, and his transfiguring of the female form as a metaphor for a conceptual statement. Like Mugler, Viktor & Rolf create pieces that are intended only for the fashion show performance, and are never meant to be worn.

● Elsa Schiaparelli

Viktor & Rolf's Spring 2008 Pierrot collection had surreal elements reminiscent of Schiaparelli. Even if the pair do not directly reference Schiaparelli, they share her use of art as a source of inspiration, draw creative energy from artistic collaborations and display a sense of the surreal in all their work.

● Yves Saint Laurent

Viktor & Rolf's Spring 2008 Pierrot collection featured large violins on the models' dresses. This brings to mind some of Saint Laurent's later collections, in which he adorned his gowns with doves, or a Picasso- or Braque-style guitar. Viktor & Rolf's heavy use of bows and frills is also reminiscent of Saint Laurent's later work in couture.

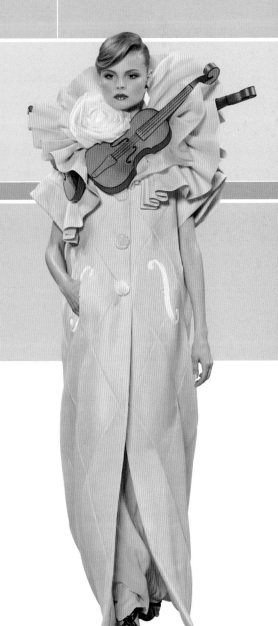

Launch men's fragrance Antidote and design a collection for the fashion retailer H&M.	*The Barbican Art Gallery in London holds a 15-year retrospective of their work; the pair re-create important looks from their collections, displayed on porcelain dolls in a large doll's house. Renzo Rosso, owner of Italian clothing company Diesel, buys a controlling stake in the house of Viktor & Rolf, allowing the designers to launch more product lines and open new stores.*
2006	**2008**

● Giles Deacon

British designer Deacon uses elements of surrealism and exaggerated shapes that are reminiscent of the work of Victor & Rolf. In his Spring 2009 collection, the models appeared on the catwalk wearing Pac-Man helmets (left); his Spring 2007 collection featured models overwhelmed by their feather headdresses — both recalling Viktor & Rolf's Spring 2005 Flowerbomb collection in which the models wore shiny black crash helmets. Beyond surrealistic references, Deacon plays with the opposites of horror versus traditional femininity, or of romantic frippery versus masculinity — also consistent inspirations for the Dutch duo.

but still has a right of existence in itself. We are torn between the hope that we can stretch the medium and mould it into something that we would like it to be — a means of expression beyond style — and exasperation that there are limits that we must accept.'

BROADENING THE SCOPE OF FASHION

In a world that already has a plethora of product available, how do designers balance the need for notoriety and acclaim with the mundane requirements of the everyday? In a society that desires self-creation and constant change, how must fashion designers meet these new challenges? For the interim, Viktor & Rolf bring our attention and that of other designers to examinations of the changing and broadening scope of fashion, and suggest that clothing should perhaps be considered in a different way.

➜ Pierrot collection

Viktor & Rolf's Spring 2008 collection was named after the French clown character whose primary trait was that of a trusting dupe, continually being taken advantage of and left for other loves, despite his devotion. The model is placed within pink ruffles and flowers, perhaps questioning women's sense of romanticism.

Hussein Chalayan has been the subject of numerous books, articles, exhibitions and shows that cite him as an intellectual and conceptual force in the fashion industry today. Examining issues of technology and our connection to it, feelings of displacement in modern society, and even concepts of space and time, Chalayan extends the discourse and traditional conceptions of fashion.

INFLUENCED BY

KEY
● fashion designer
◆ fashion house/brand
■ artistic influence
❖ cultural influence

● **Martin Margiela**
Margiela is another leading designer who examines larger issues within the context of fashion and image. Chalayan's graduation collection from London's Central Saint Martins featured fabric that had been buried, similar to Margiela's 1997 Rotterdam exhibition of bacteria-smeared fabric.

● **Nicolas Ghesquière for Balenciaga**
Ghesquière has been one of the most successful contemporary designers to blend concept with saleability. Chalayan has recently shifted a larger portion of his collections towards pieces that fashion buyers and critics can access more easily.

● **Elsa Schiaparelli**
Chalayan's Spring 2010 show featured evening dresses with porcelain hands clasping the fabric at the chest (left), which is reminiscent of Schiaparelli's work with surrealist artist Jean Cocteau.

HUSSEIN CHALAYAN
British
(1970 Nicosia, Cyprus)

	Born August 12th in Nicosia to Turkish Cypriot parents. His mother sews the family's clothing.	*His parents divorce and he moves with his father to London.*	*Graduates from London's Central Saint Martins. For his graduate collection, the clothes are buried in a friend's back garden together with metal pieces that mark the fabric, and are then dug up for display. The collection is purchased and displayed by independent fashion boutique Browns in London.*	*Designs clothing for the cover of Icelandic musician Björk's Post album. Also designs clothing for Björk's tour; in turn, she models in his show.*
CHRONOLOGY	**1970**	**1982**	**1993**	**1995**

INSPIRED

● **Haider Ackermann**
Both designers are transplants from different countries, and Ackermann says, 'There is no distinction between you and your memories, your experiences and your daily life. All that is attached in my work.' (Right: Nicosia, Chalayan's birthplace.)

● **Jonathan Saunders**
Saunders has exhibited several prints and construction techniques that are reminiscent of Chalayan's work, such as geometric shapes and colour layering within the garment.

◆ **Viktor & Rolf**
Fashion as art performance, as perfected by Chalayan, has influenced the design duo to meld concept and clothing.

Hussein Chalayan is one of the most obvious examples of a designer who straddles what fashion was, is and might become. Chalayan uses fashion to comment, examine, or suggest ideas that connect to larger issues of society, culture, aesthetics or design: 'When people talk about clothes, they don't talk about clothes in the context of society, in the social or cultural context; they just take them at face value. That's not something that interests me.'

ARTISTIC COLLABORATIONS

A true collaborator, Chalayan often works with others from various disciplines, connecting fashion with ideas from architecture, sculpture, industrial design and technology. Chalayan approaches fashion dually – as an artist who uses his work to pose open-ended rhetorical questions, but also as a designer who is focused on the body and image. The response from curators, other designers, authors and intellectuals has been enthusiastically positive and supportive. It suggests that one component that propels the fashion industry forward might be the artistic merit, scope and seriousness that encapsulate a fashion collection and show.

WEARABILITY AND FUNCTIONALITY

However, as with all other conceptual fashion designers, Hussein Chalayan constantly has to defend his ability to create wearable clothing that is saleable: 'It's so disappointing when people assume that my clothes are difficult. They're not. I love seeing people in my clothes and I often do. My clothes should be something women wear because they like them, because they enjoy the intimate space between my clothes and their bodies. That, to me, is very important.'

← Digital applications

More than any other designer, Hussein Chalayan is intrigued by the possibilities of digital applications and technology that may change the face of fashion in years to come. In his Autumn 2007 collection, he created a dress that incorporated Swarovski crystals and more than 15,000 LED lights.

● Alexander McQueen

Rather than being directly inspired by McQueen, Chalayan shares McQueen's intense interest in the intersection of technology and the natural world. Both designers have used fashion shows as centrepieces for a larger concept, expressing an abstract thought through the body, women and image.

Wins a competition for financial backing to develop a collection for London Fashion Week. Inspired by the mathematical formulas that drive pattern making, the show also features a minimalist musical score.

1995

● Thakoon Panichgul

The influence of Chalayan's Spring 2003 collection could easily be seen in the prints and simulated layers of Panichgul's Spring 2010 collection (right).

'I really do think that I am an ideas person. People often don't realize that whatever an idea is, ideas are always valuable. There is something to be respected in every given idea, no matter where it comes from.'

Hussein Chalayan

→ Earthbound

Chalayan's Autumn 2009 Earthbound collection exhibited a series of dresses with fabric innovations, such as the breastplate. The dress's fabric has similar textural qualities to earth or rock, and the breastplate encasing the chest and neck suggests a machine or robotics, as Chalayan examines the qualities of imposed attributes on an organic form.

← INFLUENCED BY

KEY
- ● fashion designer
- ◆ fashion house/brand
- ■ artistic influence
- ❖ cultural influence

● Yohji Yamamoto
Chalayan has clearly observed the relationship of fabric to the figure in the work of Yamamoto. Chalayan focuses on asymmetry and layers of fabric, much like Yamamoto.

● Cristóbal Balenciaga
Balenciaga was known for experimenting with alternative fabrications or blends, something that Chalayan also does.

● Pierre Cardin
Often using science fiction as a metaphor for the tumultuous life of the 20th century, Cardin was a forerunner in the attempt to combine innovation with business, as Chalayan strives to do.

HUSSEIN CHALAYAN CONTINUED

CHRONOLOGY	1998–2001	2001	2002	2004
	Hired as a design consultant for the New York–based knitwear company TSE.	Files for bankruptcy, but makes a quick comeback. Also begins working for British retail giant Marks & Spencer and Italian clothing manufacturer Gibo. British jeweller Asprey appoints him fashion director.	Introduces a menswear line.	Creates a diffusion line called Chalayan. Has a solo exhibition at the Groninger Museum in the Netherlands.

→ INSPIRED

● Rick Owens
In Rick Owens's Spring 2010 collection, the designer toyed with sharp shoulders and shapes that resembled Chalayan's chest breastplates from the previous season. Chalayan has always been an outsider, choosing to defy trends and work on his own terms and at his own pace, in the same way that Owens does.

● Alexandre Herchcovitch
Herchcovitch has embraced the ideas developed on the Chalayan catwalk – a blending of art, concept, worldview and saleability.

→ Feminine warrior

Rick Owens's Spring 2010 collection suggests, as his work often does, a romantic and slightly tragic sense of womanhood, utilizing much of the same visual vocabulary that Chalayan often uses, such as strong shoulders, geometric shapes or deep colours. Within this collection, Owens is thinking in terms of geometry on the figure, abstracting it away from the natural curves in order to call attention to the organic form within the man-made garment.

The fact that Chalayan is not supported by a large fashion conglomerate, such as LMVH or Gucci Group, means that he must make wearable clothing that sells. Despite his conceptual approach, Chalayan is also fully aware that to work within the fashion industry's present terms, it is essential that clothing be functional: 'I think that what makes something modern is its functionality. That's what modernism was created for. The design of something comes from its function.'

EVOLVING NEW SOLUTIONS

Hussein Chalayan has been able to balance the desire for constant change within the financially motivated industry, and his preferred slow evolution of clothing in terms of a larger concept: 'The only way to evolve your work is by seeing it as a wheel. That is the only way I can cope with the sort of horror of transience which I really hate. I can't stand it.'

→ Sculptural form

Chalayan often manipulates fabric into organic and sculptural forms, as seen in the Spring 2010 show. The entire collection has a beach resort feel, and so it only follows that he has created a dress that appears to be made of water.

■ Contemporary art

Unlike conceptual designers such as Rei Kawakubo or Martin Margiela, Chalayan does not try to distance himself from the world of fine art. Instead, he often presents his work as performance art. After watching the fashion shows that introduce his collections, it is often easier to understand the underlying meanings.

● Rei Kawakubo

The ability to separate clothing from a capricious judgement of taste in our contemporary culture is largely based on the work of Japanese designers such as Kawakubo. Chalayan has become famous for relying on an intellectual or philosophical idea to propel the dialogue of fashion and image forward. This pursuit would have undoubtedly been more difficult without the work of Kawakubo to lead the way.

Awarded an MBE (Member of the Order of the British Empire).	*Internet retailer Yoox.com buys the exclusive rights to his menswear.*	*Appointed creative director of Puma, which buys a majority stake in his label.*	*Collaborates with the J Brand jeans label to create a denim line for women.*
2006	**2007**	**2008**	**2009**

● Frida Giannini for Gucci

Giannini's layering and playing with fabric on the figure resemble many of Chalayan's experiments in his own pieces of work.

● Max Azria

Several pieces and many of the textiles in Azria's Spring 2010 collection (left) are similar in colour blocking, figural geometry and general aesthetic to Chalayan's Spring 2009 collection.

With his collections and shows, Chalayan revisits themes that interest him, but each time offers a new solution to an aesthetic problem. The designer often examines ideas of cultural representations, personal identity and the sense of self through dress as it relates to time and place. His childhood and cultural heritage play a part in his examinations, as he relates to the contemporary worldwide phenomenon of displacement and discordance.

Another common theme throughout his collections is our connection with and mastery of technology. Chalayan contrasts how we use technology with the human needs of touch, emotion and feeling. Throughout his career, Chalayan has propelled the industry forward to meet 21st-century expectations of what is to come.

BIBLIOGRAPHY

Baudot, F. *Christian Lacroix*. New York: Universe/ Vendome, 1997.

——— *Thierry Mugler*. New York: Universe/ Vendome, 1998.

——— *Fashion: The Twentieth Century*. New York: Universe, 1999.

——— *Yohji Yamamoto*. New York: Assouline, 2005.

——— *Alaïa*. New York: Assouline, 2006.

Benaïm, L. *Issey Miyake*. New York: Universe/ Vendome, 1997.

Bergé, P. *Yves Saint Laurent*. New York: Universe/ Vendome, 1997.

Berry, S. *Screen Style: Fashion and Femininity in 1930s Hollywood*. Minneapolis, MN: Minnesota Press, 2000.

Buxbaum, G. (ed.) *Icons of Fashion: The 20th Century*. New York: Prestel. 2005.

De Marly, D. *Christian Dior*. New York: Holmes & Meier, 1990.

De Osma, G. *Mariano Fortuny: His Life and Work*. New York: Rizzoli, 1980.

Deloffre, C. (ed.) *Thierry Mugler: Fashion, Fetish, Fantasy*. Santa Monica, CA: General Publication Group, 1998.

Demornex, J. *Madeleine Vionnet*. New York: Rizzoli, 1991.

Derycke, L. and Van de Veire, S. (eds.) *Belgian Fashion Design*. Ghent-Amsterdam: Ludion, 1999.

Deschodt, A. and Davanzo Poli, D. *Fortuny*. New York: Harry N. Abrams, 2000.

Deslandres, Y. *Poiret: Paul Poiret, 1879–1944*. London: Thames & Hudson, 1987.

Desveaux, D. *Fortuny*. London: Thames & Hudson, 1998.

Dior, C. translated by Fraser, A. *Christian Dior and I*. New York: Dutton, 1957.

Dresner, L., Hilberry, S. and Miro, M. (eds.) *ReFusing Fashion: Rei Kawakubo*. Detroit, MI: Museum of Contemporary Art Detroit, 2008.

Evans, C. "John Galliano: Modernity and Spectacle" chapter in book: White, N. and Griffiths, I. (eds.) *The Fashion Business: Theory, Practice, Image*. Oxford; New York: Berg, 2000.

——— "Desire and Dread: Alexander McQueen and the Contemporary Femme Fatale" chapter in book: Entwistle, J. and Wilson, E. (eds.) *Body Dressing*. Oxford; New York: Berg, 2001.

——— *Fashion at the Edge: Spectacle, Modernity and Deathliness*. New Haven, CT: Yale University Press, 2003.

———, Menkes, S., Polhemus, T. and Quinn, B. *Hussein Chalayan*. Rotterdam: NAi Publishers; Groningen: Groninger Museum, 2005.

——— and Frankel, S. *The House of Viktor & Rolf*. New York: Merrell, 2008.

Foley, B. *Marc Jacobs*. New York: Assouline, 2004.

Ford, T. and Foley, B. *Tom Ford*. New York: Rizzoli, 2004.

Galante, P. translated by Geist, E. and Wood, J. *Mademoiselle Chanel*. Chicago: Henry Regnery Company, 1973.

Gross, E. and Rottman, F. *Halston: An American Original*. New York: HarperCollins, 1999.

Haedrich, M. translated by Markmann, C. *Coco Chanel: Her Life, Her Secrets*. Boston: Little, Brown and Company, 1971.

Healy, R. *Balenciaga: Masterpiece of Fashion Design*. Melbourne, Australia: National Gallery of Victoria, 1992.

Horyn, C. "The Hands: Azzedine Alaïa." <http:// runway.blogs.nytimes.com> March 4, 2007.

——— "The Alaïa Chronicles." <http://runway. blogs.nytimes.com> August 3, 2007.

——— "Balenciaga: Flower Power." <http://runway. blogs.nytimes.com> October 2, 2007.

——— "Collection of the Season: Marc Jacobs." <http://runway.blogs.nytimes.com> October 16, 2007.

——— "The Balenciaga Line." <http://runway.blogs. nytimes.com> February 26, 2008.

——— "Paris: At Balenciaga, Light Play." <http:// runway.blogs.nytimes.com> September 30, 2008.

——— "At the Place Colette." <http://runway. blogs.nytimes.com> October 1, 2008.

——— "Paris: Piaf and Python." <http://runway. blogs.nytimes.com> October 7, 2008.

——— "Paris Arabesque." <http://runway.blogs. nytimes.com> January 28, 2009.

——— "Prada: Gone Fishin'." <http://runway.blogs. nytimes.com> March 1, 2009.

——— "Balenciaga: Paris Under the Skin." <http:// runway.blogs.nytimes.com> March 5, 2009.

——— "Paris Can-Can. Runway." <http://runway. blogs.nytimes.com> March 12, 2009.

——— "In the Mind of the Great Couturier." (Audio conversation with Karl Lagerfeld.) <http://runway.blogs.nytimes.com> July 7, 2009.

——— "Balenciaga: Au Revoir, Madame." <http:// runway.blogs.nytimes.com> October 1, 2009.

——— "A Conversation with Nicolas Ghesquière of Balenciaga." (Audio backstage interview.) <http://runway.blogs.nytimes.com> October 1, 2009.

——— "McQueen: Leaping Lizards." <http:// runway.blogs.nytimes.com> October 6, 2009.

——— "A Visit to London." <http://runway.blogs. nytimes.com> February 11, 2010.

——— "Prada: Old Dears." <http://runway.blogs. nytimes.com> February 25, 2010.

——— "Paris: McQueen Was Here." <http:// runway.blogs.nytimes.com> March 10, 2010.

Jones, T. and Rushton, S. (eds) *Fashion Now*. Italy: Taschen, 2005.

Kawamura, Y. *The Japanese Revolution in Paris Fashion*. New York: Berg, 2004.

Kirke, B. *Madeleine Vionnet*. New York: Chronicle Books, 1998.

Klensch, E. *Style [with] Elsa Klensch: Paris Collections Spring 1989*. Cable News Network, Inc.

——— *Style [with] Elsa Klensch: Paris Collections Fall 1989*. Cable News Network, Inc.

Koda, H. *Poiret*. New York: Metropolitan Museum of Art; New Haven, CT: Yale University Press, 2007.

——— and Celant, G. (eds.) *Giorgio Armani*. New York: Guggenheim Museum Publications; Harry N. Abrams, 2000.

Kojima, N. (ed.) with Margiela, M. *Maison Martin Margiela: Street Special Edition Vols. 1 & 2*. Italy: Grafiche Zanini, 1999.

Lacroix, C., Mauriès, P. and Saillard, O. *Christian Lacroix on Fashion*. London; New York: Thames & Hudson, 2008.

Lagerfeld, K. and Harlech, A. *Visions and a Decision*. London: Thames & Hudson, 2003.

Langle, E. *Pierre Cardin: Fifty Years of Fashion and Design*. New York: Vendome, 2005.

Lee, S.T. (ed.) *American Fashion: The Life and Lines of Adrian, Mainbocher, McCardell, Norell, and Trigere*. New York: Andre Deutsch, 1975.

Lynam, R. (ed.) *Couture: An Illustrated History of the Great Paris Designers and Their Creations*. New York: Doubleday & Company, Inc., 1972.

Mackrell, A. *Paul Poiret*. New York: Holmes & Meier, 1990.

Madsen, A. *Living for Design: The Yves Saint Laurent Story*. New York: Delacorte Press, 1979.

Marc Jacobs & Louis Vuitton: A Documentary by Loïc Prigent. Film distributed by Facets Video, 2007.

Marsh, L. *The House of Klein: Fashion, Controversy, and a Business Obsession*. New York: John Wiley & Sons, Inc., 2003.

Martin, R. *Gianni Versace*. New York: Metropolitan Museum of Art; Harry N. Abrams, 1997.

——— and Koda, H. *Madame Grès*. New York: Metropolitan Museum of Art; Harry N. Abrams, 1994.

——— and ——— *Haute Couture*. New York: Metropolitan Museum of Art; Harry N. Abrams, 1995.

——— and ——— *Christian Dior*. New York: Metropolitan Museum of Art; Harry N. Abrams, 1996.

Mauriès, P. *Christian Lacroix: The Diary of a Collection*. New York: Simon & Schuster, 1994.

McDowell, C. *Galliano*. New York: Sterling Publishing Co., Inc., 2001.

——— *Jean Paul Gaultier*. London: Cassell, 2003.

——— *Ralph Lauren: The Man, the Vision, the Style*. New York: Rizzoli, 2003.

Mears, P. *Madame Grès: Sphinx of Fashion*. New Haven, CT: Yale University Press; New York: Fashion Institute of Technology, 2007.

Mendes, V. *Pierre Cardin: Past, Present, Future*. London; Berlin: Dirk Nishen, 1990.

Milbank, C. R. *New York Fashion: The Evolution of American Style*. New York: Harry N. Abrams, 1989.

Miller, L. E. *Cristóbal Balenciaga (1895–1972): The Couturiers' Couturier*. London: V&A Publishing; New York: Harry N. Abrams, 2007.

Mitchell, L. (ed.) *The Cutting Edge: Fashion from Japan*. Sydney, Australia: Powerhouse Publishing, 2005.

Moffitt, P. *The Rudi Gernreich Book*. New York: Rizzoli, 1991.

Morais, R. *Pierre Cardin: The Man Who Became a Label*. London; New York: Bantam, 1991.

Mulvagh, J. *Vivienne Westwood: An Unfashionable Life*. London: HarperCollins, 1999.

Quant, M. *Quant by Quant*. New York: G.P. Putnam's Sons, 1966.

Rawsthorn, A. *Yves Saint Laurent: A Biography*. New York: Nan A. Talese/Doubleday, 1996.

Sato, K. *Issey Miyake: Making Things*. Zurich: Scalo; New York: D.A.P., 1999.

Schiaparelli, E. *Shocking Life: The Autobiography of Elsa Schiaparelli*. London: V&A Publishing, 2007.

Silva, H. "Now Honoring Dries Van Noten." <tmagazine.blogs.nytimes.com> September 8, 2009.

Sischy, I. *The Journey of a Woman: 20 Years of Donna Karan*. New York: Assouline, 2004.

——— *Donna Karan, New York*. New York: Assouline, 2005.

Troy, N. *Couture Culture: A Study in Modern Art and Fashion*. Cambridge, MA: MIT Press, 2003.

Tucker, A. *The London Fashion Book*. New York: Rizzoli, 1998.

——— *Dries Van Noten: Shape, Print and Fabric*. London: Thames & Hudson, 1999.

Vinken, B. *Fashion Zeitgeist: Trends and Cycles in the Fashion System*. New York: Berg, 2005.

White, N. *Versace*. London: Carlton, 2000.

Wilcox, C. *Vivienne Westwood*. London: V&A Publishing; New York: Harry N. Abrams, 2004.

——— (ed.) *Radical Fashion*. London: V&A Publishing; New York: Harry N. Abrams, 2001.

——— (ed.) *The Art and Craft of Gianni Versace*. London: V&A Publishing, 2002.

Wilson, E. "Q&A: Jean Paul Gaultier." <http://runway.blogs.nytimes.com> October 26, 2007.

Windels, V. *Young Belgian Fashion Design*. Ghent-Amsterdam: Ludion, 2001.

Yamamoto, Y., and Washida, K. *Talking to Myself*. Milan: Sozzani, 2002.

Yohannan, K. *Claire McCardell: Redefining Modernism*. New York: Harry N. Abrams, 1988.

DESIGNER WEBSITES

www.alexandermcqueen.com

www.anndemeulemeester.be

www.balenciaga.com

www.calvinkleininc.com

www.chanel.com

www.christian-lacroix.fr

www.courreges.com

www.dior.com

www.donnakaran.com

www.driesvannoten.be

www.fortuny.com

www.giorgioarmani.com

www.husseinchalayan.com

www.isaacmizrahiny.com

www.isseymiyake.com

www.jeanpaulgaultier.com

www.jilsander.com

www.johngalliano.com

www.karllagerfeld.com

www.katharinehamnett.com

www.maisonmartinmargiela.com

www.marcjacobs.com

www.maryquant.co.uk

www.narcisorodriguez.com

http://parfumsgres.com/history.html

www.pierrecardin.com

www.prada.com

www.ralphlauren.com

www.stellamccartney.com

www.thierrymugler.com

www.tomford.com

www.versace.com

www.viktor-rolf.com

www.viviennewestwood.com

www.yohjiyamamoto.co.jp

www.ysl.com

OTHER USEFUL WEBSITES

www.metmuseum.org/works_of_art/the_costume_institute

www.nytimes.com/pages/fashion

www.style.com

www.vam.ac.uk

INDEX

CREDITS

Key: *a* above; *b* below; *l* left; *r* right

Associated Press: John Lindsay 125*l*

Corbis: Alessandro Garofalo/Reuters 89*l* & 149*b*; Alfred/epa 140*b*; Andreea Angelescu 25*b*, 83*r* & 98; Andreu Dalmau/epa 131*al* & 133; Benoit Tessier/Reuters 107, 181*br* & 184*a*; Bettmann 22*a*, 35*l*, 39, 47*ar*, 49*a*, 67*l*, 126*a*, 127*b* & 165*a*; Charles Platiau/Reuters 180–1*a*; Condé Nast Archive 33; Davide Maestri/WWD/Condé Nast 19*r*, 70*a* &146*b*; Dominique Maitre/WWD/Condé Nast 17, 79*r* & 185*r*; Edward Steichen/Condé Nast Archive 91; Eric Robert/Sygma 124*b*; Genevieve Naylor 45, 46*a*, 95*bl* & 101; George Chinsee/WWD/Condé Nast 19*l* & 129*br*; Giovanni Giannoni/WWD/Condé Nast 27*b*; 56*a*, 71, 76, 79*l*, 81, 85*b*, 93*l*, 106*b*, 109*r*, 115, 117*r*, 119*b*, 135*l*, 137*r*, 155, 169*r*, 177*l*, 177*r*, 179, 180*b* & 184*b*; Giulio Di Mauro/epa 134*b*; Henry Clarke/Condé Nast Archive 97*l*; Ian Langsdon/epa 18*a*; Jacky Naegelen/Reuters 85*a*; Jason Szenes/epa 21*bl*; John Aquino/WWD/Condé Nast 12*b*, 29*a*, 68*b* & 119*a*; Julio Donoso/Sygma 63; Keith Bedford/Reuters 154*b*; Kourken Pakchanian/Condé Nast Archive 23*l*; Lancaster/Hulton-Deutsch Collection 61 & 123*l*; Laszlo Veres/B.D.V. 59*al*, 65*bl*, 73*a*, 111*a*, 113*a*, 141 & 142*a*; Leonard de Selva 14*a*; Les Stone/Sygma 24*b*; Lucas Dolega/epa 35*br*; Lucas Jackson/Reuters 67*r*; Lynn Goldsmith 53*b*; Martine Archambault/epa 123*r*; Matteo Bazzi/epa 27*a* & 57*r*; Mauricio Miranda/WWD/Condé Nast 57*l*; Max Rossi/Reuters 132*b*; Maxppp/Bruno Pellerin/epa 73*b*; Maya Vidon/epa 14*b*; Michel Arnaud 55 & 149*a*; Mike Reinhardt/Condé Nast Archive 49*b*; Mike Segar/Reuters 25*a*; Nick Ackerman/Condé Nast Archive 127*a*; Olivier Hoslet/epa 143; Pascal Rossignol/Reuters 168*b*; Peter Harholdt 34*a*; Petre Buzoianu 50*b*; Philadelphia Museum of Art 15, 163*l* & 164*r*; Philippe Wojazer/Reuters 59*r*; Pierre Vauthey/Sygma 29*b*, 105*bl*, 131*r* & 176*a*; Robert Mitra/WWD/Condé Nast 21*a*; Stefano Rellandini/Reuters 165*b*; Stephane Cardinale/People Avenue 40*b*, 75, 77*r* & 156*a*; Stephane Tavoularis/Bettmann 43; Steve Eichner/WWD/Condé Nast Archive 65*r*; Talaya Centeno WWD/Condé Nast 159*b*; Thierry Orban/Sygma 104 & 108; Thomas Iannaccone/WWD/Condé Nast 82*a*, 117*bl* & 153*b*; Underwood & Underwood 13 & 37; WWD/Condé Nast 24*a* & 82*bl*; Xavier Lhospice/Reuters 77*l*

Getty Images: Albin Guillot/Roger Viollet 2*l*; Apic/Hulton Archive 90*a*, 92*a*, 96*a* & 162*a*; Bill Brandt/Hulton Archive 95*ar*; Dirck Halstead/Time & Life Pictures 51; Fernanda Calfat for IMG 38*b*; Francois Guillot/AFP 173*ar*; Keystone 53*a*; Mark Mainz 151*l*; Pierre Verdy/AFP 113*b* & 172*a*; Rabbani and Solimene Photography/Wirelmage 89*r*; Randy Brooke/Wirelmage 159*a*; Sasha 32*a* & *b*

Mary Evans Picture Library: 8

Reuters: Charles Platiau 168*a* &173*bl*; Jean-Paul Pelissier 116*a*; Paolo Cocco 145; Peter Morgan 153*a*; Stefano Rellandini 146*a* & 147*r*; Stephen Hird 151*r*; STR New 105*ar* & 132*a*

Rex Features: 41, 42*ar*, 60*b*, 167, 171 & 175; Cavan Pawson 96*b*; Corpet 69; Everett Collection 38*ar*; Mark Large 111*b*; NBCU Photo Bank 50*a*; NTI Media Ltd 157*r*; Richard Young 140*a*; Roger-Viollet 58*a*, 93*r*, 99, 100*ar* & 100*bl*; Sharok Hatami 129*al*; Sipa Press 2*r*, 47*bl*, 64*a*, 103 & 136; Cavan Pawson/Associated Newspapers 183*l*

St. Edmundsbury Borough Council: 12*a*

All other photographs and illustrations are the copyright of Quarto Publishing plc. While every effort has been made to credit contributors, Quarto would like to apologize should there have been any errors or omissions – and would be pleased to make the appropriate correction for future editions of the book.

Author's acknowledgements

I would like to thank Edith Serkownek, librarian in the fashion library of Kent State University, for all her invaluable help in the research of this book.

The many people from Quarto Publishing, specifically Michelle Pickering, editor, for their outstanding work.

And, of course, my family and friends, who were largely ignored throughout the writing of this book, yet never failed to voice support.